THE MASSIVE ™

"This is making for an impressive run of a terrific and thought-provoking comic."

— DigitalNoob/EGMNOW

"THE STORY SERVES AS A TRIBUTE TO MEN WHO PAY THE HEAVY PRICE OF PUTTING THE GREATER GOOD BEFORE THEMSELVES, PITTING RAW HUMAN EMOTION AGAINST A MERCILESS WORLD. GARRY BROWN AND JORDIE BELLAIRE SIMPLY ROCK THIS BOOK'S ARTWORK; EVERY PAGE SEEMS SO RUGGED AND CALCULATED IT'S SCARILY GOOD."

—GEEKS UNLEASHED

"This series continues to uphold my faith that there are genuinely original comics out there that deal with topics rarely seen in comics today and *The Massive* does it in spades every single month. Hats off to Brian Wood, Garry Brown and Dark Horse Comics."

— Comics: The Gathering

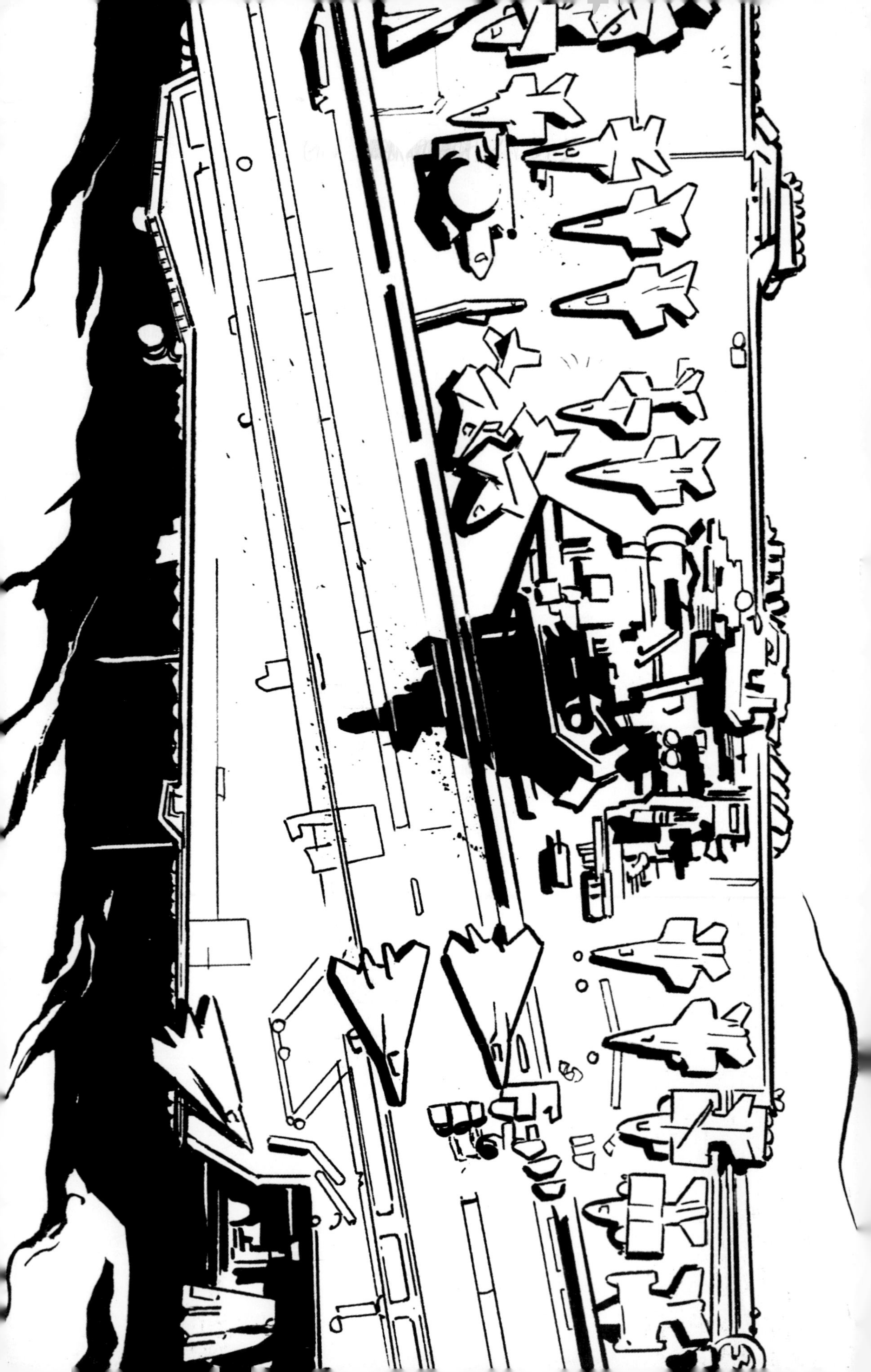

THE MASSIVE™

LONGSHIP

BRIAN WOOD
STORY

GARRY BROWN
ART

JORDIE BELLAIRE
COLORS

JARED K. FLETCHER
LETTERING

J. P. LEON
COVER ART

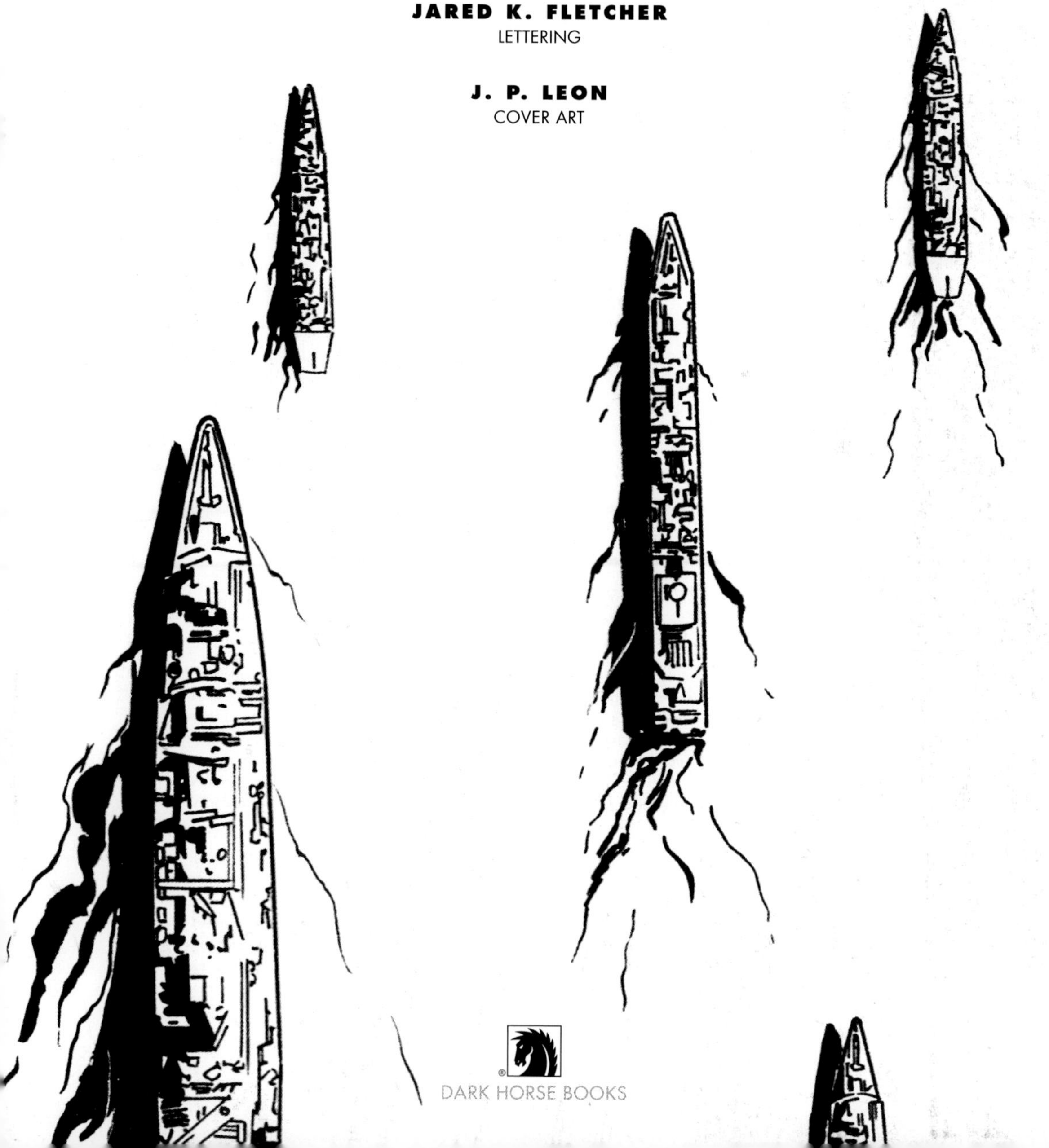

DARK HORSE BOOKS

GN WOOD v.3

MIKE RICHARDSON
PRESIDENT & PUBLISHER

SIERRA HAHN
EDITOR

JIM GIBBONS
ASSOCIATE EDITOR

SPENCER CUSHING
ASSISTANT EDITOR

JUSTIN COUCH
COLLECTION DESIGNER

Special thanks to Meredith, Audrey, and Ian.

Published by **DARK HORSE BOOKS**
A division of Dark Horse Comics, Inc.
10956 SE Main Street, Milwaukie, OR 97222

DARKHORSE.COM

First edition: June 2014
ISBN 978-1-61655-446-0

1 3 5 7 9 10 8 6 4 2

To find a comics shop in your area, call the
Comic Shop Locator Service toll-free at (888) 266-4226.
International Licensing: (503) 905-2377

Neil Hankerson Executive Vice President · Tom Weddle Chief Financial Officer · Randy Stradley Vice President of Publishing · Michael Martens Vice President of Book Trade Sales · Anita Nelson Vice President of Business Affairs · Scott Allie Editor in Chief · Matt Parkinson Vice President of Marketing · David Scroggy Vice President of Product Development · Dale LaFountain Vice President of Information Technology · Darlene Vogel Senior Director of Print, Design, and Production · Ken Lizzi General Counsel · Davey Estrada Editorial Director · Chris Warner Senior Books Editor · Diana Schutz Executive Editor · Cary Grazzini Director of Print and Development · Lia Ribacchi Art Director · Cara Niece Director of Scheduling · Tim Wiesch Director of International Licensing · Mark Bernardi Director of Digital Publishing

This volume reprints the comic-book series *The Massive* #13–#18 from Dark Horse Comics.

APOCALYP-SEA: SAILING INTO THE HEART OF CONSEQUENCE

JOHNNY COLT

Hold up.

Stop for a moment, draw a deep breath, and listen . . .

Can you feel it?

Let me tell you right now, you won't feel a thing as long as you're tethered to that smartphone, head down and numbly punching away at your three-hundred-dollar anchor while the world and your place in it are being snatched away from you.

If, however, you can slip free from your technochains and find just a moment of stillness, there's a message waiting for you. You won't just hear it, though—you'll feel it. You'll feel it in the vibrations of your bones, between the manic palpitations of your heart all the way up to those imperceptible hairs standing at attention on the back of your neck. Something is very, very wrong.

In the Gulf of Mexico, an imperious multinational oil conglomerate recklessly tunnels a mile into the ocean floor, without any viable disaster response plan. Of course, disaster does strike. Big time. BP's Deepwater Horizon drilling rig explodes, killing eleven workers and resulting in millions of gallons of crude oil gushing into the ocean for nearly three full months. In a haughty attempt to conceal the extent of the damage, a private corporation uses military aircraft to drop a nasty chemical dispersant into the ocean in order to push the oil down to the ocean floor, jacking up toxicity levels beyond all human comprehension. Out of sight and out of mind.

Nepalese UN peacekeepers stationed in Haiti cavalierly dump their own human waste directly into that country's most vital river, contaminating this critical water source with the deadly bacteria known as cholera. In a country that is 90 percent deforested, the rainy season brings torrential floods, and as these coursing waters spread the life-threatening disease throughout the country, the people of Haiti spiral into a decimating epidemic that will kill eight thousand and sicken a jaw-dropping six hundred thousand others. While the disease is normally curable with antibiotics, in a poverty-stricken country like Haiti, even the most basic of life-sustaining care is a remote luxury.

Sitting halfway around the world on the tiny Pacific island nation of Nauru, what was once a lush, tropical paradise is now a ruinous, rocky atoll as a result of ruthless strip-mining efforts to remove rich phosphate deposits from beneath the surface. As water levels rise, valuable coral dies and the local population suffer a paralyzing lack of natural resources. Residents subsist on processed foods imported from neighboring countries, resulting in marked spikes in obesity and diabetes. The people's primary source of food is literally killing them.

On another island nation, an incomprehensibly massive tsunami the size of something out of a Saturday afternoon monster movie wipes out vast ranges of Japan's northeastern coast. In addition to the fifteen thousand deaths, the tsunami all but destroys the Fukushima nuclear reactor complex, resulting in not one but three reactor meltdowns that—three years later—continue to leak lethal amounts of radiation into the Pacific Ocean.

Sounds like a bunch of far-fetched plots of summer blockbuster movies, right?

Wrong.

These terrifying vignettes are all very real, and they are events that I personally experienced as a conflict journalist. Consequently, Brian Wood's *The Massive* resonates with me on a deep and personal level because what I have seen from my viewpoint, camped out on the frontlines of these incomprehensible tragedies, is precisely the world that Brian has created in his new collection. With *The Massive*, Brian Wood has conceived a slate of dramatic and perhaps inevitable climate-change scenarios in which mankind's future is anything but assured.

For me personally, *The Massive* is no far-fetched sci-fi thriller set in a distant future. Brian has tapped into not just the experiences but also the feelings that accompany such mind-blowing levels of tragedy. Thumbing through each rich, evocative page felt as though Brian had crawled inside my brain and foretold planet Earth's demise as the natural conclusion of the events that I have seen firsthand.

With *The Massive* (as well as previous works such as *DMZ* and *Northlanders*), Brian Wood taps into that sublime realm of creativity known only to the world's greatest artists; he has not simply created a great piece of art, but he has advanced the entire art form of sequential storytelling.

Beyond question, Wood has constructed a thoroughly engaging plot, rich with detail and authenticity, with characters who not only drive the story forward, but who are also easy to relate to, with attitudes and emotions that pull the reader deep into the narrative.

Brian's works have earned him dramatic levels of critical and popular acclaim, and *The Massive* stands among his finest efforts yet, but what I love most about his work is that it's so damn readable. Not to mention that *The Massive* has, well, it has it all: A mercenary with a heart of gold, whose redemption sees him finding unusual and downright noble uses for blood money. One of Brian's classic female characters, complex and independent. A post-war, post-Crash, post-disaster, post-everything dying world. Oh, and did I mention the mystery ship?

Sign me up.

With *The Massive*, Brian Wood does not simply predict our future; he tells us how it's going to feel.

Johnny Colt began his career as an original member of the Black Crowes and continues his musical life as a current member of the legendary southern rock band Lynyrd Skynyrd. Parallel to his musical career, Colt plays a role as unlikely as it is genuinely rock 'n' roll: Colt can be seen on CNN and the Weather Channel traversing landscapes of disaster and conflict, in pursuit of his deep passion for journalism. Special thanks to Joe Daly. **JohnnyColtJournalist.com**

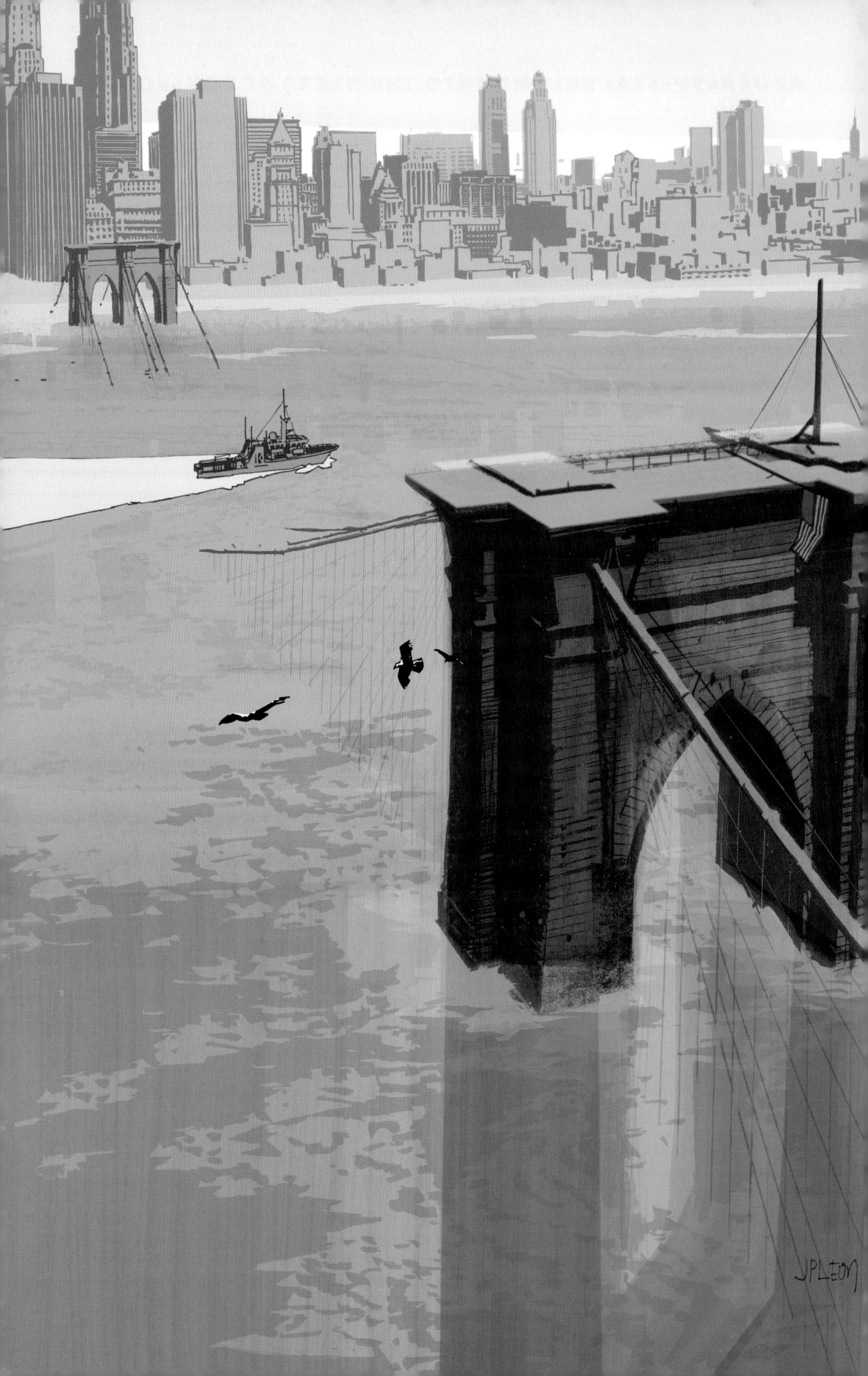
JPLEON

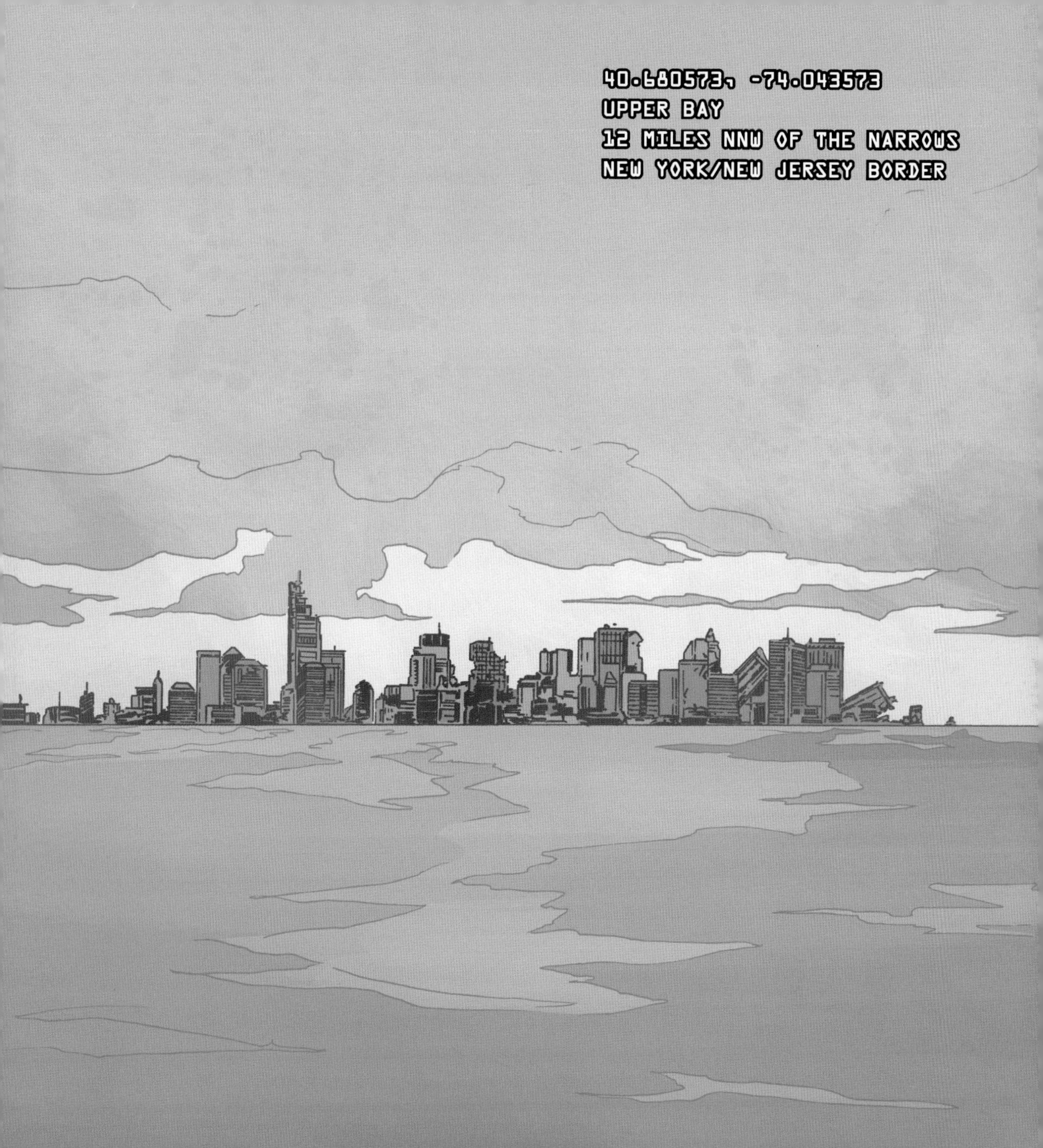
40.680573, -74.043573
UPPER BAY
12 MILES NNW OF THE NARROWS
NEW YORK/NEW JERSEY BORDER

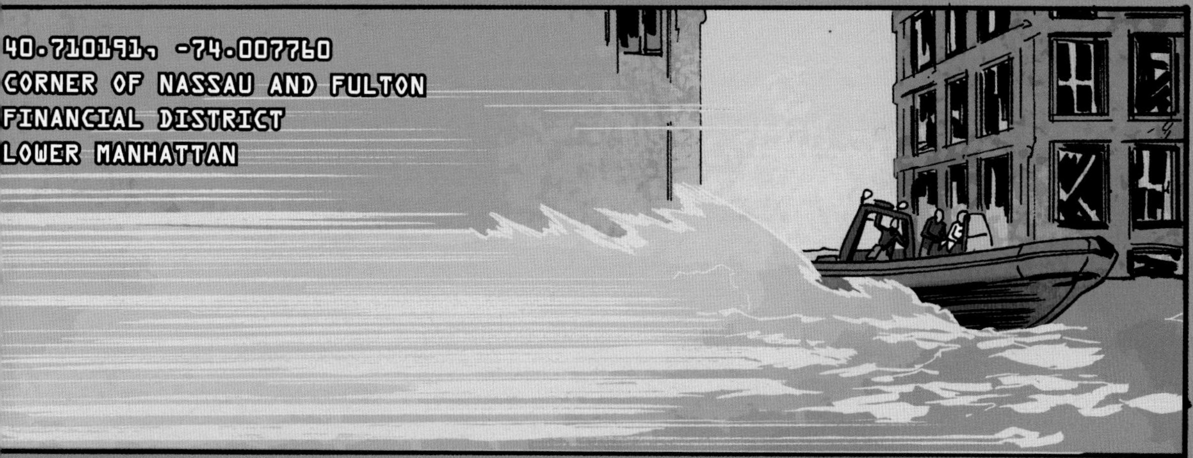
40.710191, -74.007760
CORNER OF NASSAU AND FULTON
FINANCIAL DISTRICT
LOWER MANHATTAN

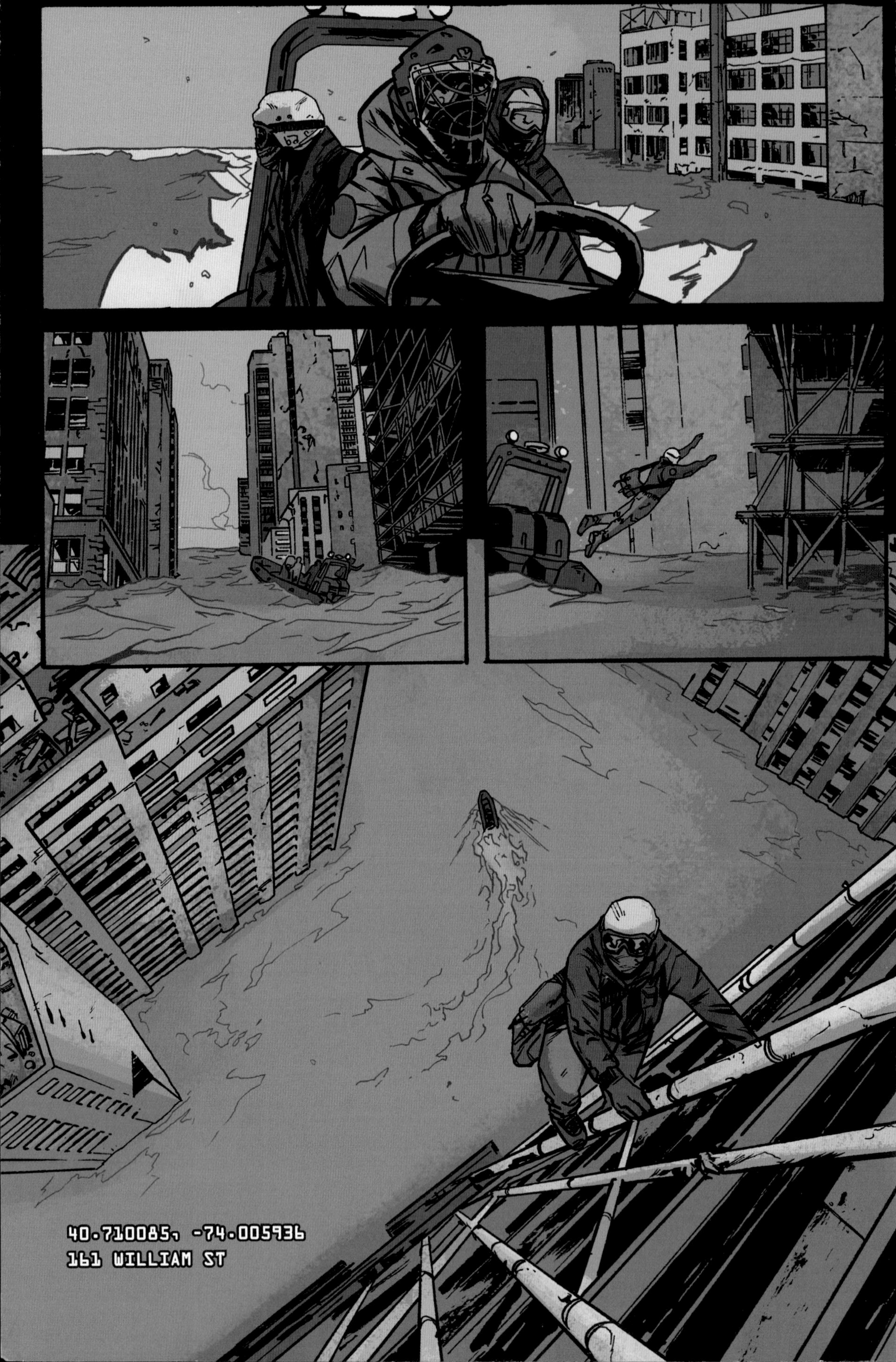
40.710085, -74.005936
161 WILLIAM ST

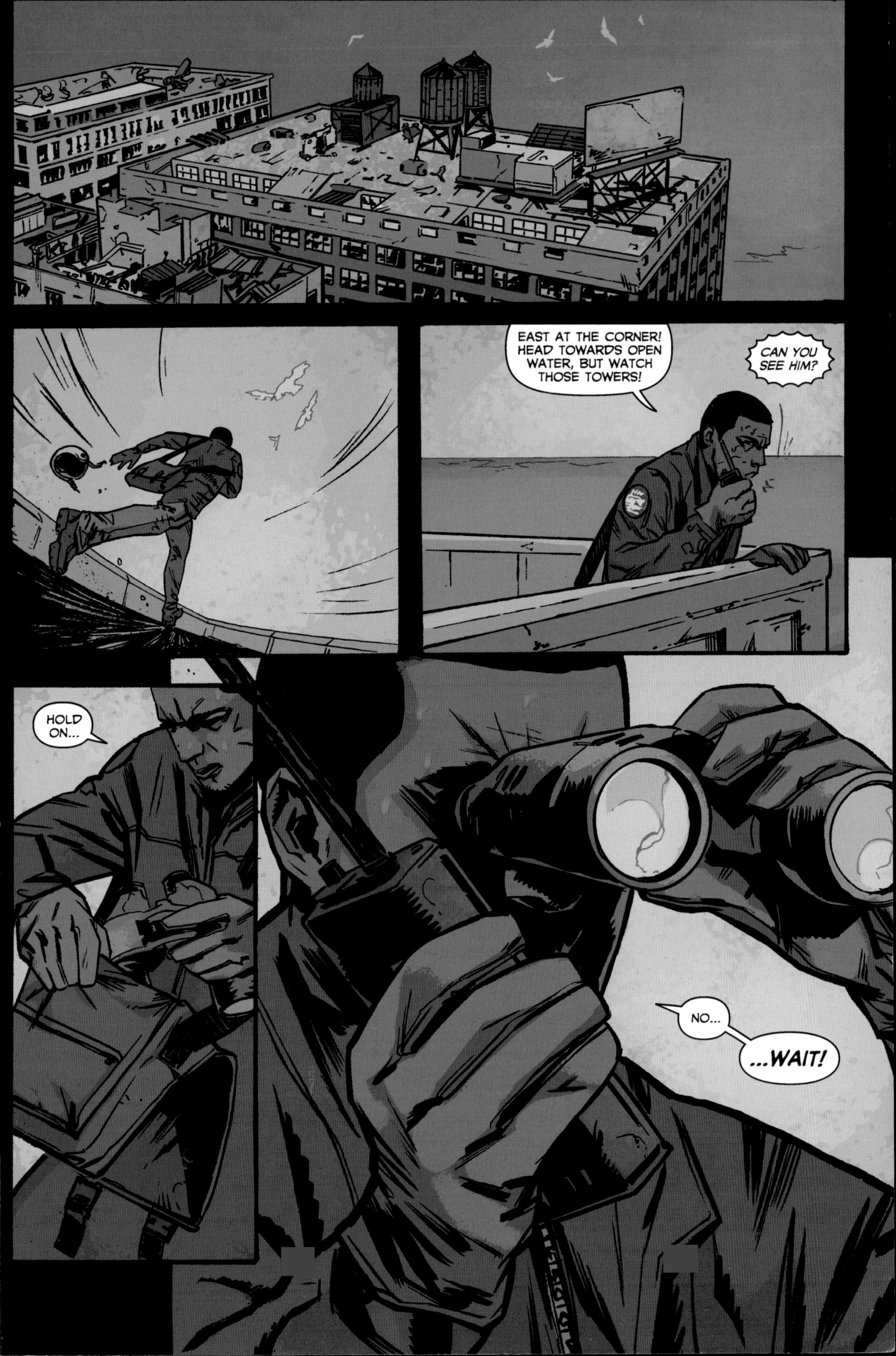
EAST AT THE CORNER! HEAD TOWARDS OPEN WATER, BUT WATCH THOSE TOWERS!
CAN YOU SEE HIM?
HOLD ON...
NO...
...WAIT!

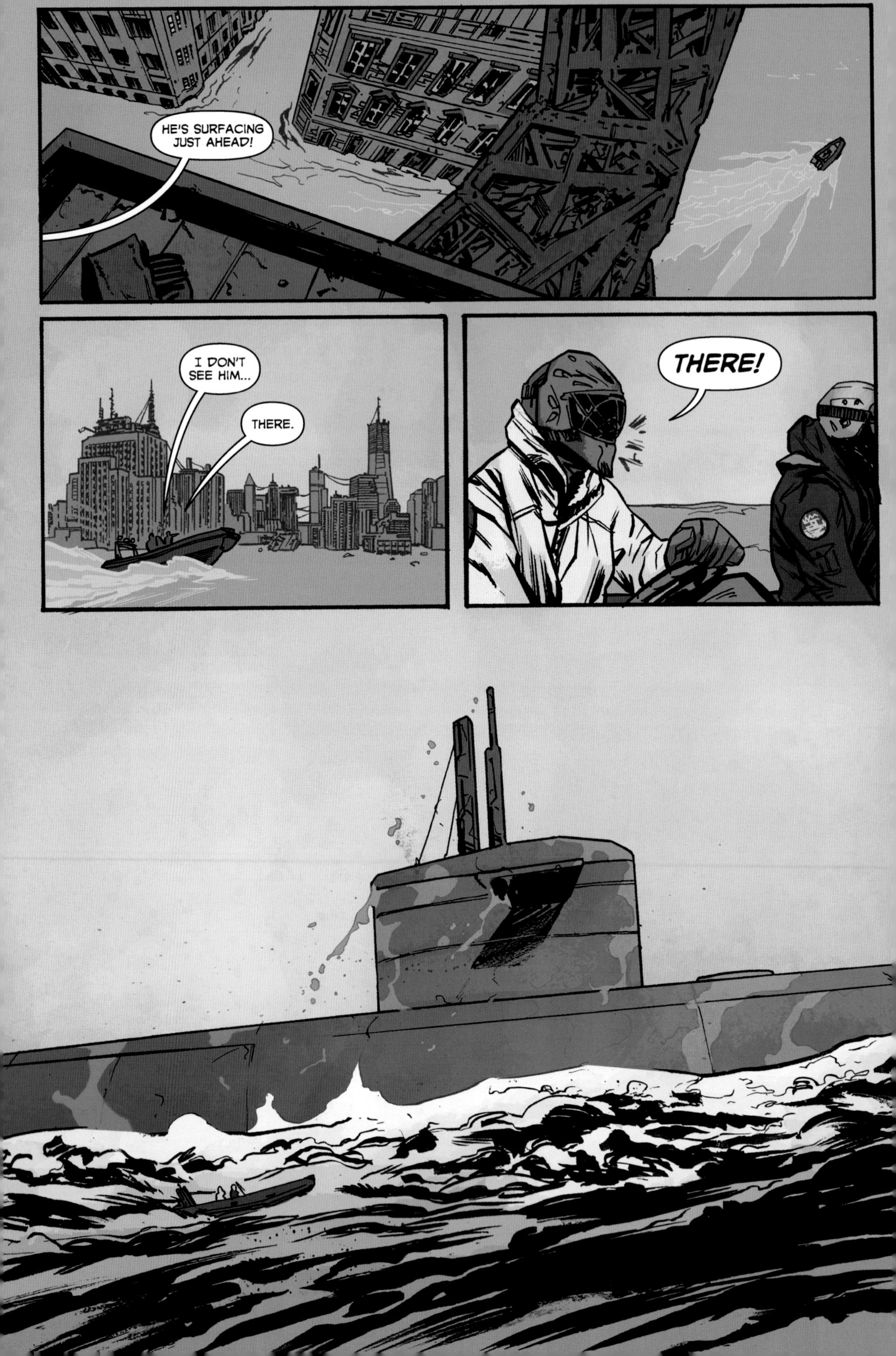
HE'S SURFACING JUST AHEAD!
I DON'T SEE HIM...
THERE.
THERE!

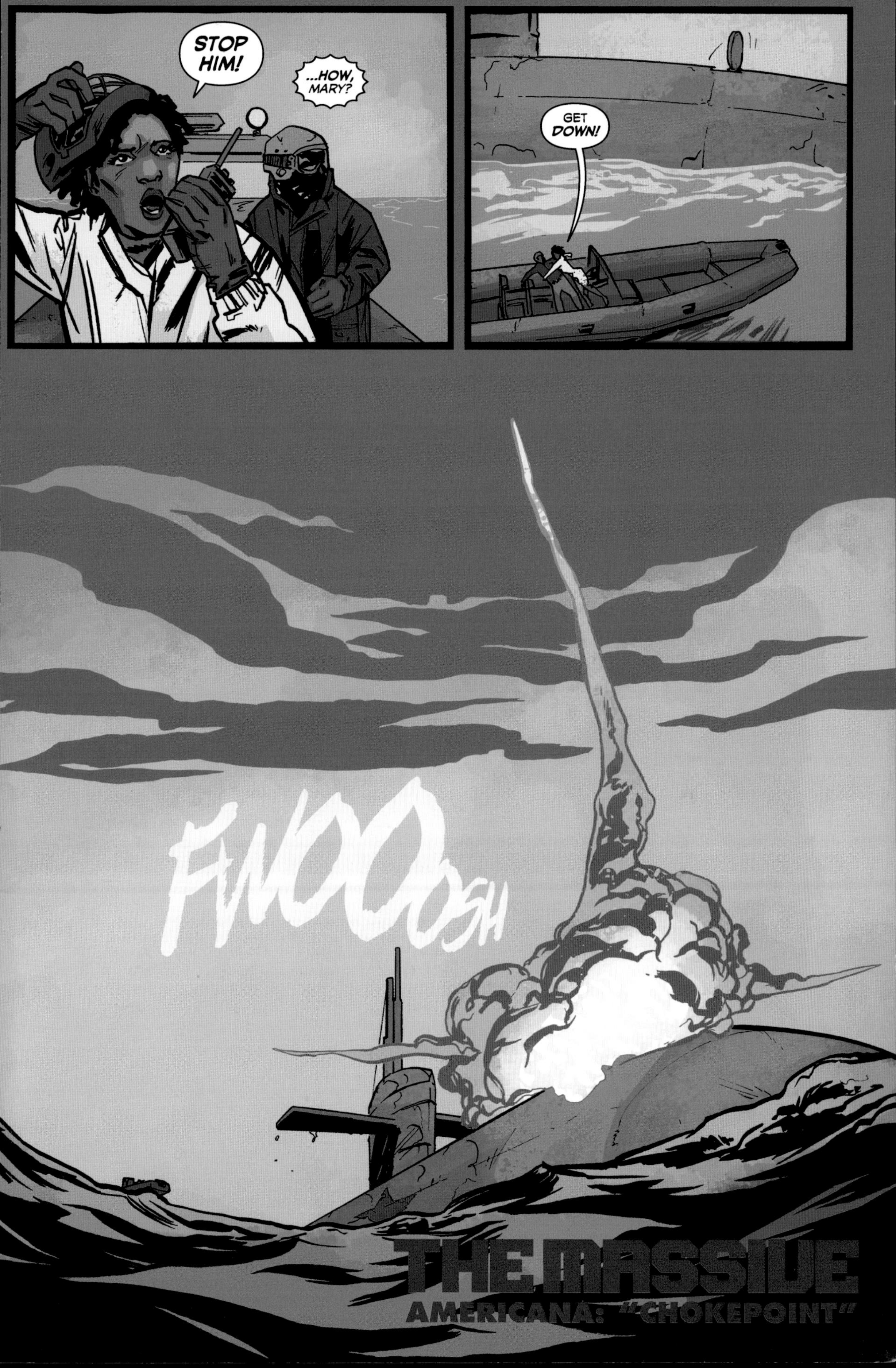
STOP HIM!
...HOW, MARY?
GET DOWN!
FWOOOSH
THE MASSIVE
AMERICANA: "CHOKEPOINT"

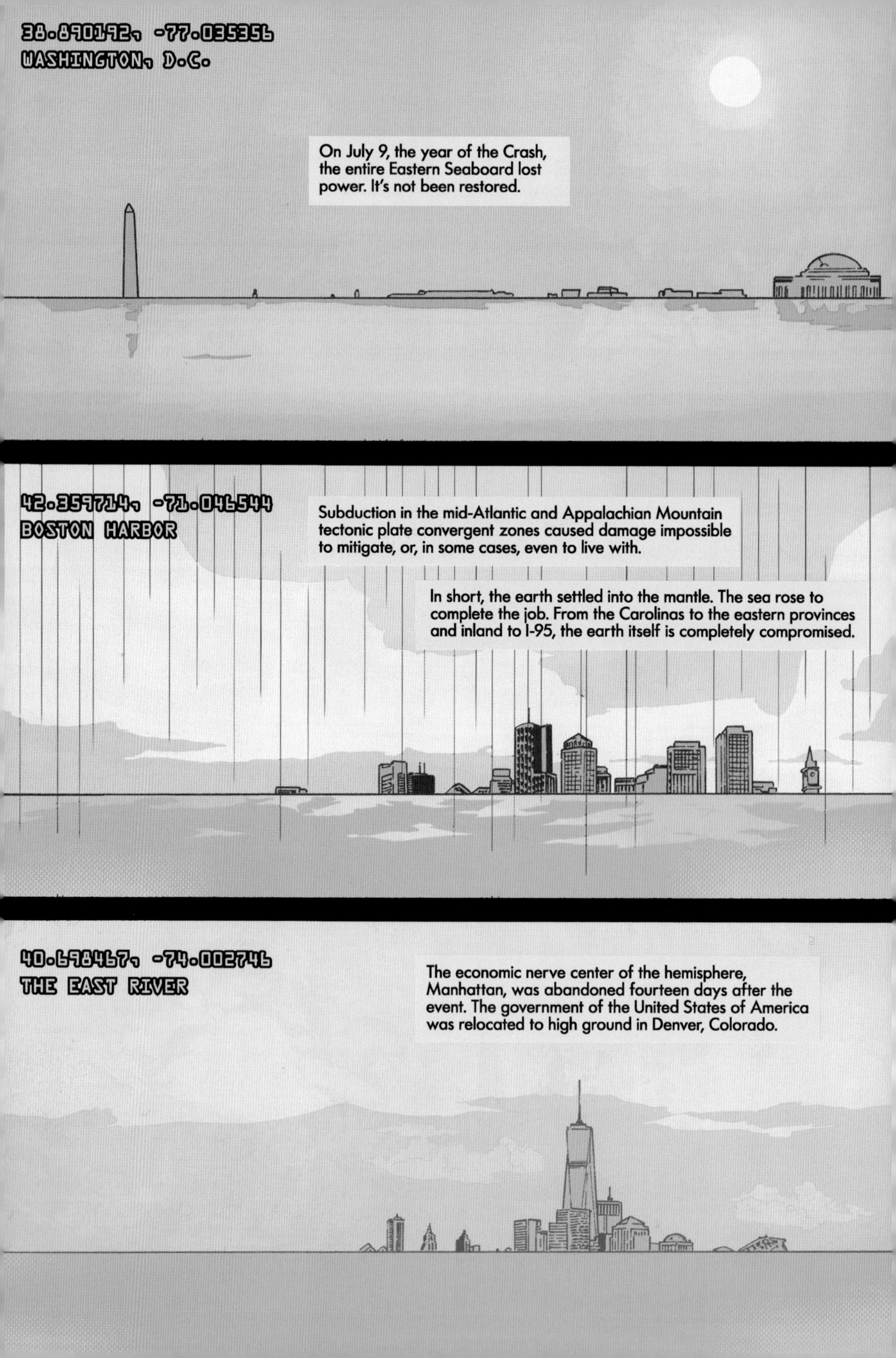

On July 9, the year of the Crash, the entire Eastern Seaboard lost power. It's not been restored.

42.359714, -71.046544
BOSTON HARBOR

Subduction in the mid-Atlantic and Appalachian Mountain tectonic plate convergent zones caused damage impossible to mitigate, or, in some cases, even to live with.

In short, the earth settled into the mantle. The sea rose to complete the job. From the Carolinas to the eastern provinces and inland to I-95, the earth itself is completely compromised.

40.678467, -74.002746
THE EAST RIVER

The economic nerve center of the hemisphere, Manhattan, was abandoned fourteen days after the event. The government of the United States of America was relocated to high ground in Denver, Colorado.

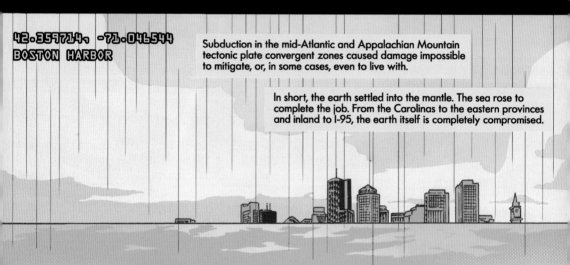

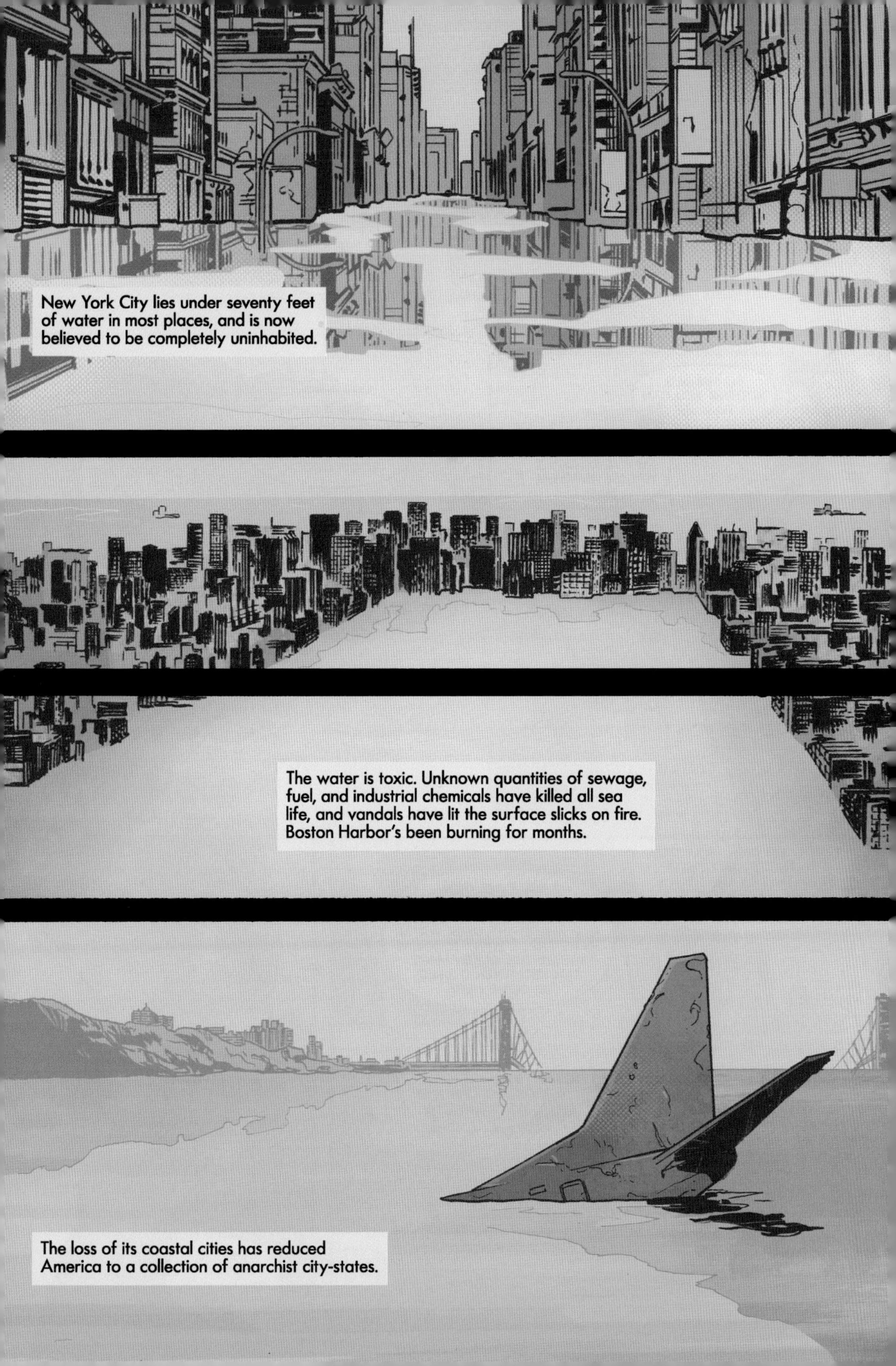
New York City lies under seventy feet of water in most places, and is now believed to be completely uninhabited.
The water is toxic. Unknown quantities of sewage, fuel, and industrial chemicals have killed all sea life, and vandals have lit the surface slicks on fire. Boston Harbor's been burning for months.
The loss of its coastal cities has reduced America to a collection of anarchist city-states.

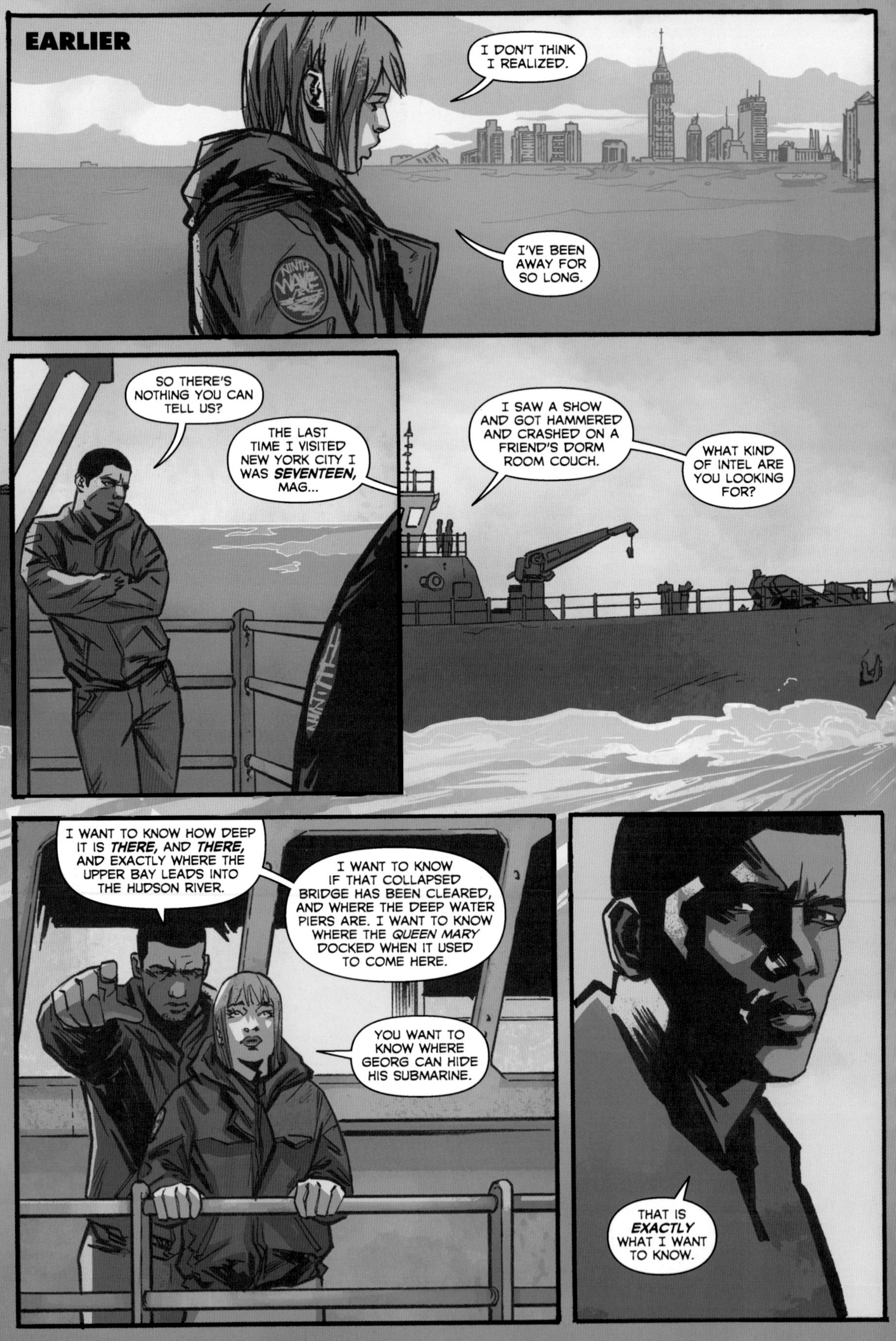
EARLIER
I DON'T THINK I REALIZED.
I'VE BEEN AWAY FOR SO LONG.
SO THERE'S NOTHING YOU CAN TELL US?
THE LAST TIME I VISITED NEW YORK CITY I WAS SEVENTEEN, MAG...
I SAW A SHOW AND GOT HAMMERED AND CRASHED ON A FRIEND'S DORM ROOM COUCH.
WHAT KIND OF INTEL ARE YOU LOOKING FOR?
I WANT TO KNOW HOW DEEP IT IS THERE, AND THERE, AND EXACTLY WHERE THE UPPER BAY LEADS INTO THE HUDSON RIVER.
I WANT TO KNOW IF THAT COLLAPSED BRIDGE HAS BEEN CLEARED, AND WHERE THE DEEP WATER PIERS ARE. I WANT TO KNOW WHERE THE QUEEN MARY DOCKED WHEN IT USED TO COME HERE.
YOU WANT TO KNOW WHERE GEORG CAN HIDE HIS SUBMARINE.
THAT IS EXACTLY WHAT I WANT TO KNOW.

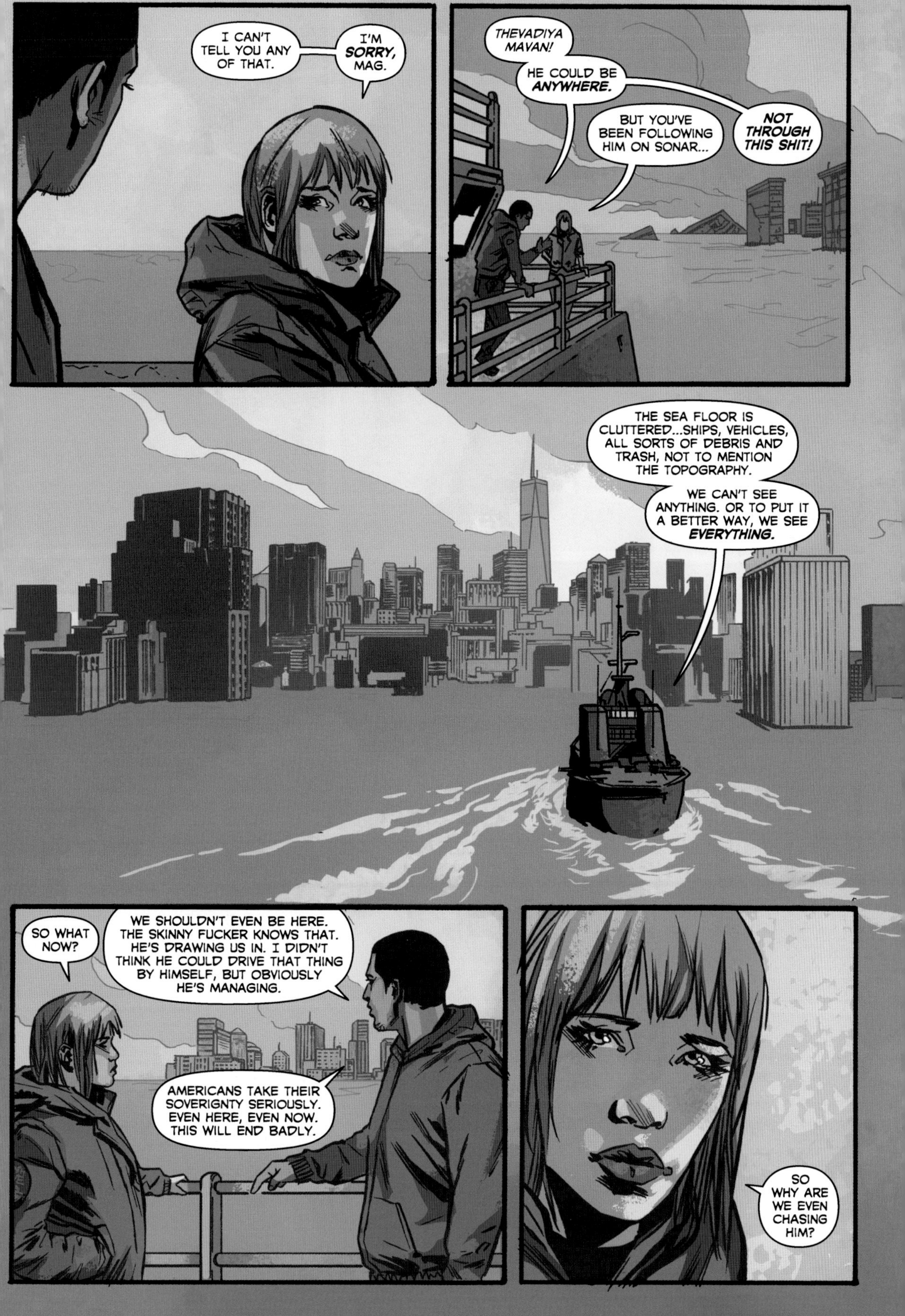

I CAN'T TELL YOU ANY OF THAT.
I'M **SORRY,** MAG.
THEVADIYA MAVAN!
HE COULD BE ***ANYWHERE.***
BUT YOU'VE BEEN FOLLOWING HIM ON SONAR...
NOT THROUGH THIS SHIT!
THE SEA FLOOR IS CLUTTERED...SHIPS, VEHICLES, ALL SORTS OF DEBRIS AND TRASH, NOT TO MENTION THE TOPOGRAPHY.
WE CAN'T SEE ANYTHING. OR TO PUT IT A BETTER WAY, WE SEE ***EVERYTHING.***
SO WHAT NOW?
WE SHOULDN'T EVEN BE HERE. THE SKINNY FUCKER KNOWS THAT. HE'S DRAWING US IN. I DIDN'T THINK HE COULD DRIVE THAT THING BY HIMSELF, BUT OBVIOUSLY HE'S MANAGING.
AMERICANS TAKE THEIR SOVERIGNTY SERIOUSLY. EVEN HERE, EVEN NOW. THIS WILL END BADLY.
SO WHY ARE WE EVEN CHASING HIM?

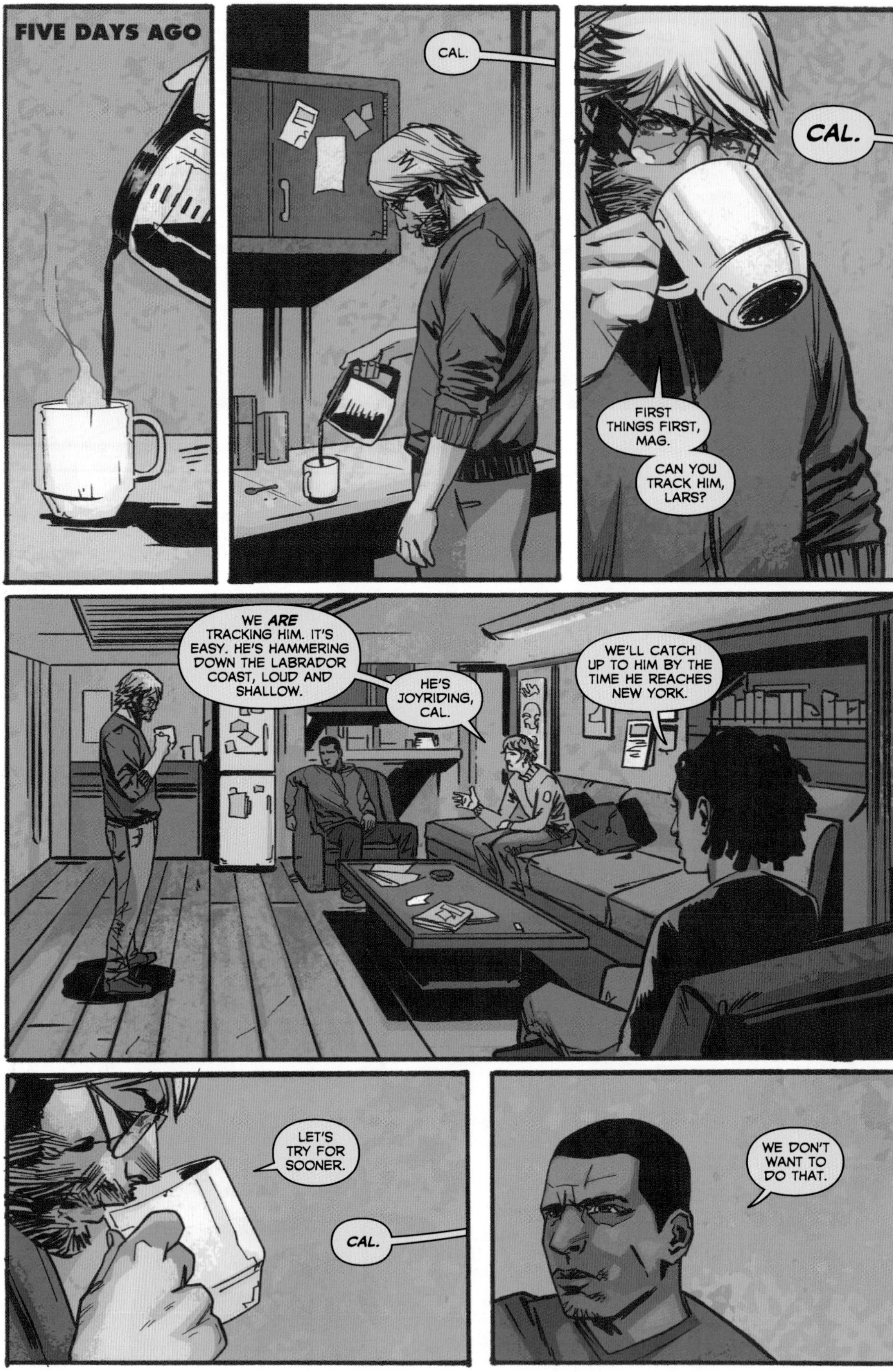
FIVE DAYS AGO
CAL.
CAL.
FIRST THINGS FIRST, MAG.
CAN YOU TRACK HIM, LARS?
WE ARE TRACKING HIM. IT'S EASY. HE'S HAMMERING DOWN THE LABRADOR COAST, LOUD AND SHALLOW.
HE'S JOYRIDING, CAL.
WE'LL CATCH UP TO HIM BY THE TIME HE REACHES NEW YORK.
LET'S TRY FOR SOONER.
CAL.
WE DON'T WANT TO DO THAT.

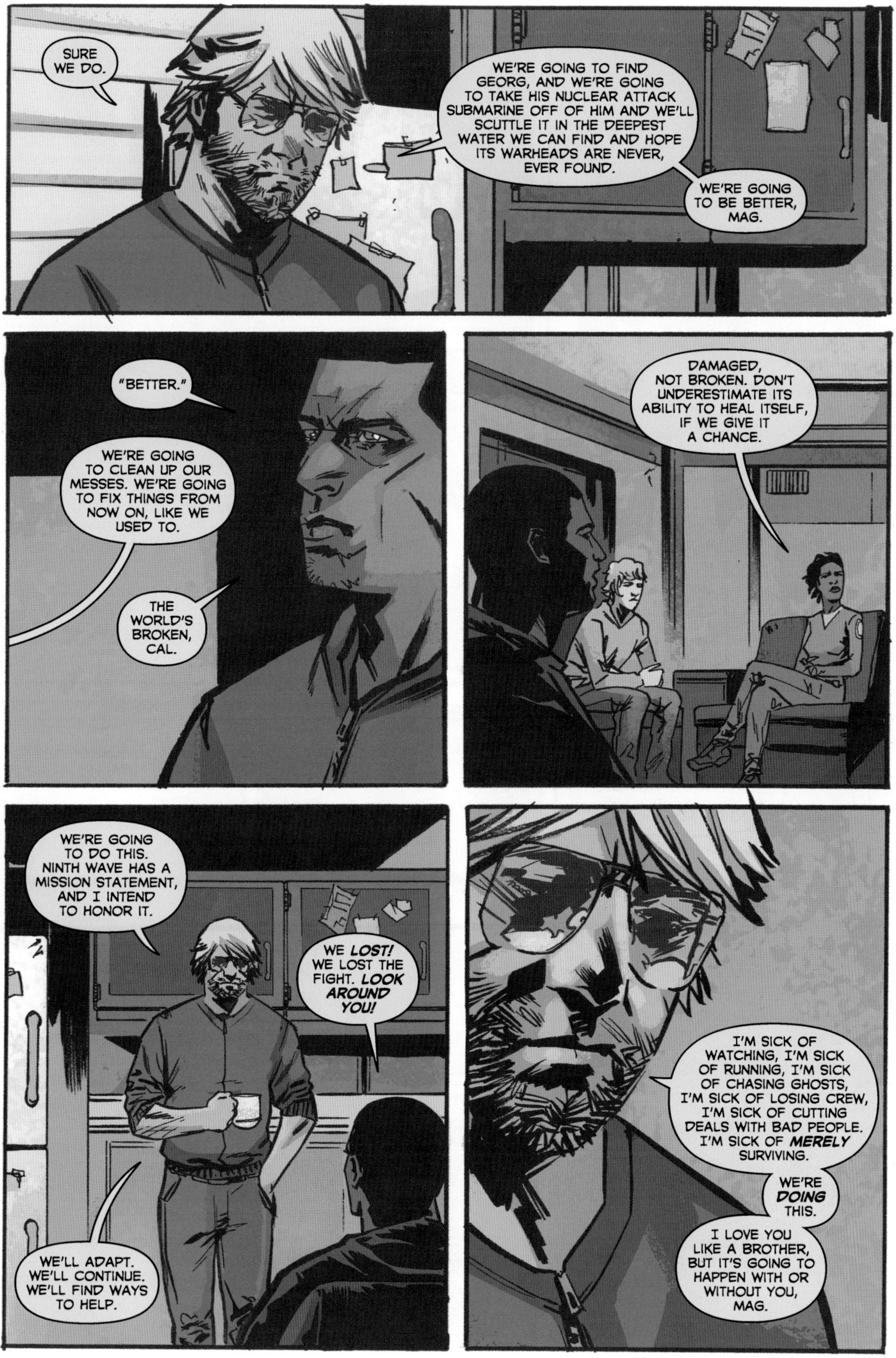
SURE WE DO.
WE'RE GOING TO FIND GEORG, AND WE'RE GOING TO TAKE HIS NUCLEAR ATTACK SUBMARINE OFF OF HIM AND WE'LL SCUTTLE IT IN THE DEEPEST WATER WE CAN FIND AND HOPE ITS WARHEADS ARE NEVER, EVER FOUND.
WE'RE GOING TO BE BETTER, MAG.
"BETTER."
WE'RE GOING TO CLEAN UP OUR MESSES. WE'RE GOING TO FIX THINGS FROM NOW ON, LIKE WE USED TO.
THE WORLD'S BROKEN, CAL.
DAMAGED, NOT BROKEN. DON'T UNDERESTIMATE ITS ABILITY TO HEAL ITSELF, IF WE GIVE IT A CHANCE.
WE'RE GOING TO DO THIS. NINTH WAVE HAS A MISSION STATEMENT, AND I INTEND TO HONOR IT.
WE ***LOST!*** WE LOST THE FIGHT. ***LOOK AROUND YOU!***
WE'LL ADAPT. WE'LL CONTINUE. WE'LL FIND WAYS TO HELP.
I'M SICK OF WATCHING, I'M SICK OF RUNNING, I'M SICK OF CHASING GHOSTS, I'M SICK OF LOSING CREW, I'M SICK OF CUTTING DEALS WITH BAD PEOPLE. I'M SICK OF ***MERELY*** SURVIVING.
WE'RE ***DOING*** THIS.
I LOVE YOU LIKE A BROTHER, BUT IT'S GOING TO HAPPEN WITH OR WITHOUT YOU, MAG.

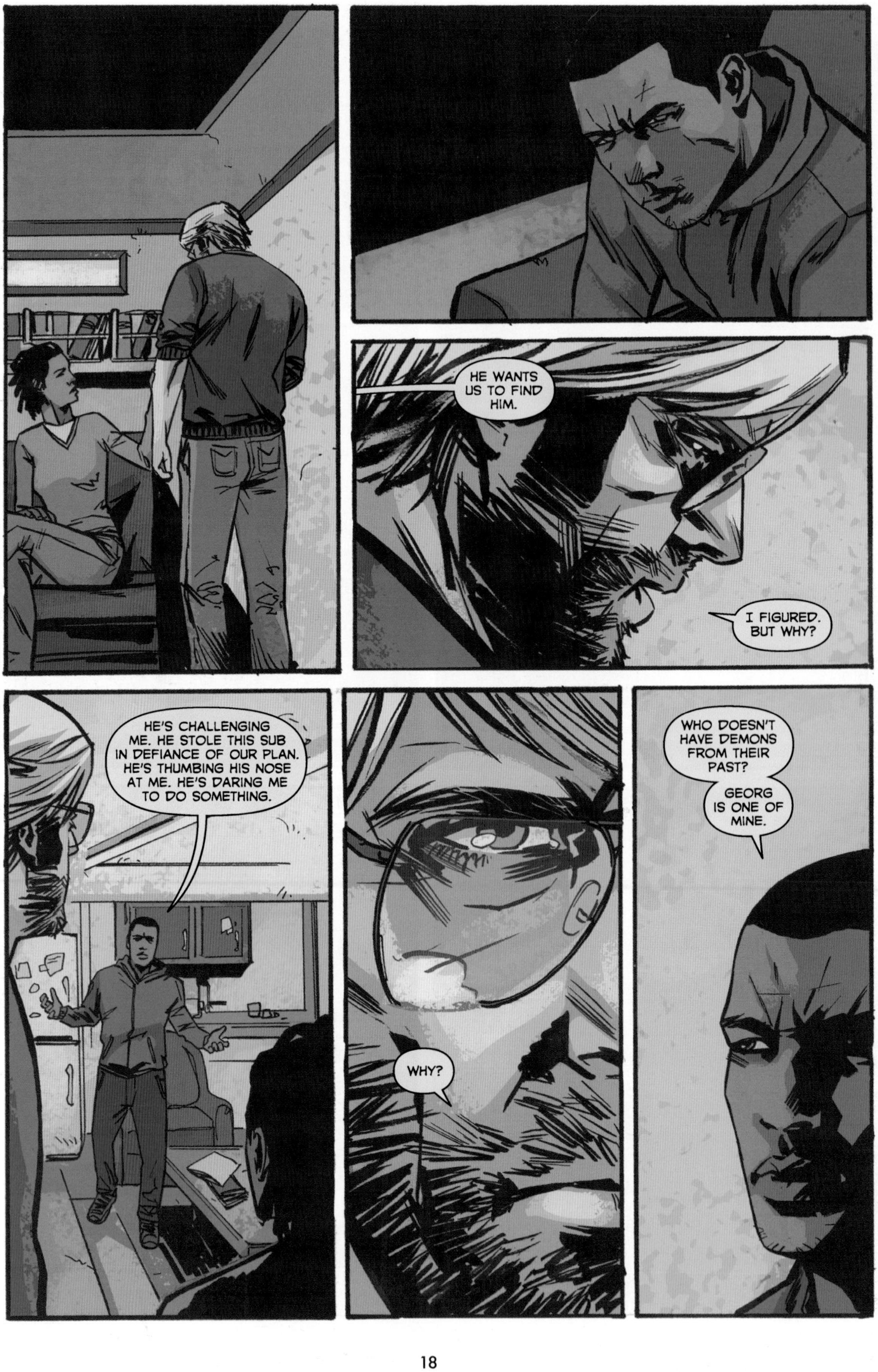
HE WANTS US TO FIND HIM.
I FIGURED. BUT WHY?
HE'S CHALLENGING ME. HE STOLE THIS SUB IN DEFIANCE OF OUR PLAN. HE'S THUMBING HIS NOSE AT ME. HE'S DARING ME TO DO SOMETHING.
WHY?
WHO DOESN'T HAVE DEMONS FROM THEIR PAST?
GEORG IS ONE OF MINE.

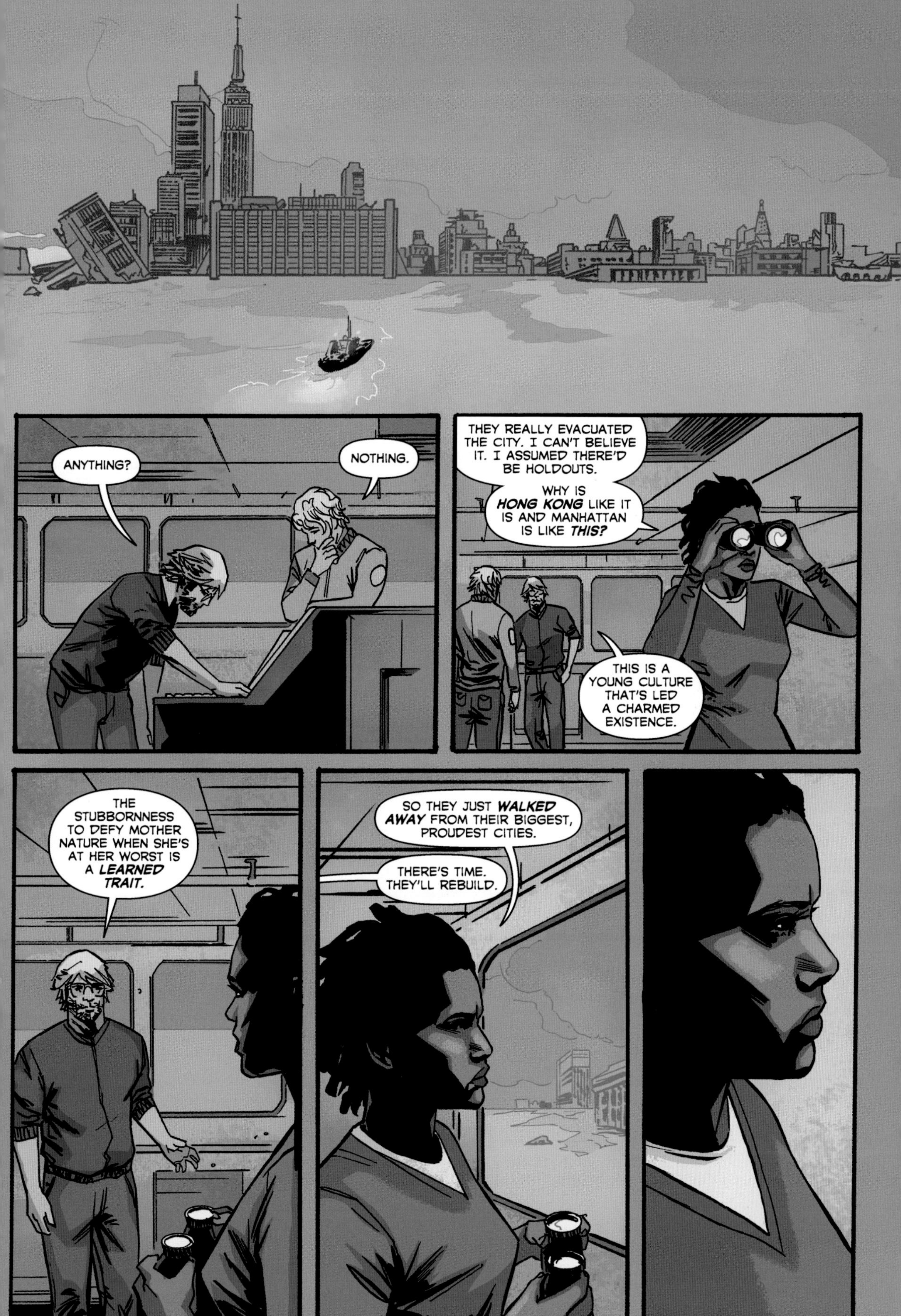
ANYTHING?
NOTHING.
THEY REALLY EVACUATED THE CITY. I CAN'T BELIEVE IT. I ASSUMED THERE'D BE HOLDOUTS.
WHY IS HONG KONG LIKE IT IS AND MANHATTAN IS LIKE THIS?
THIS IS A YOUNG CULTURE THAT'S LED A CHARMED EXISTENCE.
THE STUBBORNNESS TO DEFY MOTHER NATURE WHEN SHE'S AT HER WORST IS A LEARNED TRAIT.
SO THEY JUST WALKED AWAY FROM THEIR BIGGEST, PROUDEST CITIES.
THERE'S TIME. THEY'LL REBUILD.

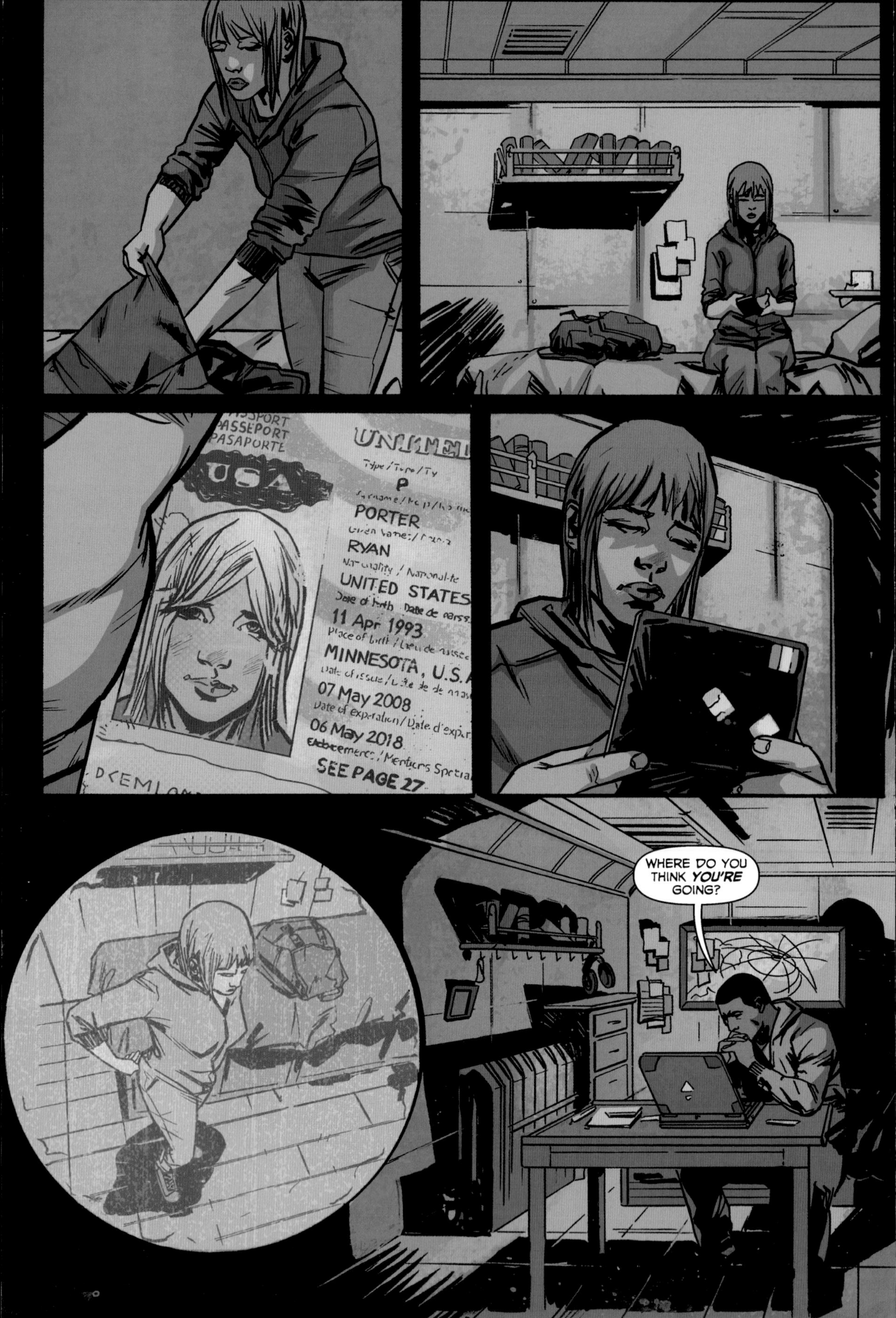
PASSEPORT
PASAPORTE
USA
PORTER
RYAN
UNITED STATES
11 Apr 1993
MINNESOTA, U.S.A
07 May 2008
06 May 2018
SEE PAGE 27
WHERE DO YOU THINK *YOU'RE* GOING?

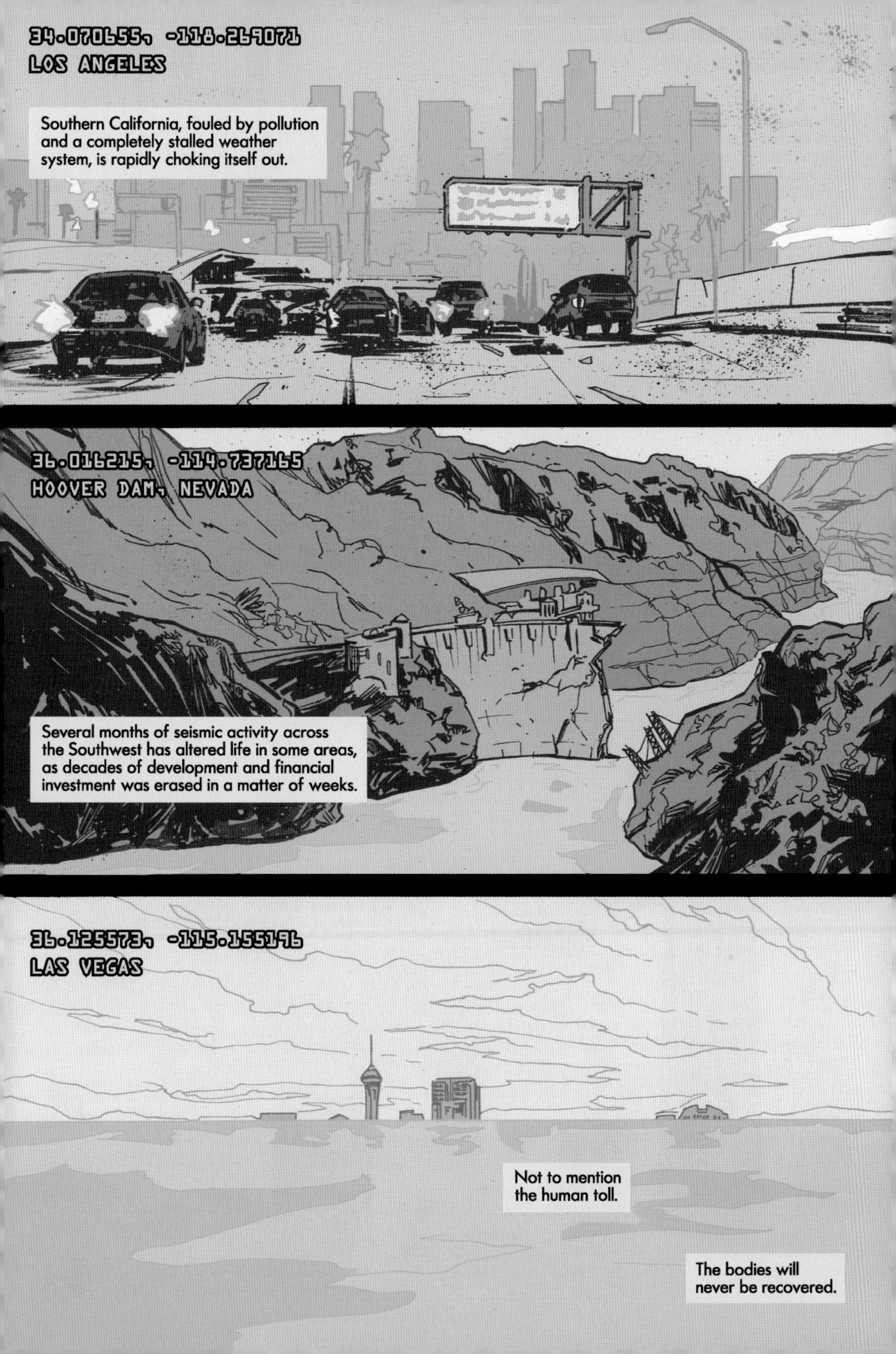
34.070655, -118.269071
LOS ANGELES
Southern California, fouled by pollution and a completely stalled weather system, is rapidly choking itself out.
36.016215, -114.737165
HOOVER DAM, NEVADA
Several months of seismic activity across the Southwest has altered life in some areas, as decades of development and financial investment was erased in a matter of weeks.
36.125573, -115.155196
LAS VEGAS
Not to mention the human toll.
The bodies will never be recovered.

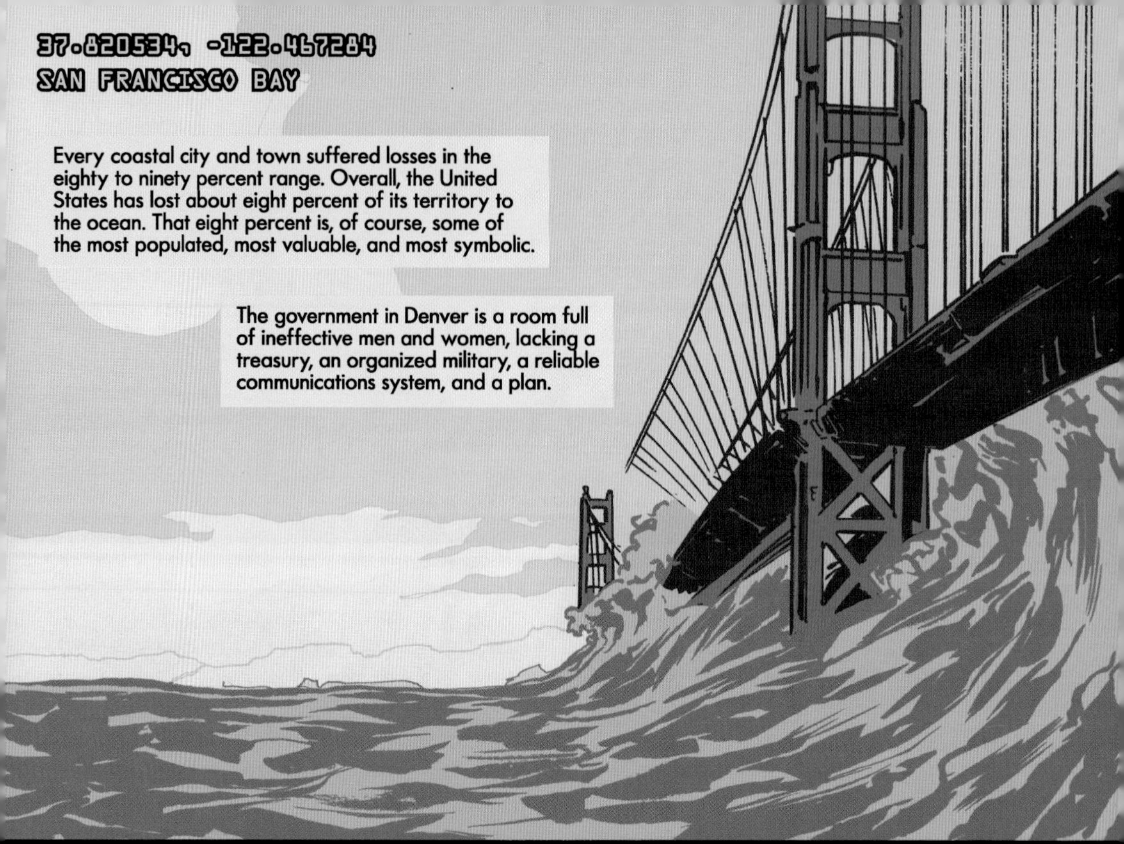
37.820534, -122.467284
SAN FRANCISCO BAY
Every coastal city and town suffered losses in the eighty to ninety percent range. Overall, the United States has lost about eight percent of its territory to the ocean. That eight percent is, of course, some of the most populated, most valuable, and most symbolic.
The government in Denver is a room full of ineffective men and women, lacking a treasury, an organized military, a reliable communications system, and a plan.

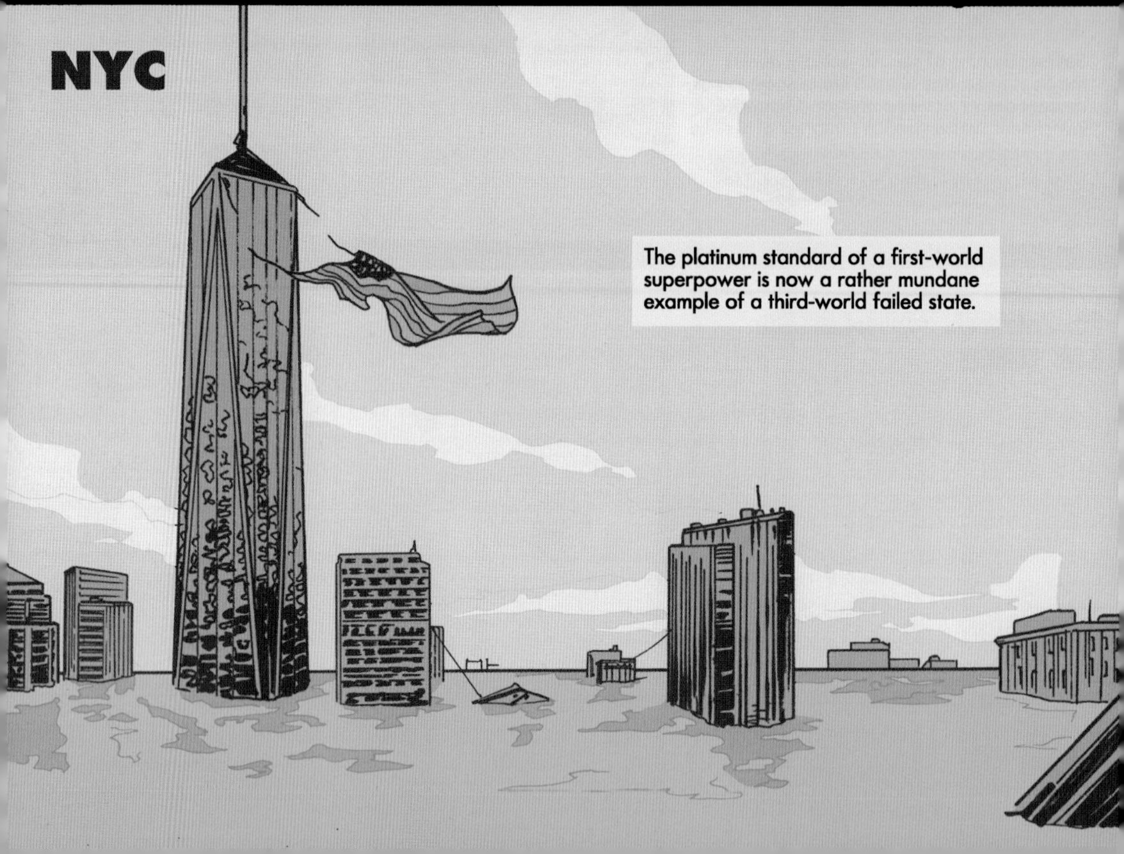
NYC
The platinum standard of a first-world superpower is now a rather mundane example of a third-world failed state.

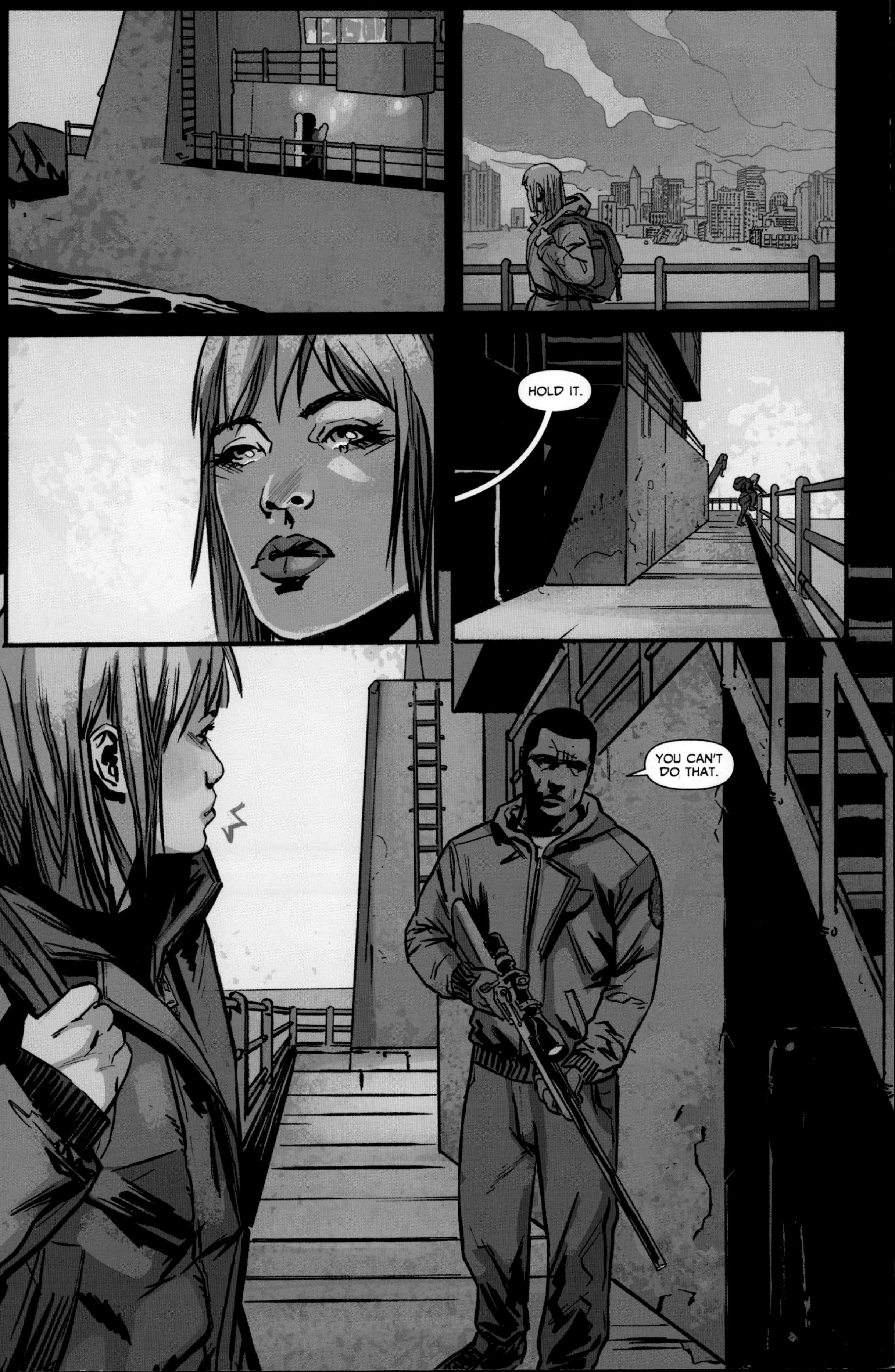
HOLD IT.
YOU CAN'T DO THAT.

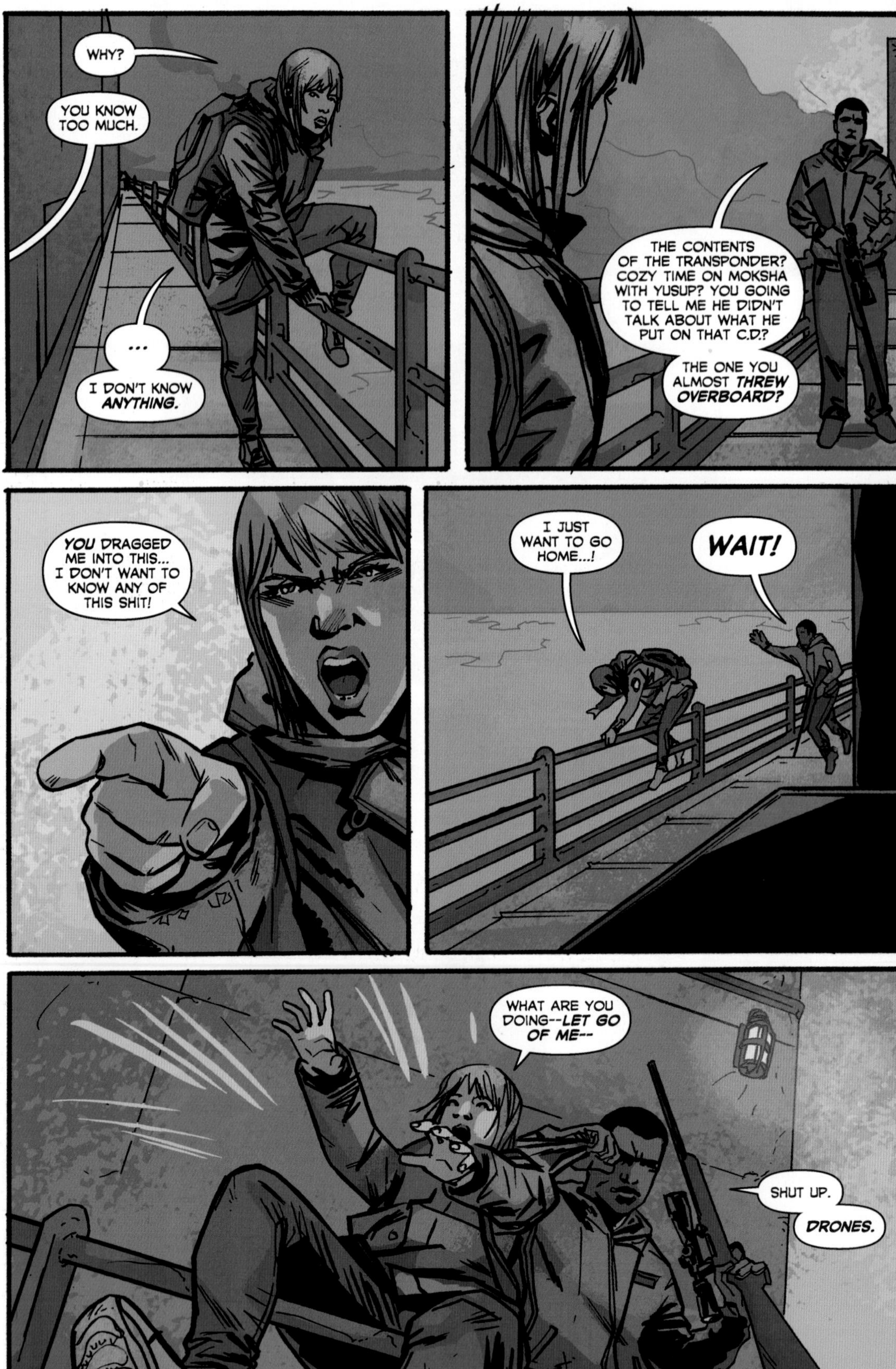
WHY?
YOU KNOW TOO MUCH.
...
I DON'T KNOW *ANYTHING.*
THE CONTENTS OF THE TRANSPONDER? COZY TIME ON MOKSHA WITH YUSUP? YOU GOING TO TELL ME HE DIDN'T TALK ABOUT WHAT HE PUT ON THAT C.D.?
THE ONE YOU ALMOST *THREW OVERBOARD?*
YOU DRAGGED ME INTO THIS... I DON'T WANT TO KNOW ANY OF THIS SHIT!
I JUST WANT TO GO HOME...!
WAIT!
WHAT ARE YOU DOING--*LET GO OF ME--*
SHUT UP.
DRONES.

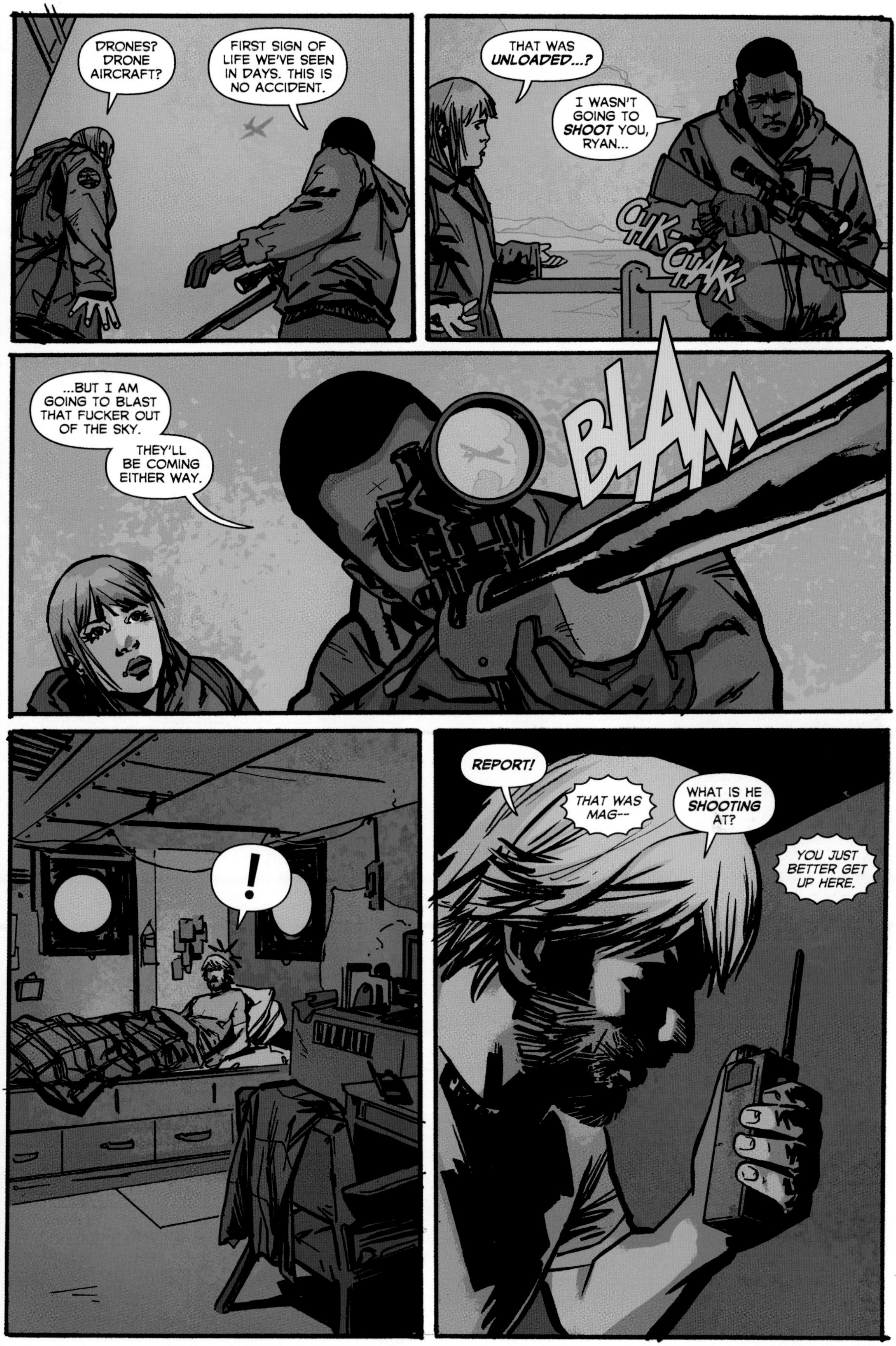
DRONES? DRONE AIRCRAFT?
FIRST SIGN OF LIFE WE'VE SEEN IN DAYS. THIS IS NO ACCIDENT.
THAT WAS UNLOADED...?
I WASN'T GOING TO SHOOT YOU, RYAN...
CHK-CHAKK
...BUT I AM GOING TO BLAST THAT FUCKER OUT OF THE SKY.
THEY'LL BE COMING EITHER WAY.
BLAM
!
REPORT!
THAT WAS MAG--
WHAT IS HE SHOOTING AT?
YOU JUST BETTER GET UP HERE.

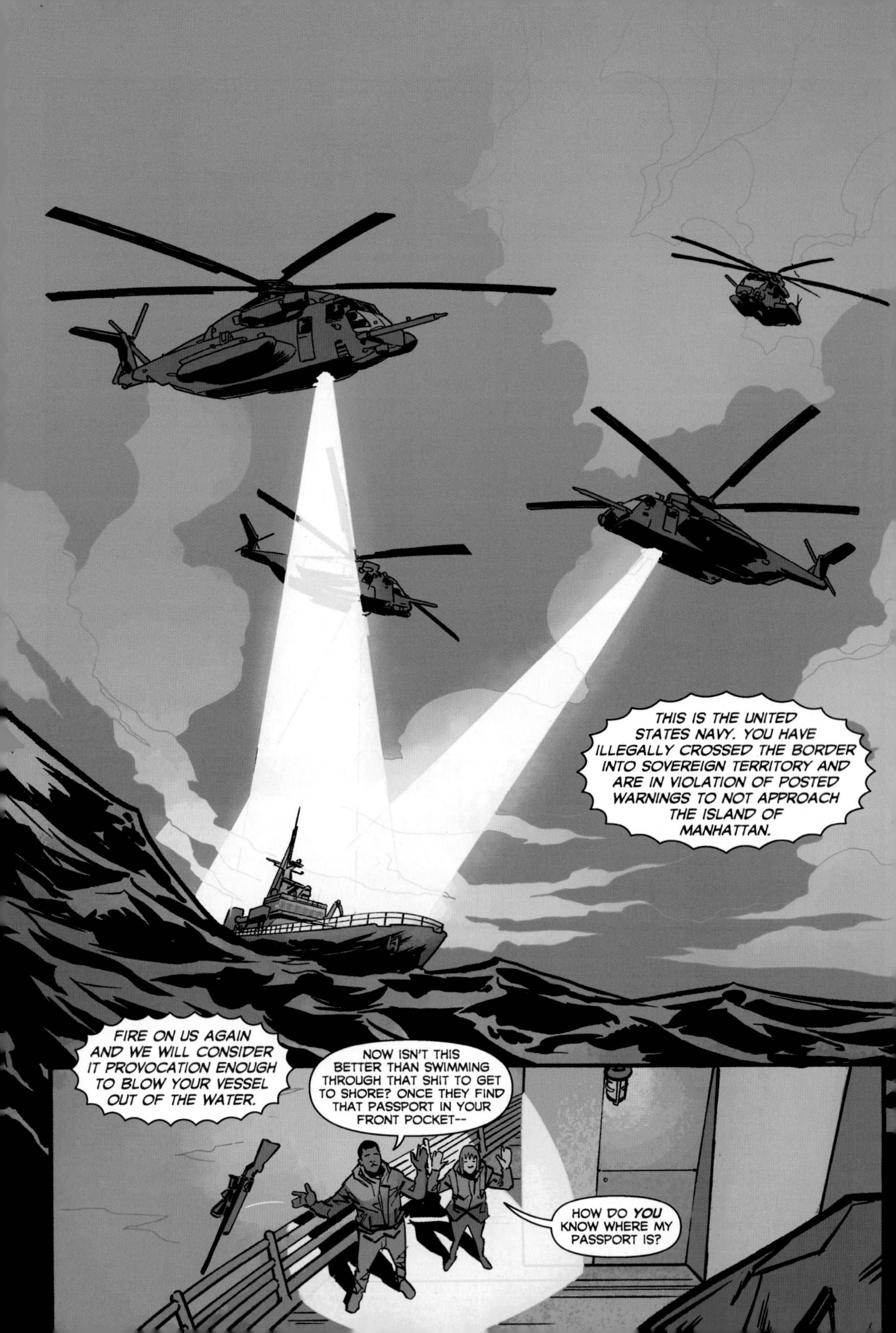
THIS IS THE UNITED STATES NAVY. YOU HAVE ILLEGALLY CROSSED THE BORDER INTO SOVEREIGN TERRITORY AND ARE IN VIOLATION OF POSTED WARNINGS TO NOT APPROACH THE ISLAND OF MANHATTAN.
FIRE ON US AGAIN AND WE WILL CONSIDER IT PROVOCATION ENOUGH TO BLOW YOUR VESSEL OUT OF THE WATER.
NOW ISN'T THIS BETTER THAN SWIMMING THROUGH THAT SHIT TO GET TO SHORE? ONCE THEY FIND THAT PASSPORT IN YOUR FRONT POCKET--
HOW DO *YOU* KNOW WHERE MY PASSPORT IS?

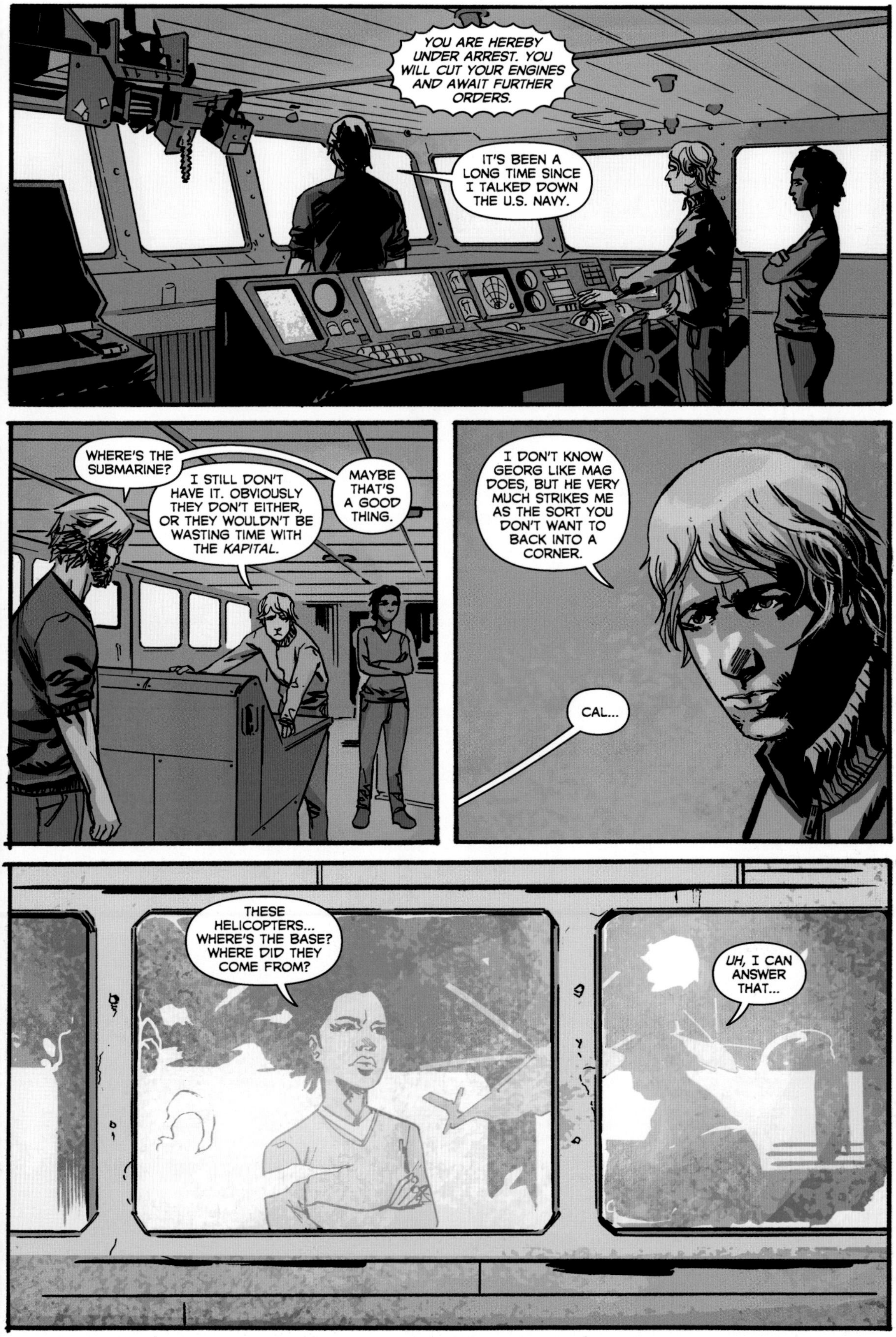
YOU ARE HEREBY UNDER ARREST. YOU WILL CUT YOUR ENGINES AND AWAIT FURTHER ORDERS.
IT'S BEEN A LONG TIME SINCE I TALKED DOWN THE U.S. NAVY.
WHERE'S THE SUBMARINE?
I STILL DON'T HAVE IT. OBVIOUSLY THEY DON'T EITHER, OR THEY WOULDN'T BE WASTING TIME WITH THE *KAPITAL.*
MAYBE THAT'S A GOOD THING.
I DON'T KNOW GEORG LIKE MAG DOES, BUT HE VERY MUCH STRIKES ME AS THE SORT YOU DON'T WANT TO BACK INTO A CORNER.
CAL...
THESE HELICOPTERS... WHERE'S THE BASE? WHERE DID THEY COME FROM?
UH, I CAN ANSWER THAT...

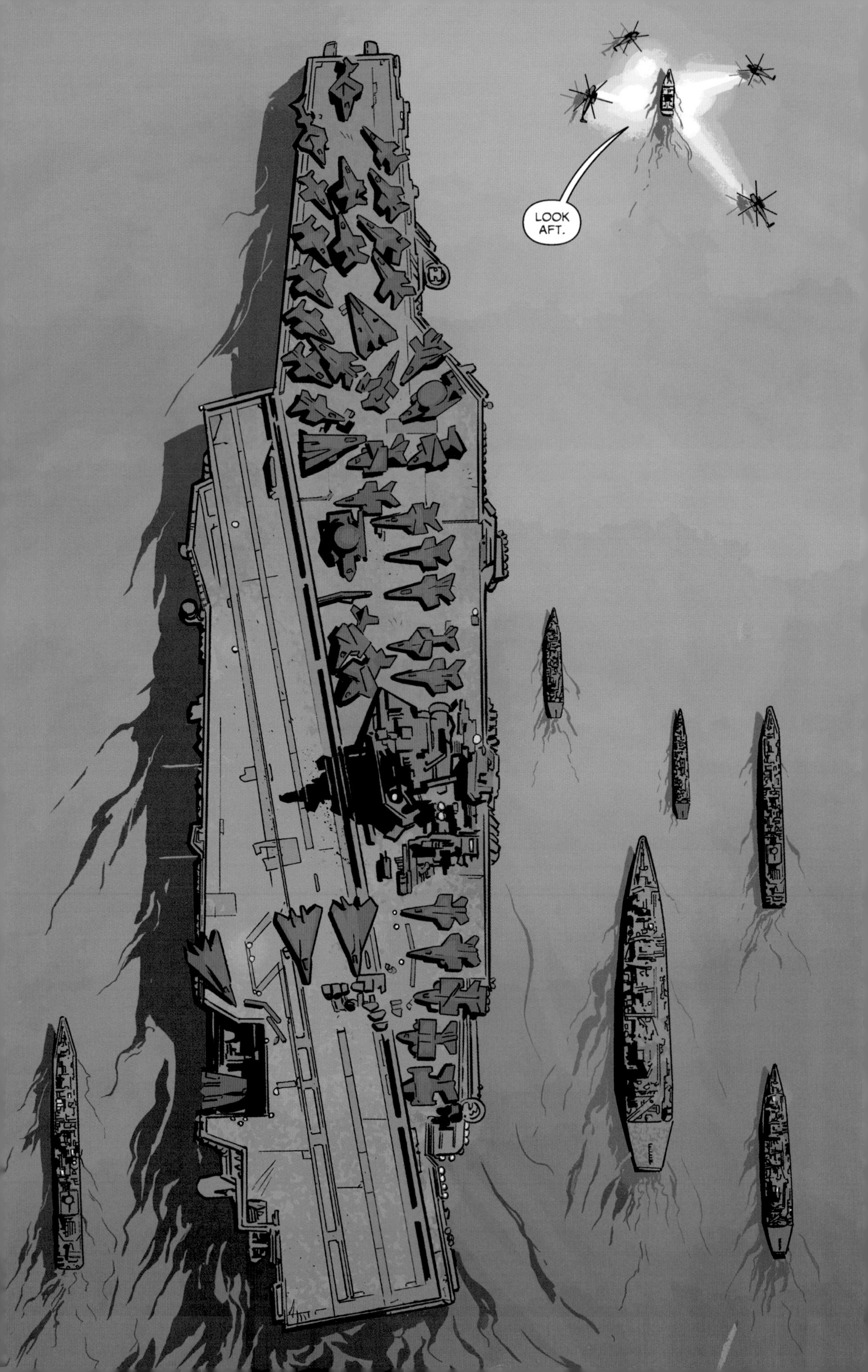
LOOK AFT.

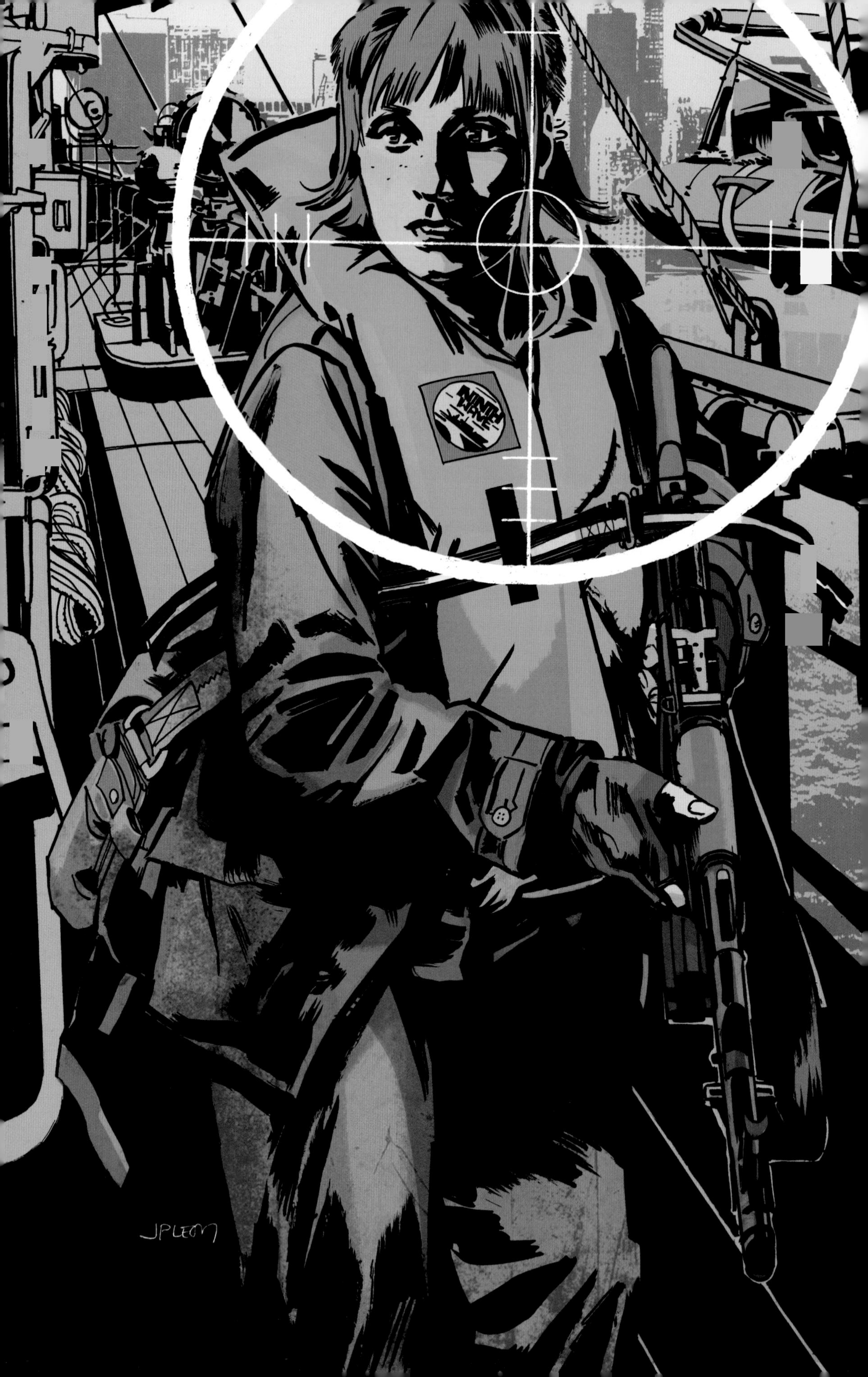
NINTH WAVE
JPLEON

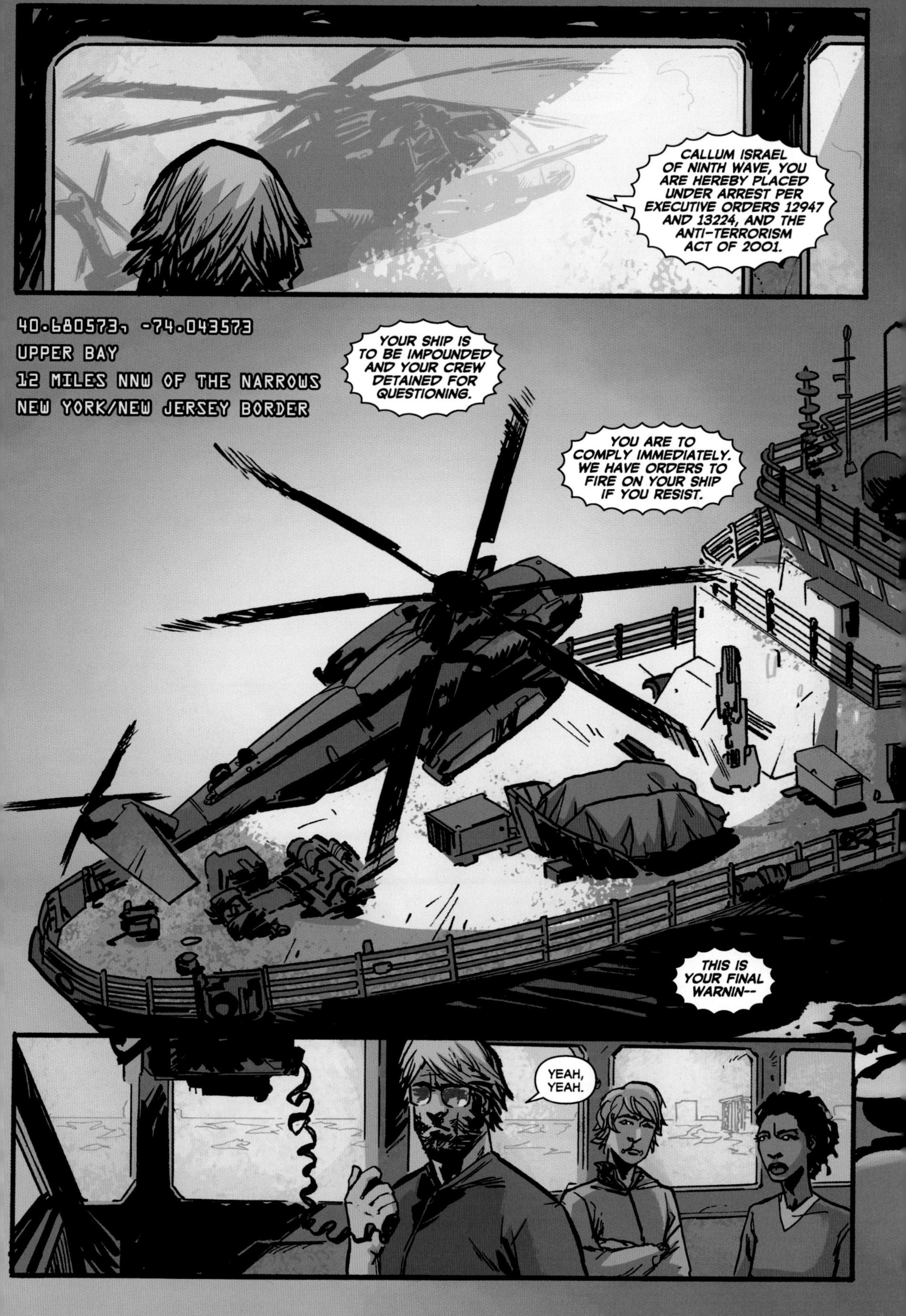
CALLUM ISRAEL OF NINTH WAVE, YOU ARE HEREBY PLACED UNDER ARREST PER EXECUTIVE ORDERS 12947 AND 13224, AND THE ANTI-TERRORISM ACT OF 2001.
40.680573, -74.043573
UPPER BAY
12 MILES NNW OF THE NARROWS
NEW YORK/NEW JERSEY BORDER
YOUR SHIP IS TO BE IMPOUNDED AND YOUR CREW DETAINED FOR QUESTIONING.
YOU ARE TO COMPLY IMMEDIATELY. WE HAVE ORDERS TO FIRE ON YOUR SHIP IF YOU RESIST.
THIS IS YOUR FINAL WARNIN--
YEAH, YEAH.

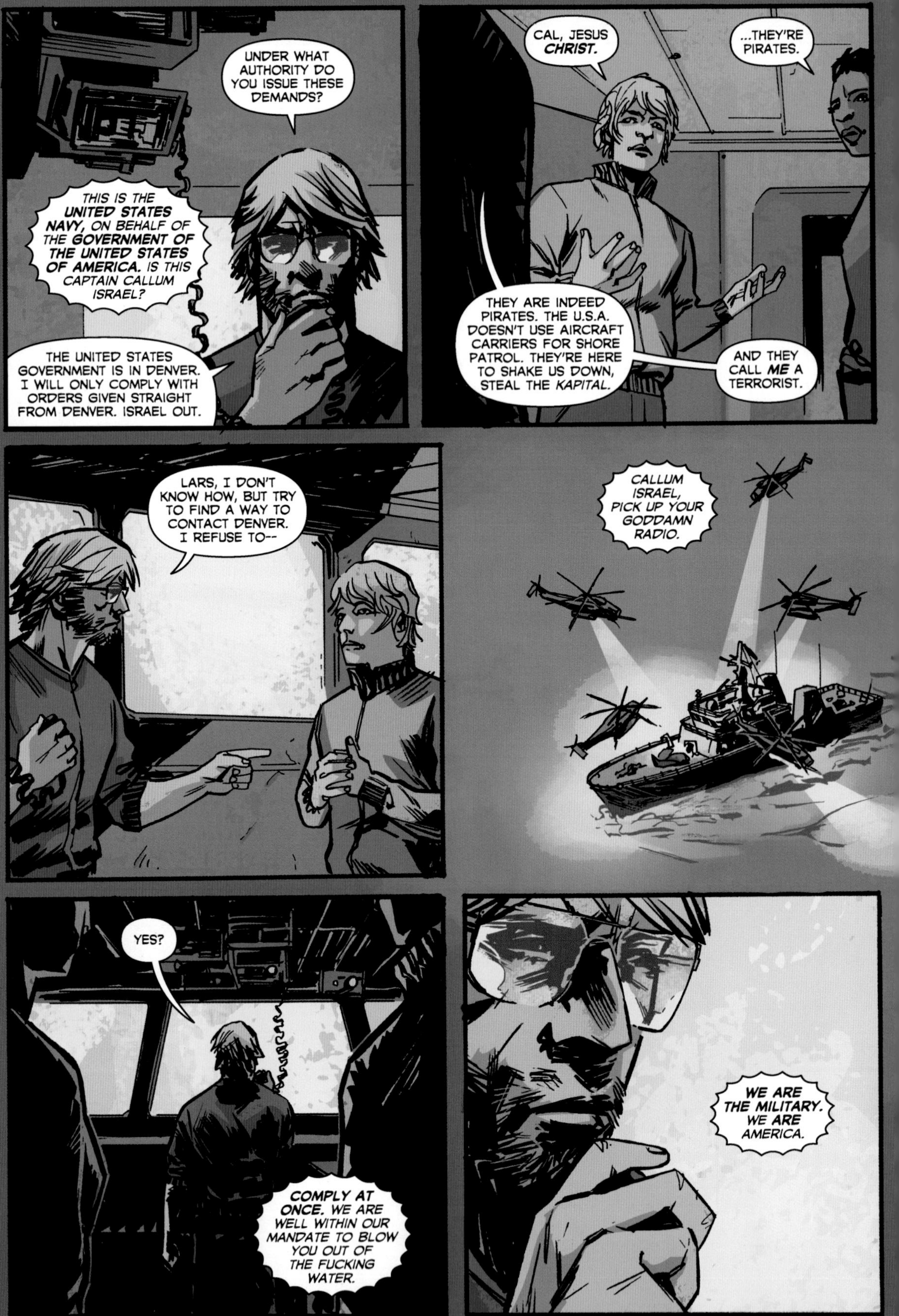
UNDER WHAT AUTHORITY DO YOU ISSUE THESE DEMANDS?
THIS IS THE UNITED STATES NAVY, ON BEHALF OF THE GOVERNMENT OF THE UNITED STATES OF AMERICA. IS THIS CAPTAIN CALLUM ISRAEL?
THE UNITED STATES GOVERNMENT IS IN DENVER. I WILL ONLY COMPLY WITH ORDERS GIVEN STRAIGHT FROM DENVER. ISRAEL OUT.
CAL, JESUS CHRIST.
...THEY'RE PIRATES.
THEY ARE INDEED PIRATES. THE U.S.A. DOESN'T USE AIRCRAFT CARRIERS FOR SHORE PATROL. THEY'RE HERE TO SHAKE US DOWN, STEAL THE KAPITAL.
AND THEY CALL ME A TERRORIST.
LARS, I DON'T KNOW HOW, BUT TRY TO FIND A WAY TO CONTACT DENVER. I REFUSE TO--
CALLUM ISRAEL, PICK UP YOUR GODDAMN RADIO.
YES?
COMPLY AT ONCE. WE ARE WELL WITHIN OUR MANDATE TO BLOW YOU OUT OF THE FUCKING WATER.
WE ARE THE MILITARY. WE ARE AMERICA.

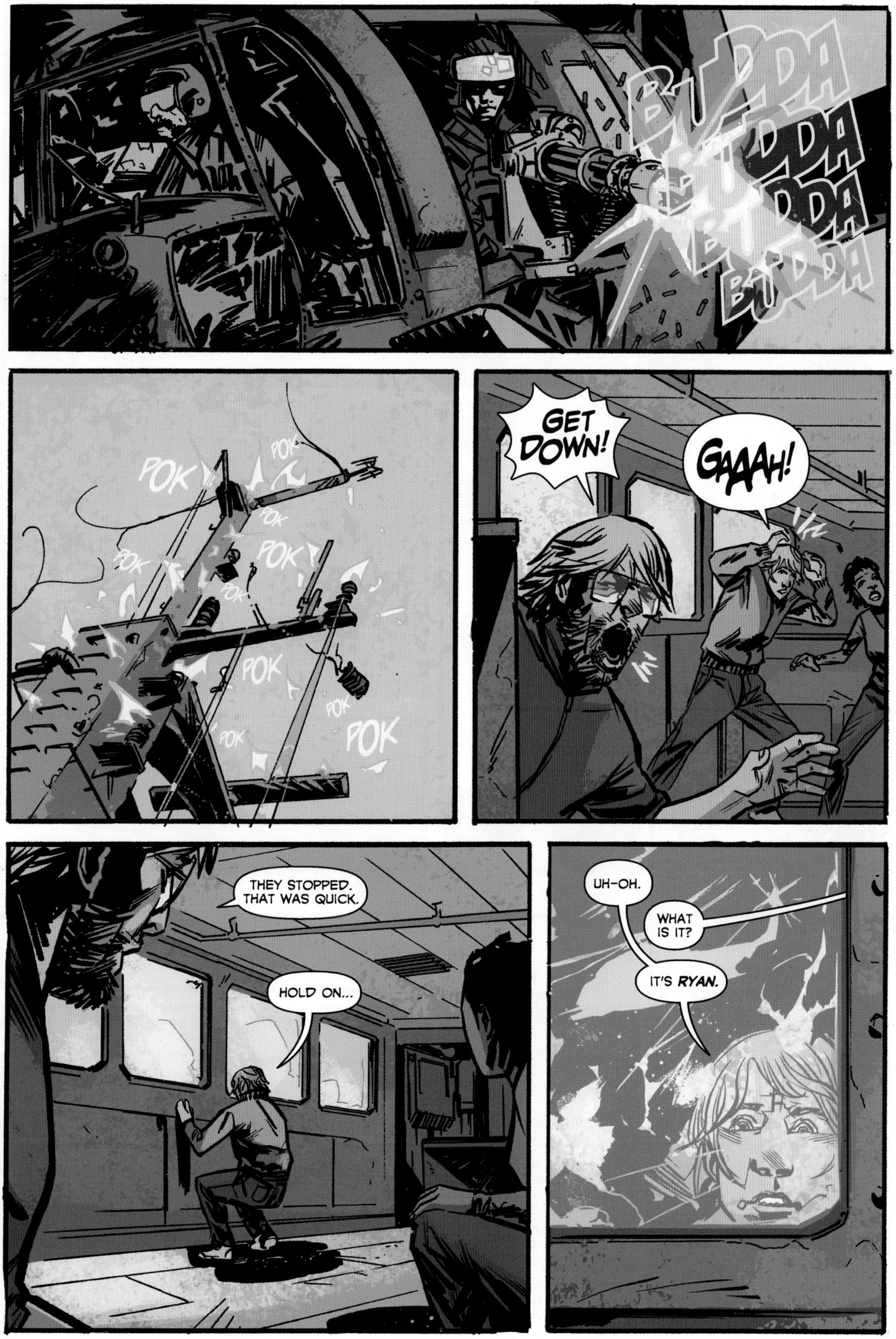
BUDDA BUDDA BUDDA BUDDA
POK POK POK POK POK POK POK POK POK
GET DOWN!
GAAAH!
THEY STOPPED. THAT WAS QUICK.
HOLD ON...
UH-OH.
WHAT IS IT?
IT'S *RYAN.*

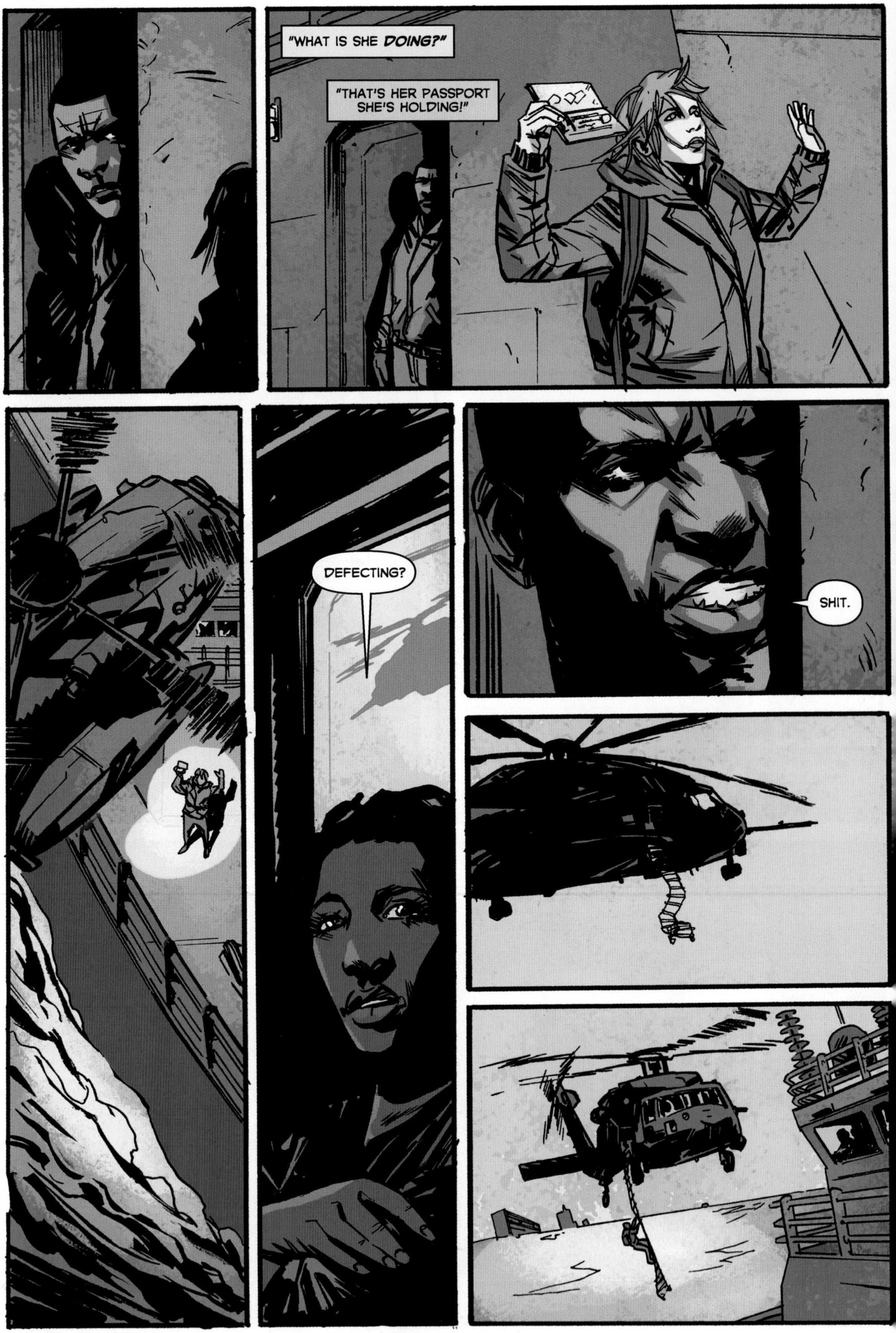
"WHAT IS SHE DOING?"
"THAT'S HER PASSPORT SHE'S HOLDING!"
DEFECTING?
SHIT.

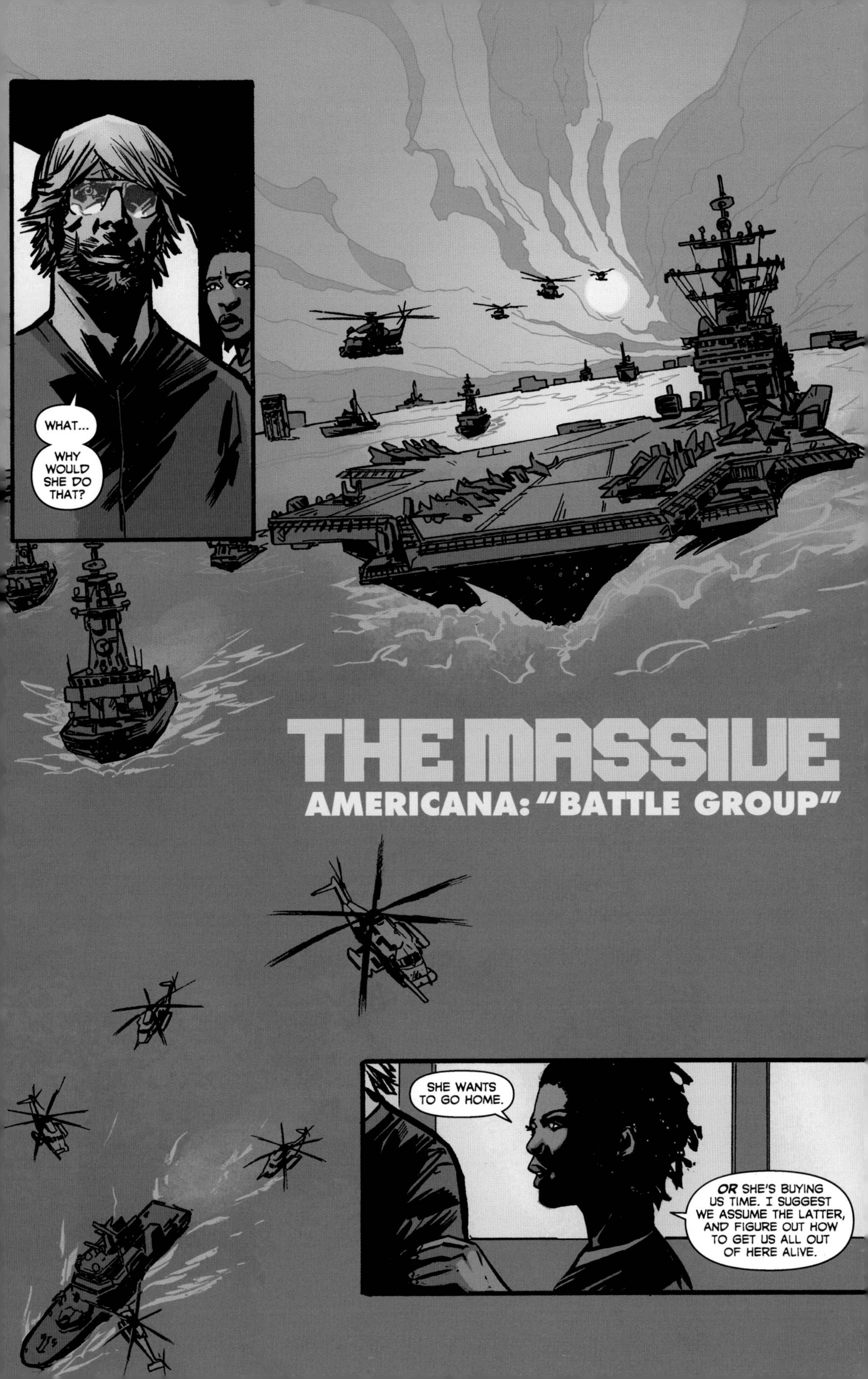
WHAT...
WHY WOULD SHE DO THAT?
THE MASSIVE
AMERICANA: "BATTLE GROUP"
SHE WANTS TO GO HOME.
OR SHE'S BUYING US TIME. I SUGGEST WE ASSUME THE LATTER, AND FIGURE OUT HOW TO GET US ALL OUT OF HERE ALIVE.

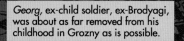

Georg, ex-child soldier, ex-Brodyagi, was about as far removed from his childhood in Grozny as is possible.

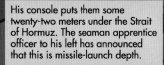

His console puts them some twenty-two meters under the Strait of Hormuz. The seaman apprentice officer to his left has announced that this is missile-launch depth.

This is a Tariq-class submarine retrofitted to hold nuclear arms.

They have their target.

Enemy contacts closing. They have mere seconds.

Georg hears the captain order the missile tubes flooded, and the doors opened.

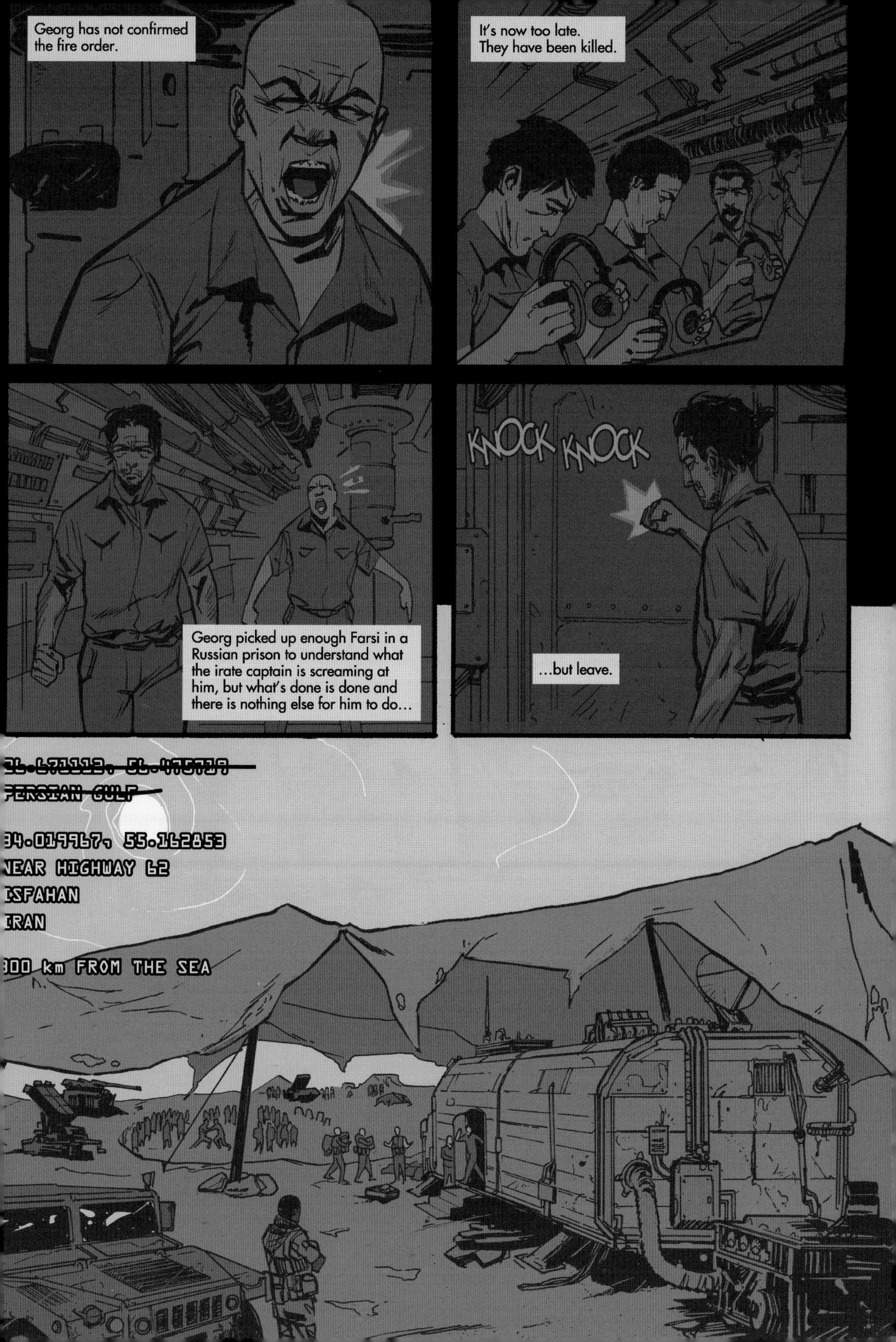
Georg has not confirmed the fire order.
It's now too late. They have been killed.
Georg picked up enough Farsi in a Russian prison to understand what the irate captain is screaming at him, but what's done is done and there is nothing else for him to do…
KNOCK KNOCK
…but leave.
~~6.671112, 56.475719~~
~~PERSIAN GULF~~
34.019967, 55.162853
NEAR HIGHWAY 62
ISFAHAN
IRAN
300 km FROM THE SEA

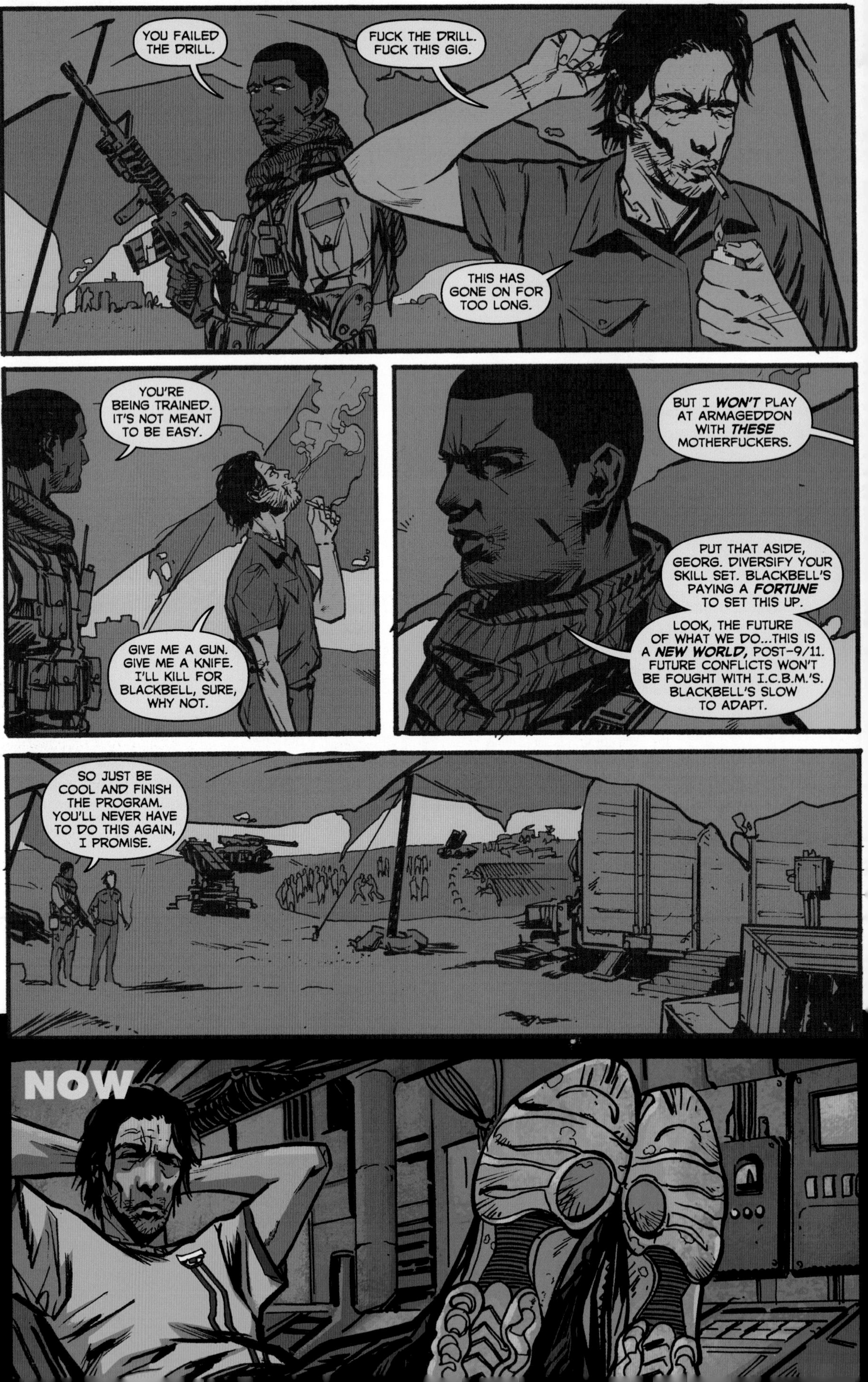
YOU FAILED THE DRILL.
FUCK THE DRILL. FUCK THIS GIG.
THIS HAS GONE ON FOR TOO LONG.
YOU'RE BEING TRAINED. IT'S NOT MEANT TO BE EASY.
GIVE ME A GUN. GIVE ME A KNIFE. I'LL KILL FOR BLACKBELL, SURE, WHY NOT.
BUT I WON'T PLAY AT ARMAGEDDON WITH THESE MOTHERFUCKERS.
PUT THAT ASIDE, GEORG. DIVERSIFY YOUR SKILL SET. BLACKBELL'S PAYING A FORTUNE TO SET THIS UP.
LOOK, THE FUTURE OF WHAT WE DO...THIS IS A NEW WORLD, POST-9/11. FUTURE CONFLICTS WON'T BE FOUGHT WITH I.C.B.M.'S. BLACKBELL'S SLOW TO ADAPT.
SO JUST BE COOL AND FINISH THE PROGRAM. YOU'LL NEVER HAVE TO DO THIS AGAIN, I PROMISE.
NOW

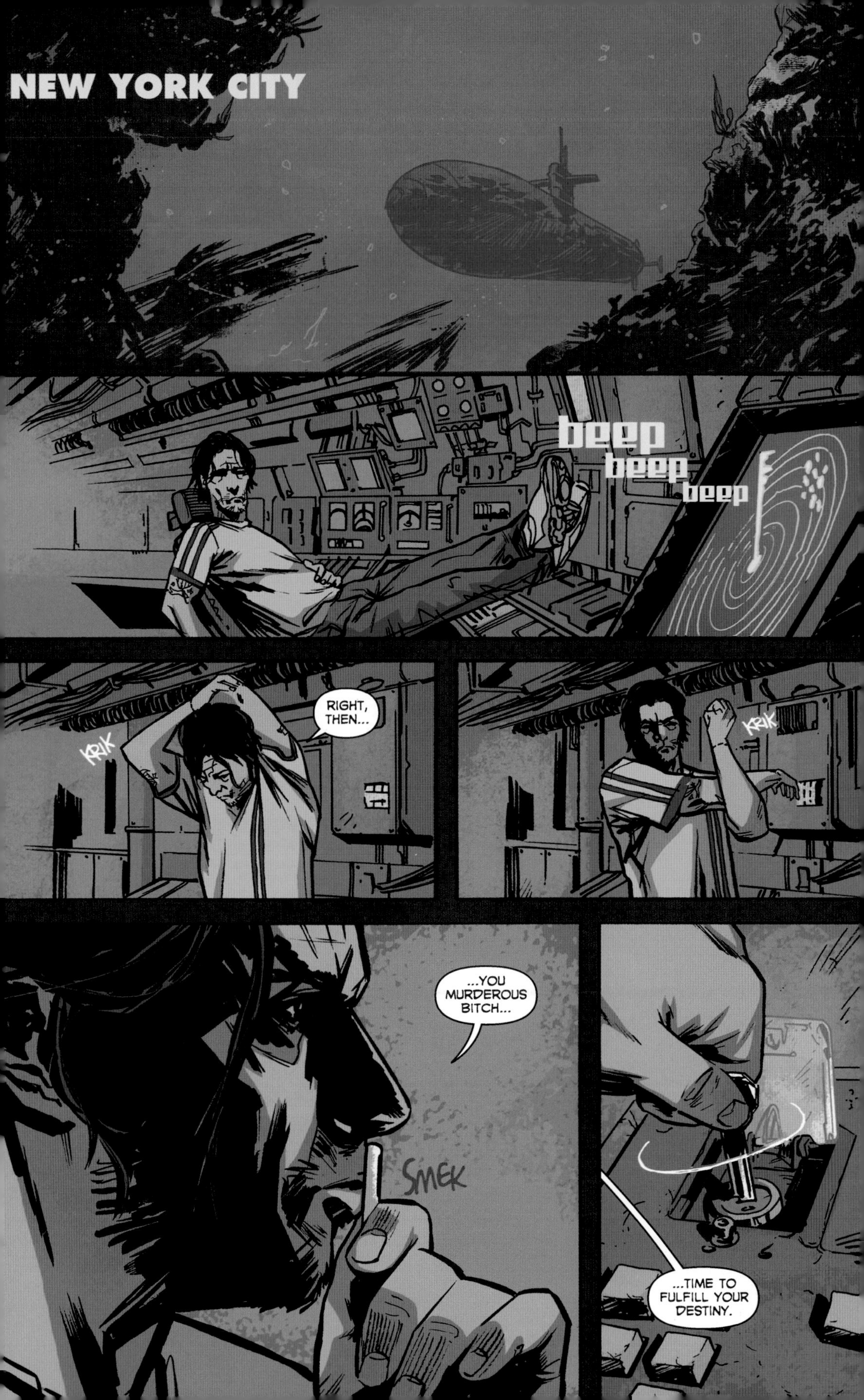
NEW YORK CITY
beep
beep
beep
RIGHT, THEN...
KRIK
KRIK
...YOU MURDEROUS BITCH...
SMEK
...TIME TO FULFILL YOUR DESTINY.

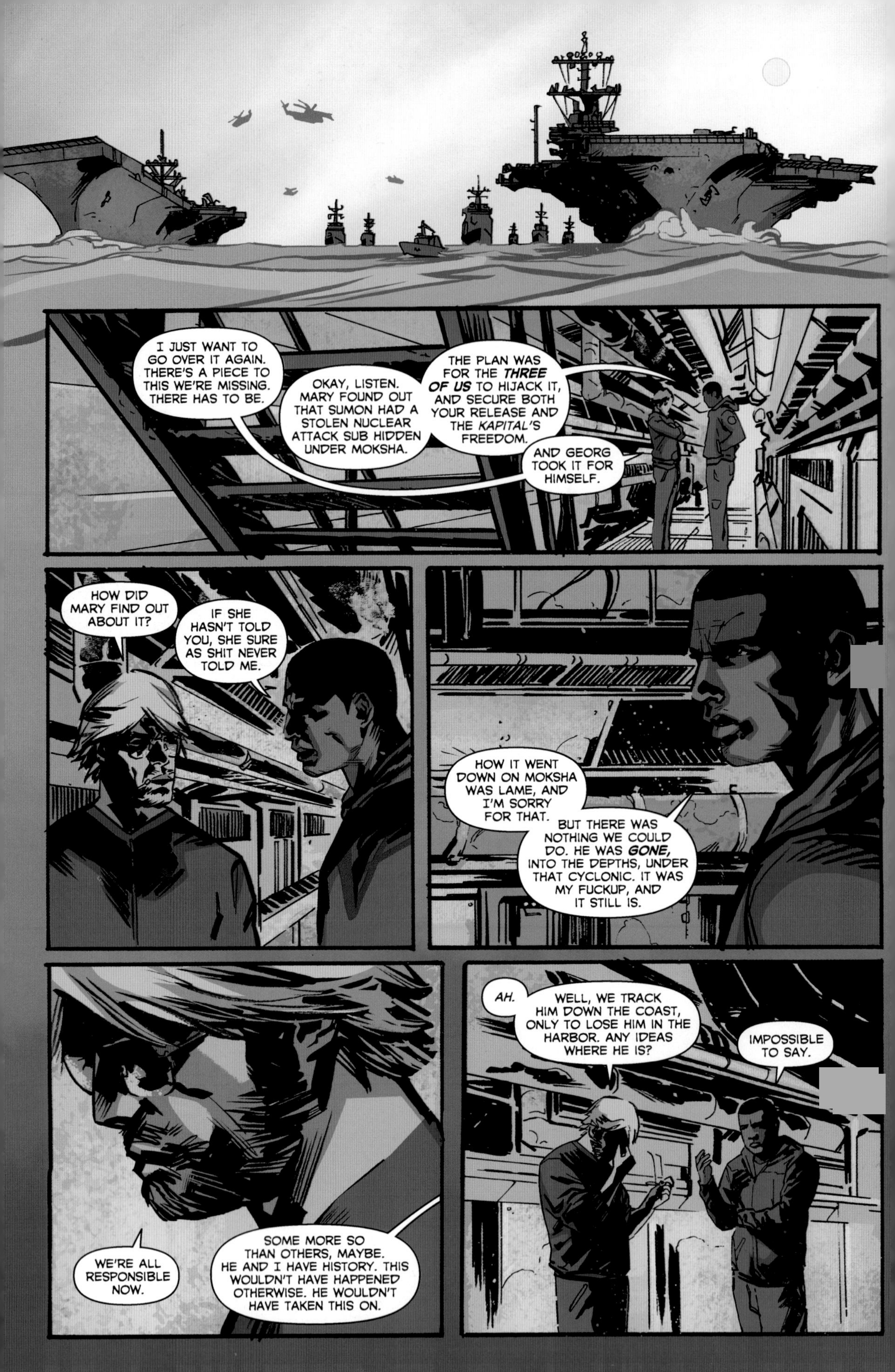
I JUST WANT TO GO OVER IT AGAIN. THERE'S A PIECE TO THIS WE'RE MISSING. THERE HAS TO BE.
OKAY, LISTEN. MARY FOUND OUT THAT SUMON HAD A STOLEN NUCLEAR ATTACK SUB HIDDEN UNDER MOKSHA.
THE PLAN WAS FOR THE THREE OF US TO HIJACK IT, AND SECURE BOTH YOUR RELEASE AND THE KAPITAL'S FREEDOM.
AND GEORG TOOK IT FOR HIMSELF.
HOW DID MARY FIND OUT ABOUT IT?
IF SHE HASN'T TOLD YOU, SHE SURE AS SHIT NEVER TOLD ME.
HOW IT WENT DOWN ON MOKSHA WAS LAME, AND I'M SORRY FOR THAT.
BUT THERE WAS NOTHING WE COULD DO. HE WAS GONE, INTO THE DEPTHS, UNDER THAT CYCLONIC. IT WAS MY FUCKUP, AND IT STILL IS.
WE'RE ALL RESPONSIBLE NOW.
SOME MORE SO THAN OTHERS, MAYBE. HE AND I HAVE HISTORY. THIS WOULDN'T HAVE HAPPENED OTHERWISE. HE WOULDN'T HAVE TAKEN THIS ON.
AH.
WELL, WE TRACK HIM DOWN THE COAST, ONLY TO LOSE HIM IN THE HARBOR. ANY IDEAS WHERE HE IS?
IMPOSSIBLE TO SAY.

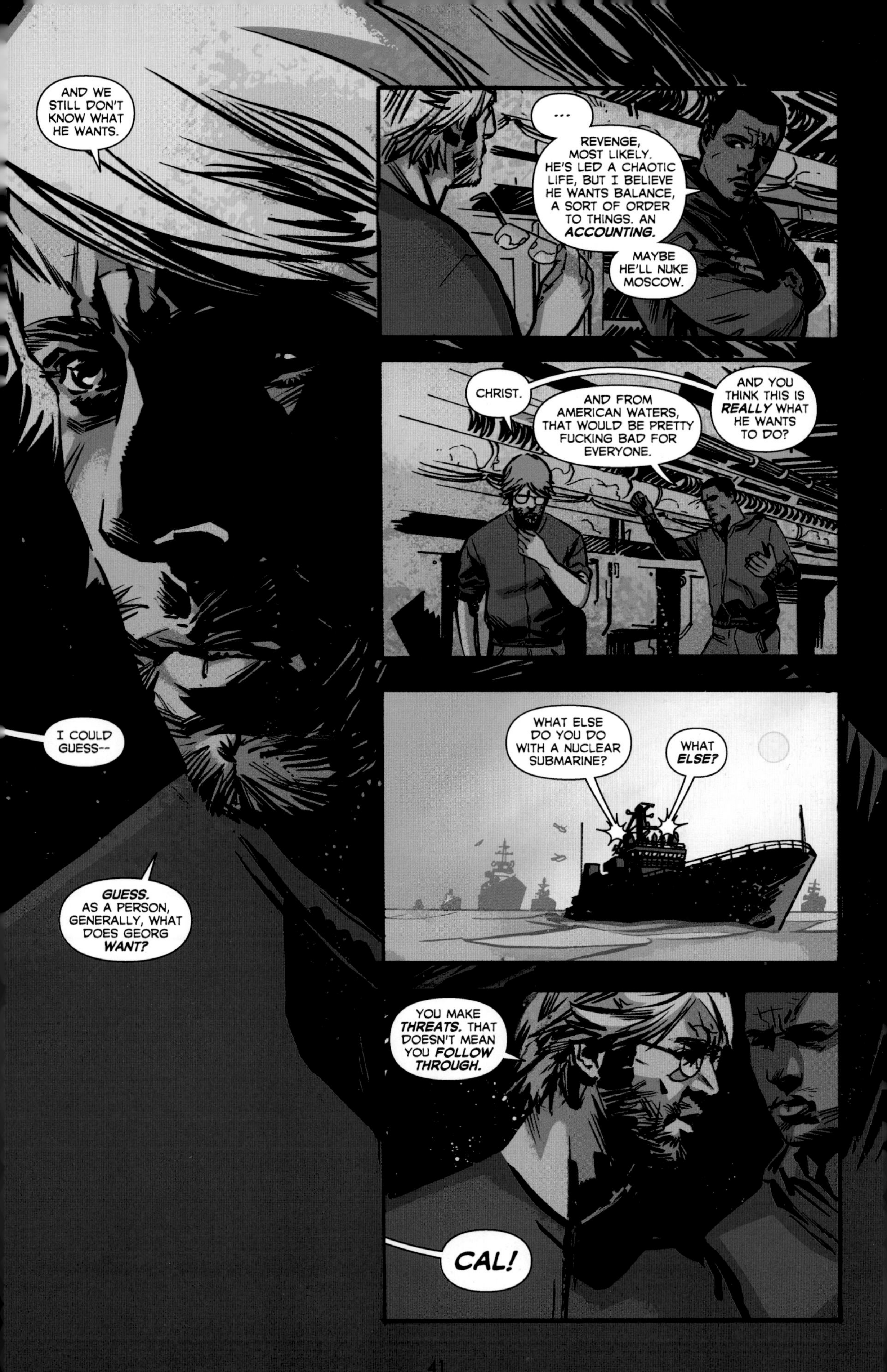
AND WE STILL DON'T KNOW WHAT HE WANTS.
...
REVENGE, MOST LIKELY. HE'S LED A CHAOTIC LIFE, BUT I BELIEVE HE WANTS BALANCE, A SORT OF ORDER TO THINGS. AN ACCOUNTING.
MAYBE HE'LL NUKE MOSCOW.
CHRIST.
AND FROM AMERICAN WATERS, THAT WOULD BE PRETTY FUCKING BAD FOR EVERYONE.
AND YOU THINK THIS IS REALLY WHAT HE WANTS TO DO?
I COULD GUESS--
GUESS. AS A PERSON, GENERALLY, WHAT DOES GEORG WANT?
WHAT ELSE DO YOU DO WITH A NUCLEAR SUBMARINE?
WHAT ELSE?
YOU MAKE THREATS. THAT DOESN'T MEAN YOU FOLLOW THROUGH.
CAL!

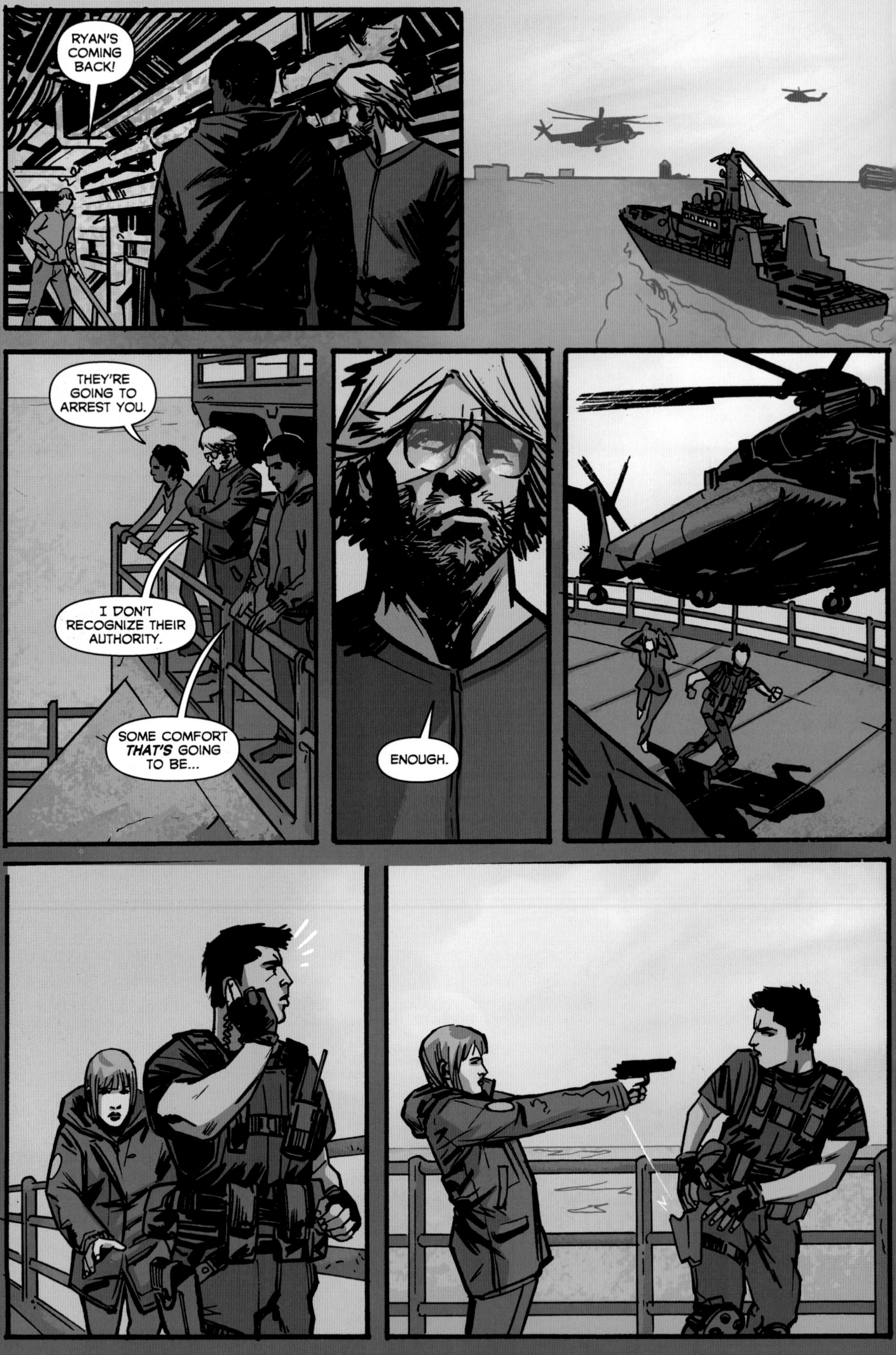
RYAN'S COMING BACK!
THEY'RE GOING TO ARREST YOU.
I DON'T RECOGNIZE THEIR AUTHORITY.
SOME COMFORT *THAT'S* GOING TO BE...
ENOUGH.

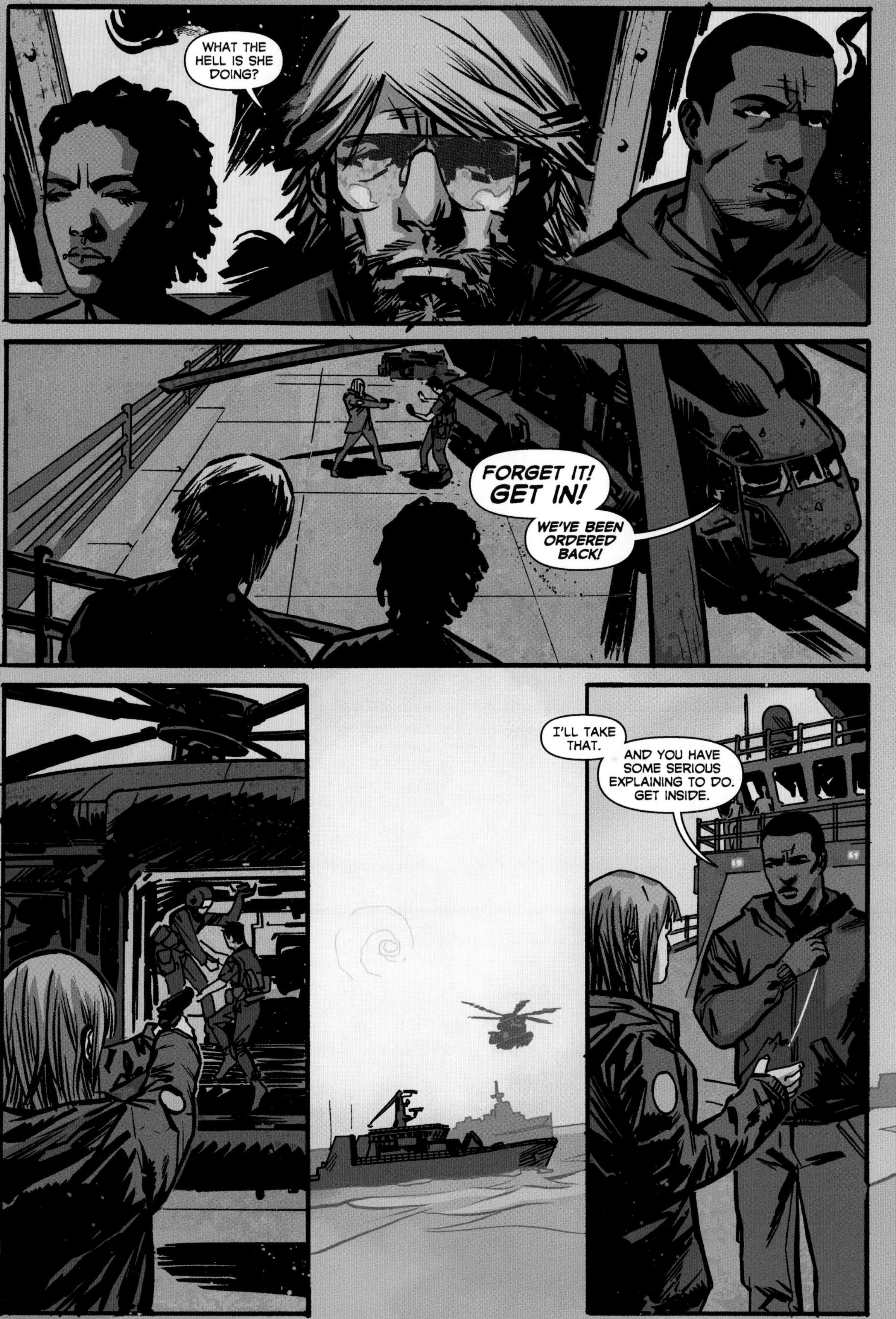
WHAT THE HELL IS SHE DOING?
FORGET IT! GET IN!
WE'VE BEEN ORDERED BACK!
I'LL TAKE THAT.
AND YOU HAVE SOME SERIOUS EXPLAINING TO DO. GET INSIDE.

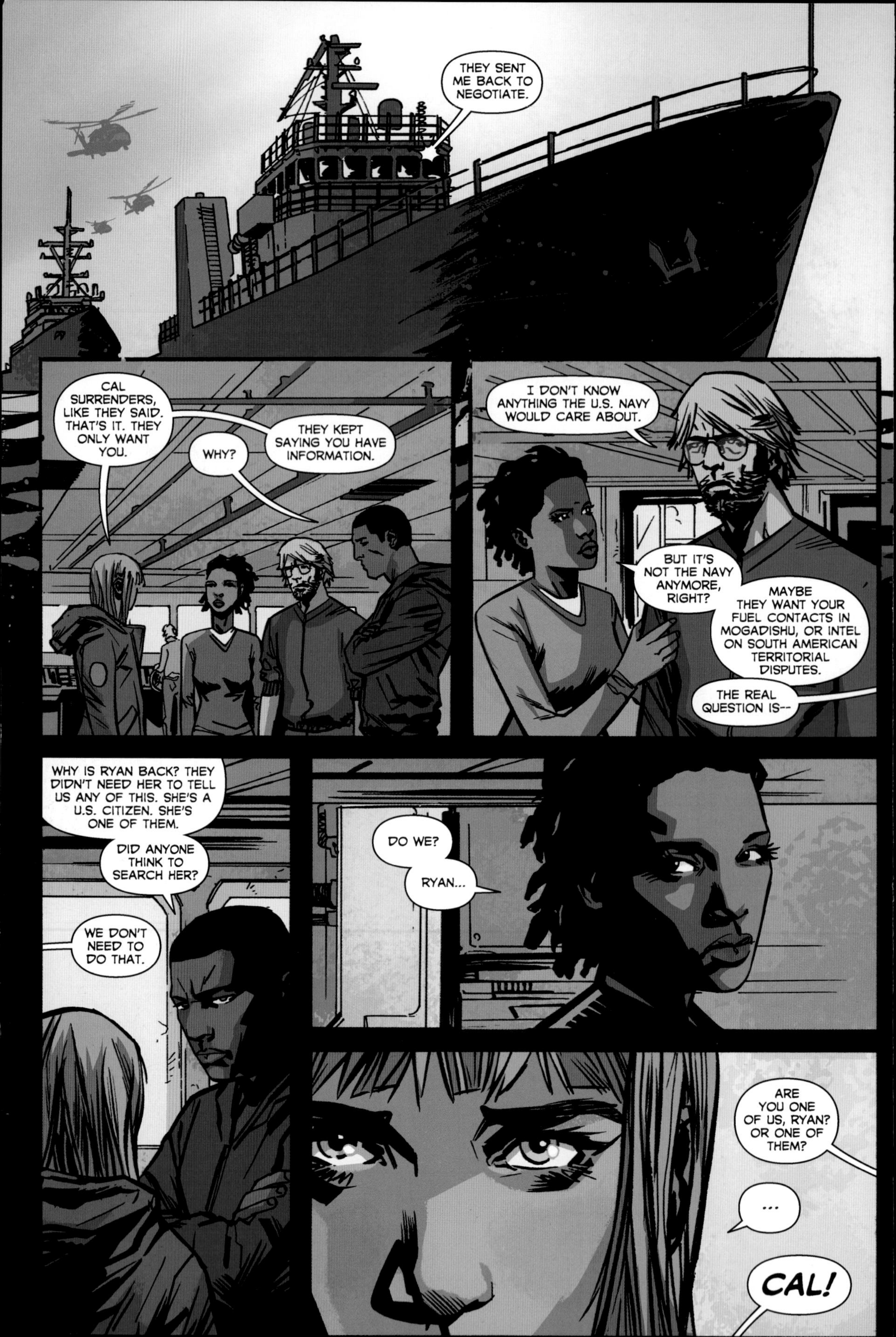
THEY SENT ME BACK TO NEGOTIATE.
CAL SURRENDERS, LIKE THEY SAID. THAT'S IT. THEY ONLY WANT YOU.
WHY?
THEY KEPT SAYING YOU HAVE INFORMATION.
I DON'T KNOW ANYTHING THE U.S. NAVY WOULD CARE ABOUT.
BUT IT'S NOT THE NAVY ANYMORE, RIGHT?
MAYBE THEY WANT YOUR FUEL CONTACTS IN MOGADISHU, OR INTEL ON SOUTH AMERICAN TERRITORIAL DISPUTES.
THE REAL QUESTION IS--
WHY IS RYAN BACK? THEY DIDN'T NEED HER TO TELL US ANY OF THIS. SHE'S A U.S. CITIZEN. SHE'S ONE OF THEM.
DID ANYONE THINK TO SEARCH HER?
WE DON'T NEED TO DO THAT.
DO WE?
RYAN...
ARE YOU ONE OF US, RYAN? OR ONE OF THEM?
...
CAL!

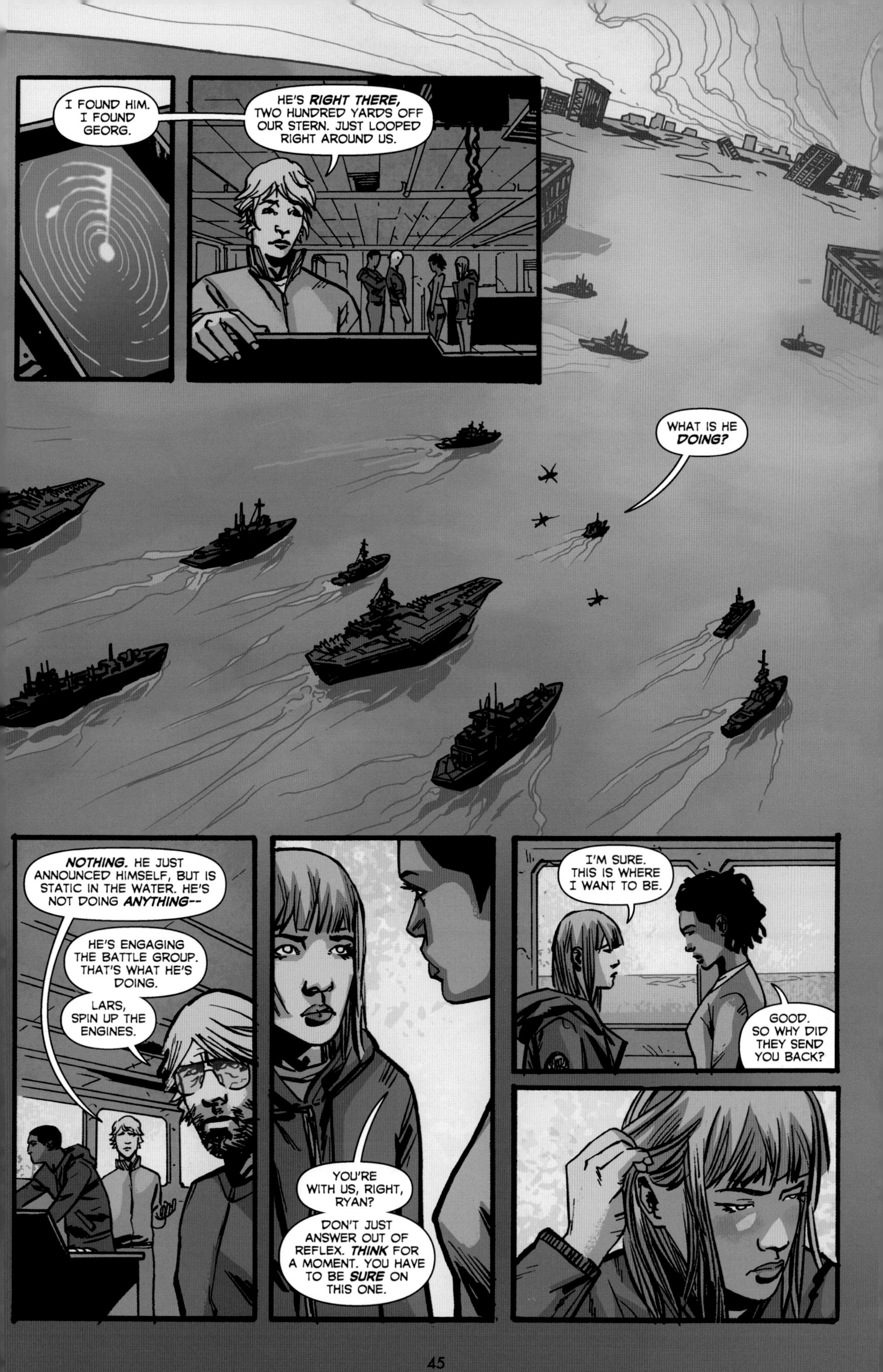
I FOUND HIM. I FOUND GEORG.
HE'S **RIGHT THERE,** TWO HUNDRED YARDS OFF OUR STERN. JUST LOOPED RIGHT AROUND US.
WHAT IS HE **DOING?**
NOTHING. HE JUST ANNOUNCED HIMSELF, BUT IS STATIC IN THE WATER. HE'S NOT DOING **ANYTHING--**
HE'S ENGAGING THE BATTLE GROUP. THAT'S WHAT HE'S DOING.
LARS, SPIN UP THE ENGINES.
YOU'RE WITH US, RIGHT, RYAN?
DON'T JUST ANSWER OUT OF REFLEX. **THINK** FOR A MOMENT. YOU HAVE TO BE **SURE** ON THIS ONE.
I'M SURE. THIS IS WHERE I WANT TO BE.
GOOD. SO WHY DID THEY SEND YOU BACK?

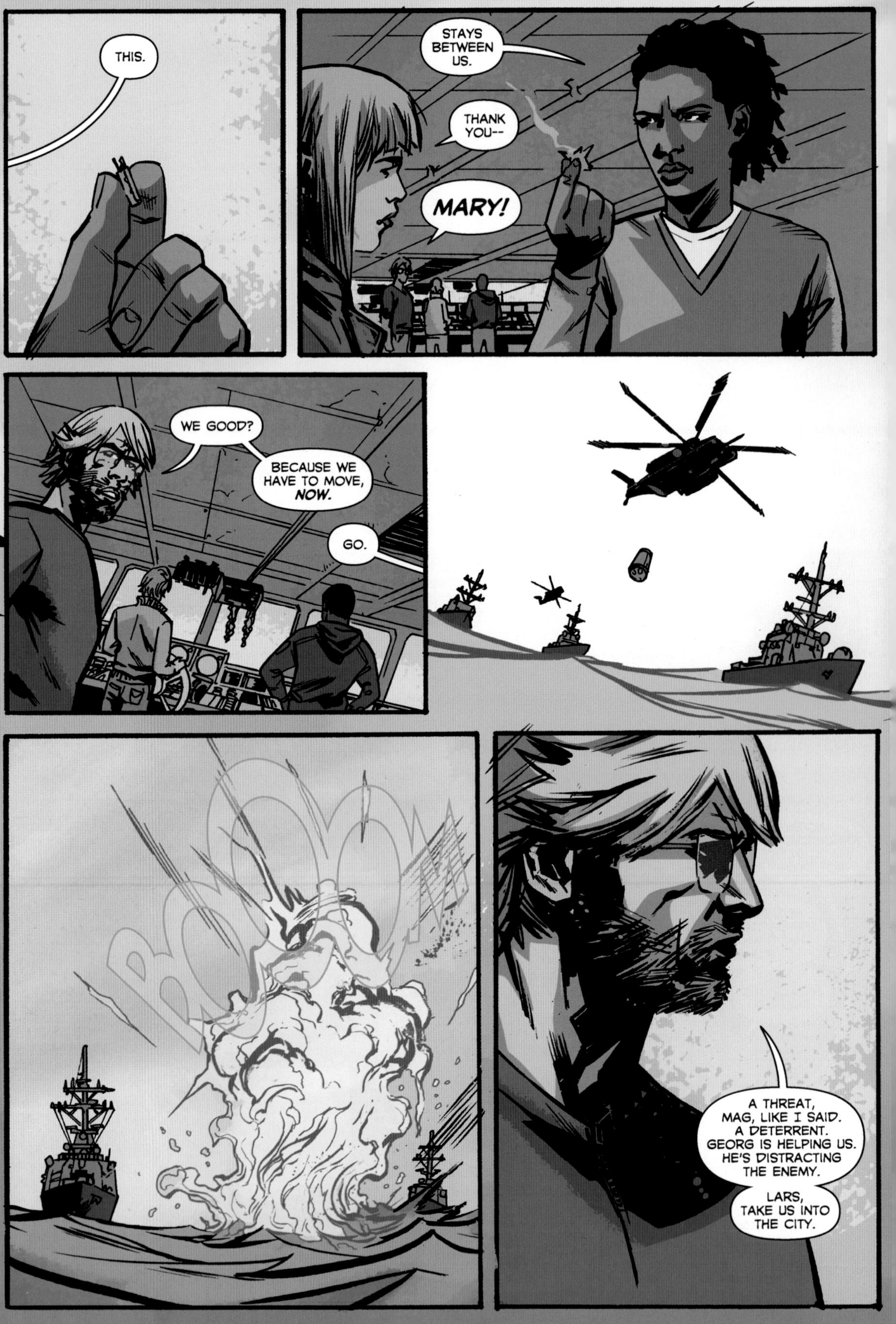
THIS.
STAYS BETWEEN US.
THANK YOU--
MARY!
WE GOOD?
BECAUSE WE HAVE TO MOVE, NOW.
GO.
A THREAT, MAG, LIKE I SAID. A DETERRENT. GEORG IS HELPING US. HE'S DISTRACTING THE ENEMY.
LARS, TAKE US INTO THE CITY.

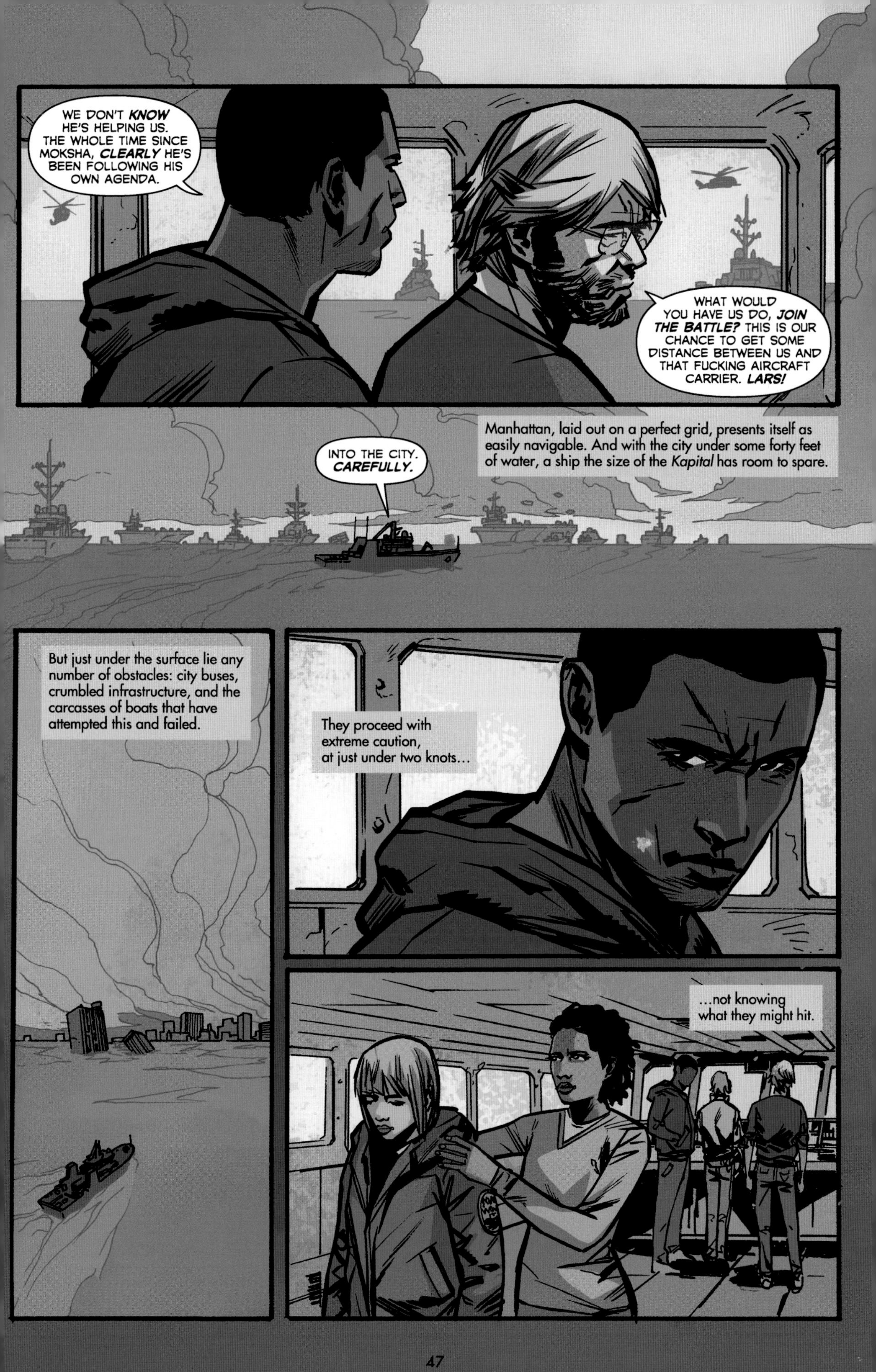
WE DON'T *KNOW* HE'S HELPING US. THE WHOLE TIME SINCE MOKSHA, *CLEARLY* HE'S BEEN FOLLOWING HIS OWN AGENDA.
WHAT WOULD YOU HAVE US DO, *JOIN THE BATTLE?* THIS IS OUR CHANCE TO GET SOME DISTANCE BETWEEN US AND THAT FUCKING AIRCRAFT CARRIER. *LARS!*
INTO THE CITY. *CAREFULLY.*
Manhattan, laid out on a perfect grid, presents itself as easily navigable. And with the city under some forty feet of water, a ship the size of the *Kapital* has room to spare.
But just under the surface lie any number of obstacles: city buses, crumbled infrastructure, and the carcasses of boats that have attempted this and failed.
They proceed with extreme caution, at just under two knots…
…not knowing what they might hit.

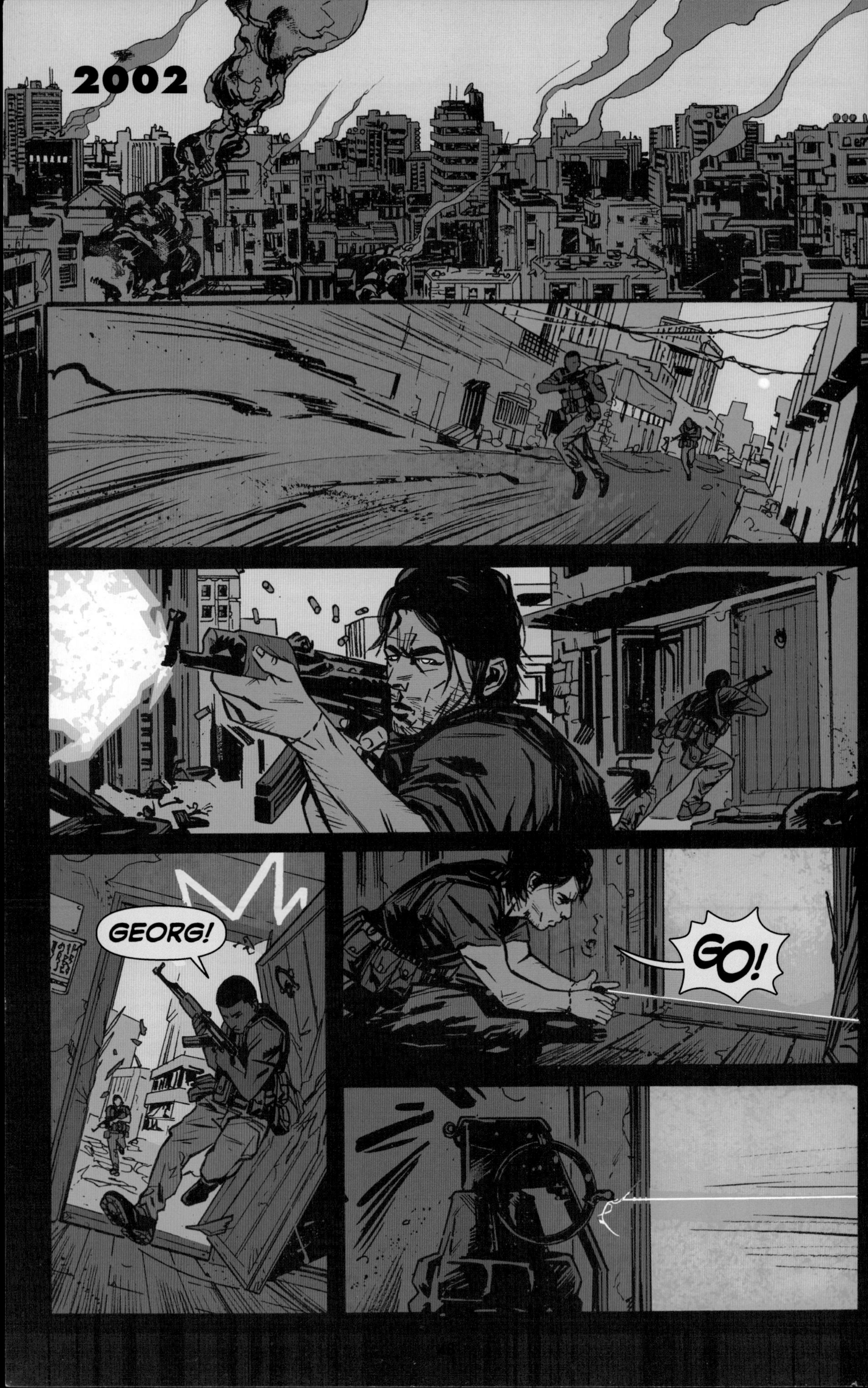
2002
GEORG!
GO!

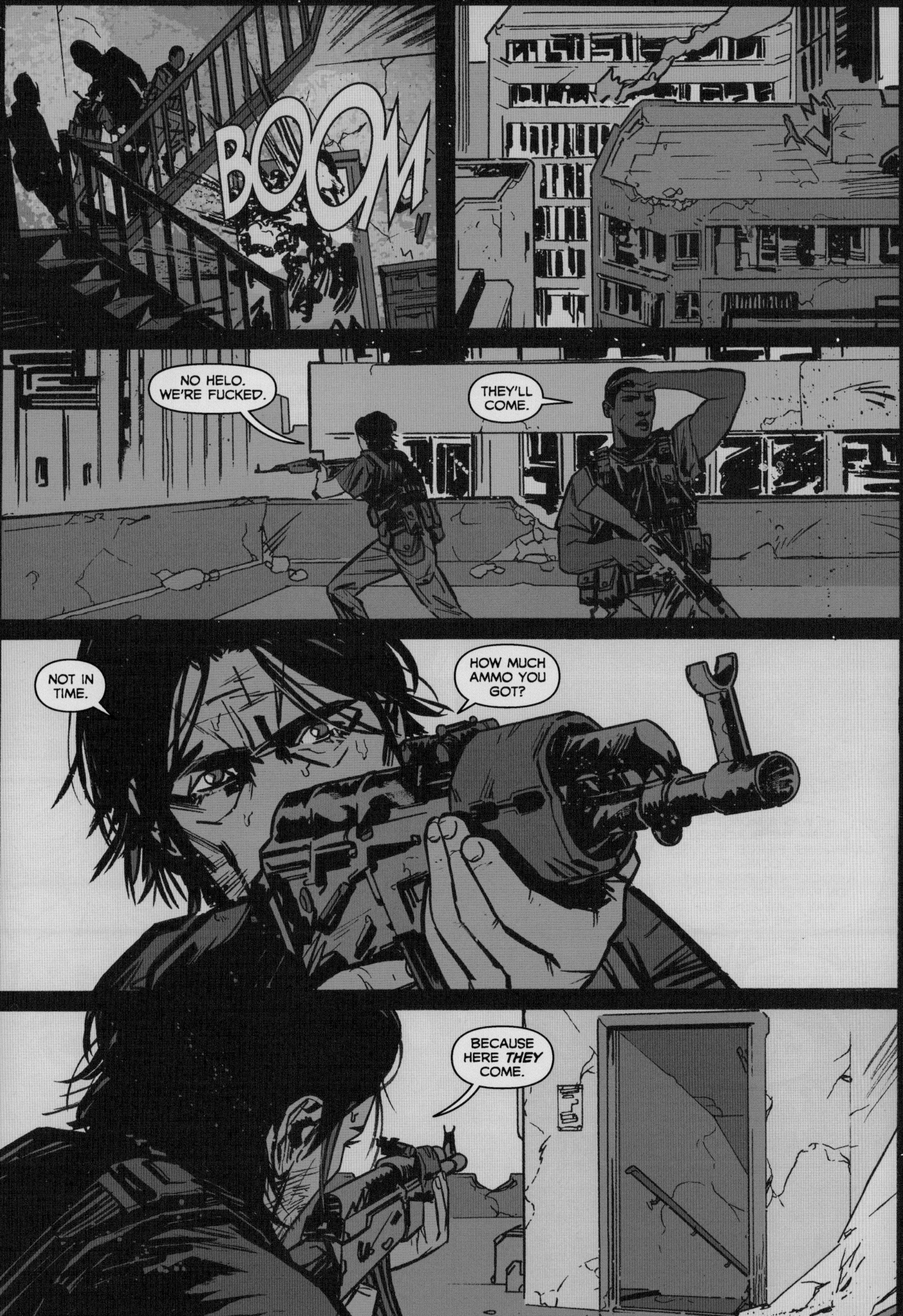
BOOM
NO HELO. WE'RE FUCKED.
THEY'LL COME.
NOT IN TIME.
HOW MUCH AMMO YOU GOT?
BECAUSE HERE ***THEY*** COME.

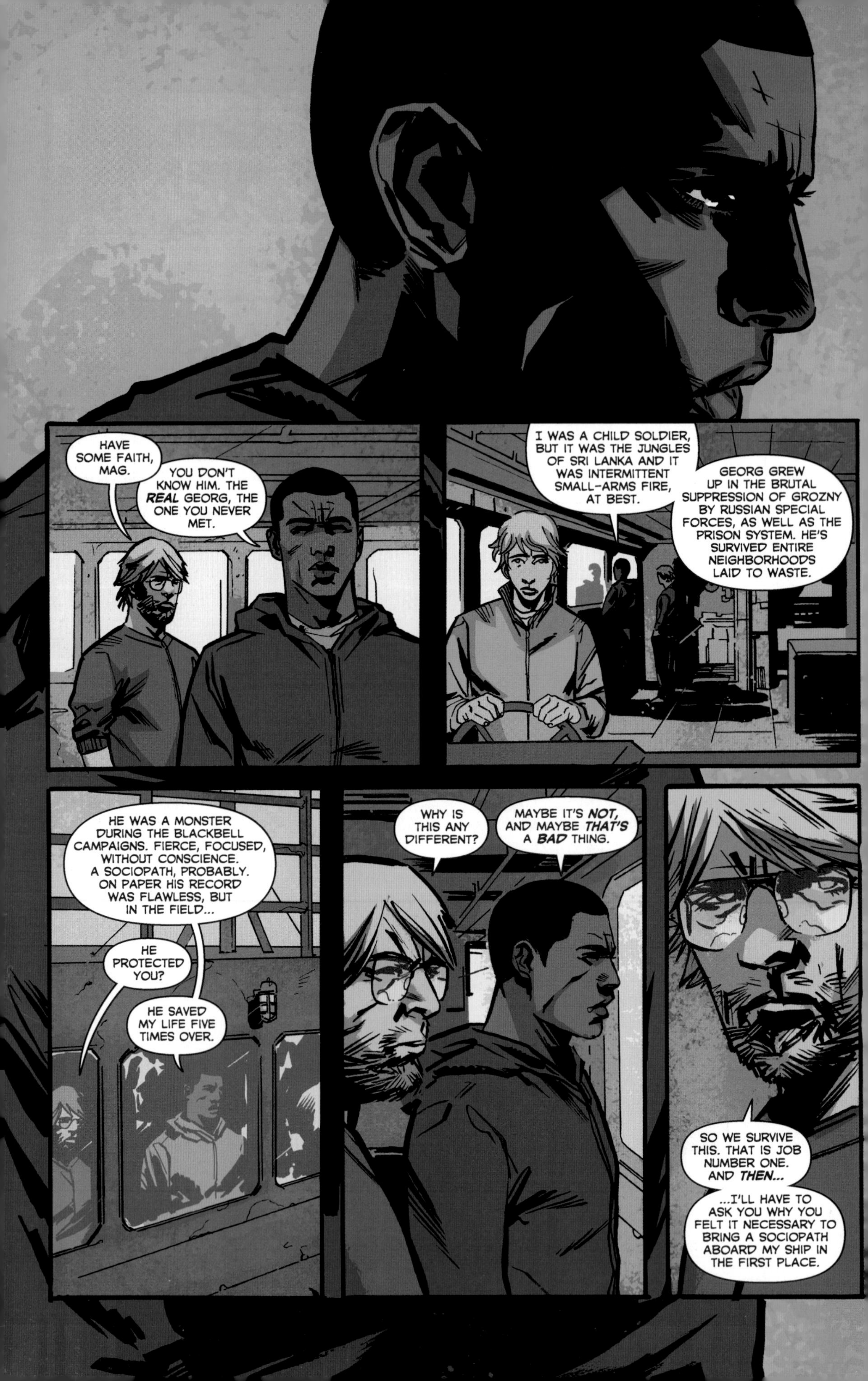

HAVE SOME FAITH, MAG.
YOU DON'T KNOW HIM. THE REAL GEORG, THE ONE YOU NEVER MET.
I WAS A CHILD SOLDIER, BUT IT WAS THE JUNGLES OF SRI LANKA AND IT WAS INTERMITTENT SMALL-ARMS FIRE, AT BEST.
GEORG GREW UP IN THE BRUTAL SUPPRESSION OF GROZNY BY RUSSIAN SPECIAL FORCES, AS WELL AS THE PRISON SYSTEM. HE'S SURVIVED ENTIRE NEIGHBORHOODS LAID TO WASTE.
HE WAS A MONSTER DURING THE BLACKBELL CAMPAIGNS. FIERCE, FOCUSED, WITHOUT CONSCIENCE. A SOCIOPATH, PROBABLY. ON PAPER HIS RECORD WAS FLAWLESS, BUT IN THE FIELD...
HE PROTECTED YOU?
HE SAVED MY LIFE FIVE TIMES OVER.
WHY IS THIS ANY DIFFERENT?
MAYBE IT'S NOT, AND MAYBE THAT'S A BAD THING.
SO WE SURVIVE THIS. THAT IS JOB NUMBER ONE. AND THEN...
...I'LL HAVE TO ASK YOU WHY YOU FELT IT NECESSARY TO BRING A SOCIOPATH ABOARD MY SHIP IN THE FIRST PLACE.

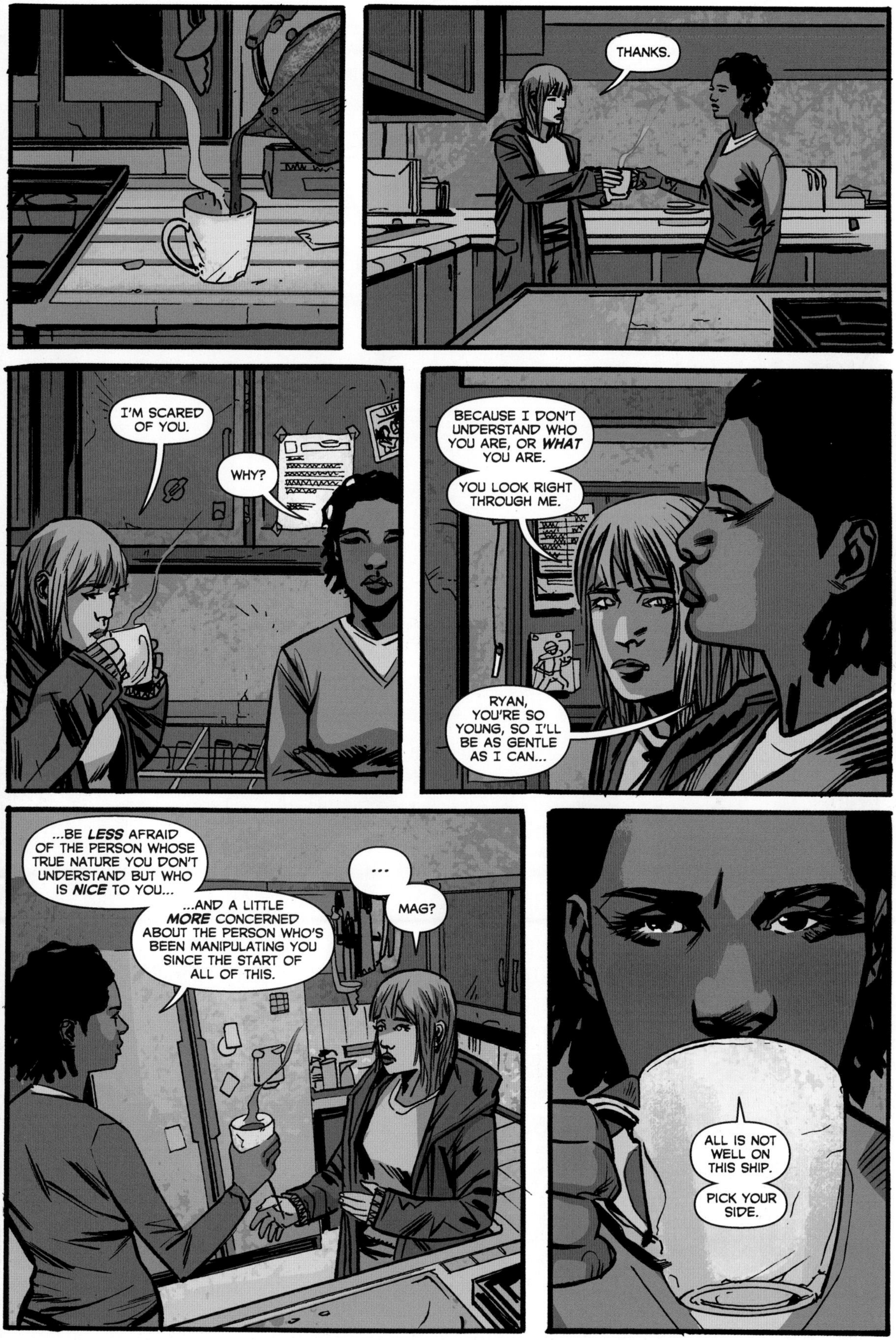
THANKS.
I'M SCARED OF YOU.
WHY?
BECAUSE I DON'T UNDERSTAND WHO YOU ARE, OR *WHAT* YOU ARE.
YOU LOOK RIGHT THROUGH ME.
RYAN, YOU'RE SO YOUNG, SO I'LL BE AS GENTLE AS I CAN...
...BE *LESS* AFRAID OF THE PERSON WHOSE TRUE NATURE YOU DON'T UNDERSTAND BUT WHO IS *NICE* TO YOU...
...AND A LITTLE *MORE* CONCERNED ABOUT THE PERSON WHO'S BEEN MANIPULATING YOU SINCE THE START OF ALL OF THIS.
...
MAG?
ALL IS NOT WELL ON THIS SHIP.
PICK YOUR SIDE.

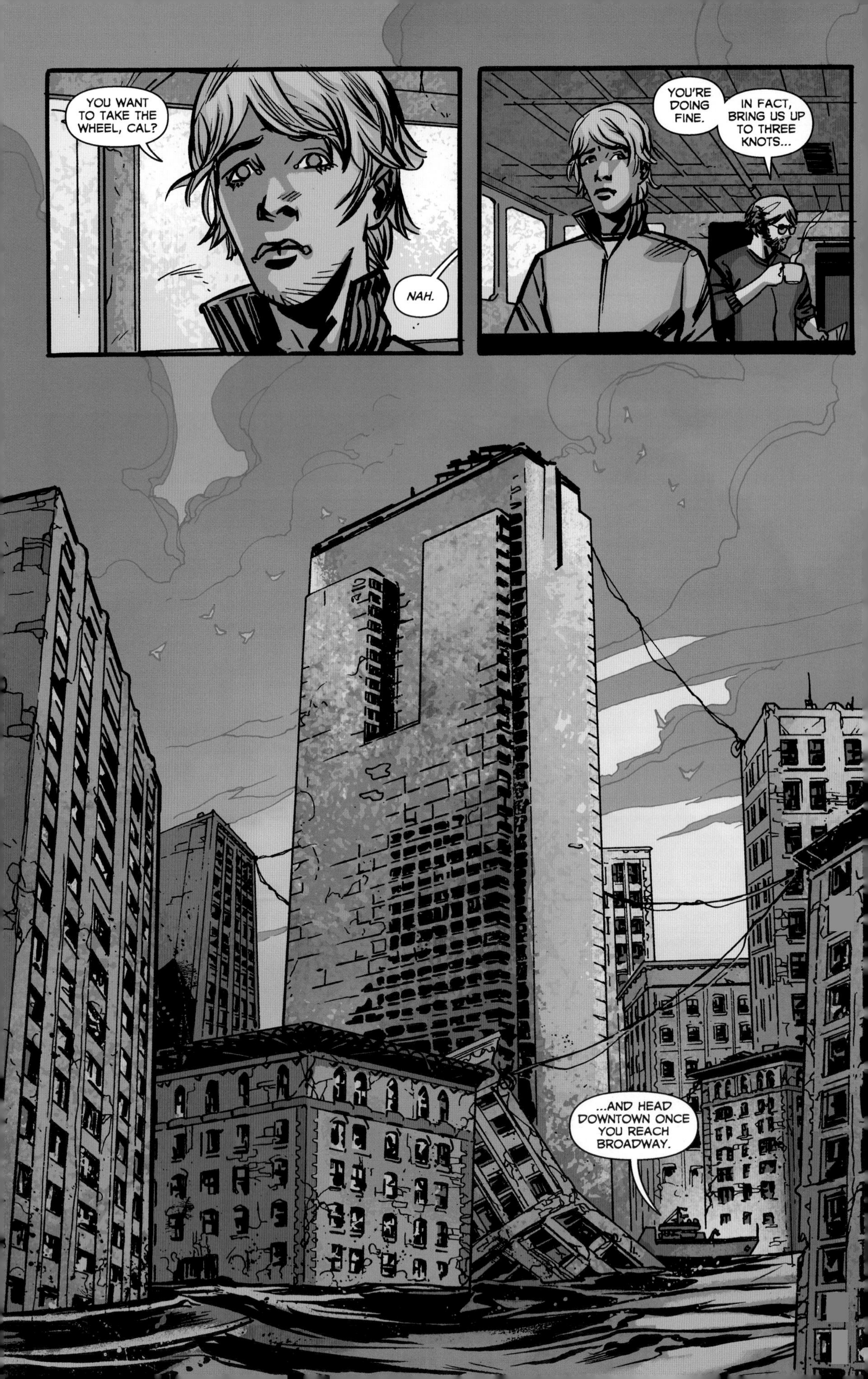
YOU WANT TO TAKE THE WHEEL, CAL?
NAH.
YOU'RE DOING FINE.
IN FACT, BRING US UP TO THREE KNOTS...
...AND HEAD DOWNTOWN ONCE YOU REACH BROADWAY.

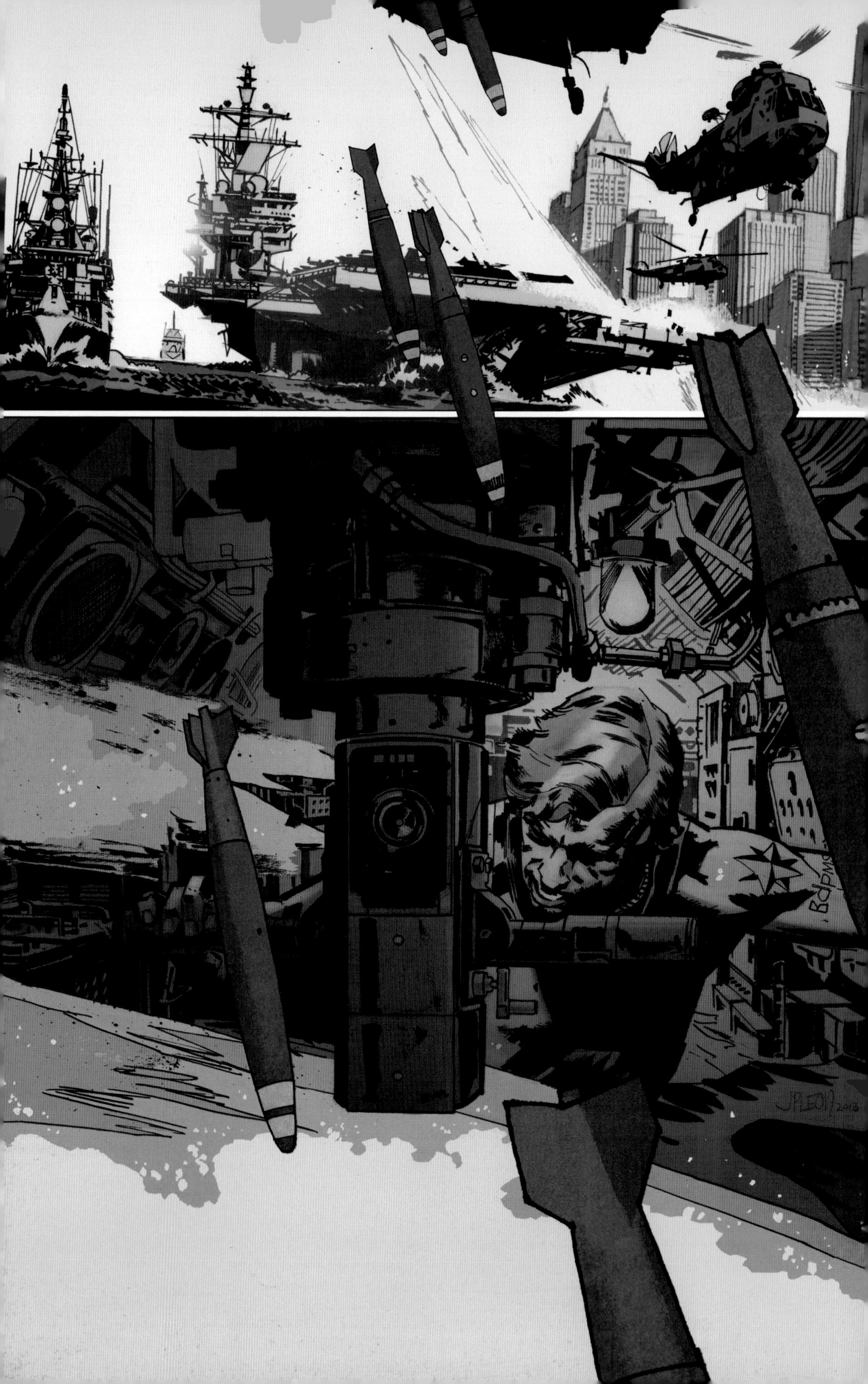

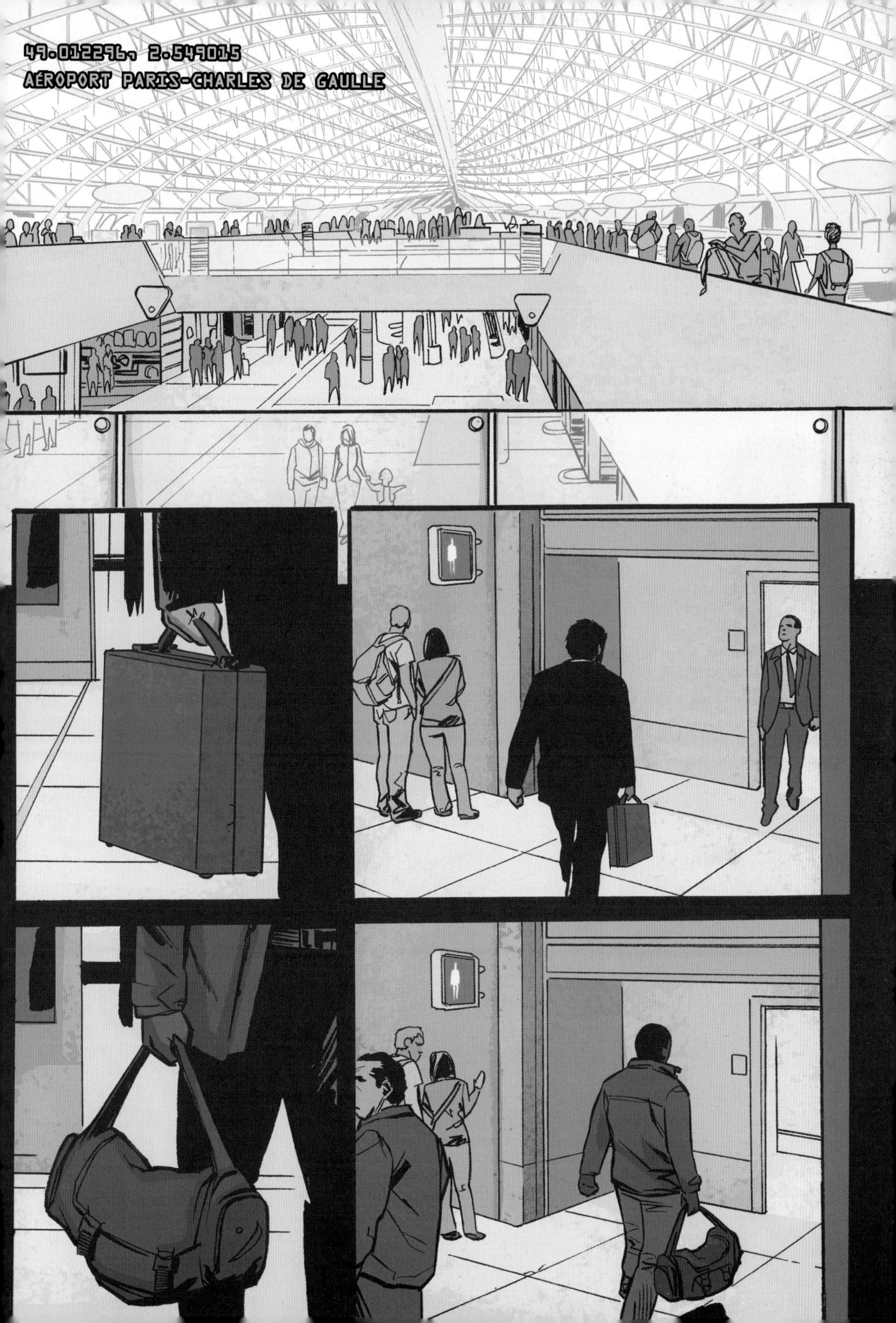
49.012296, 2.549015
AÉROPORT PARIS-CHARLES DE GAULLE

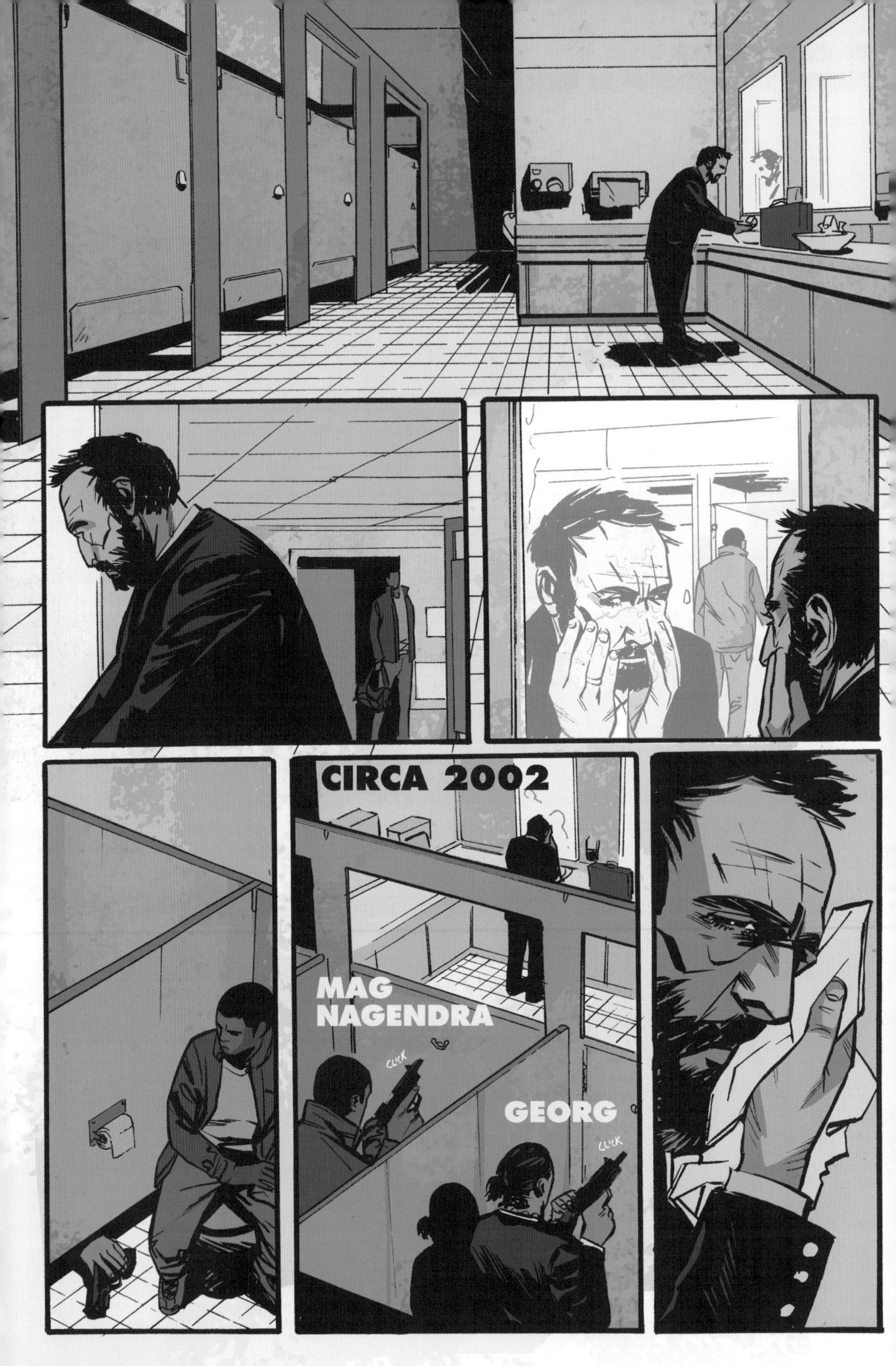
CIRCA 2002
MAG NAGENDRA
CLICK
GEORG
CLICK

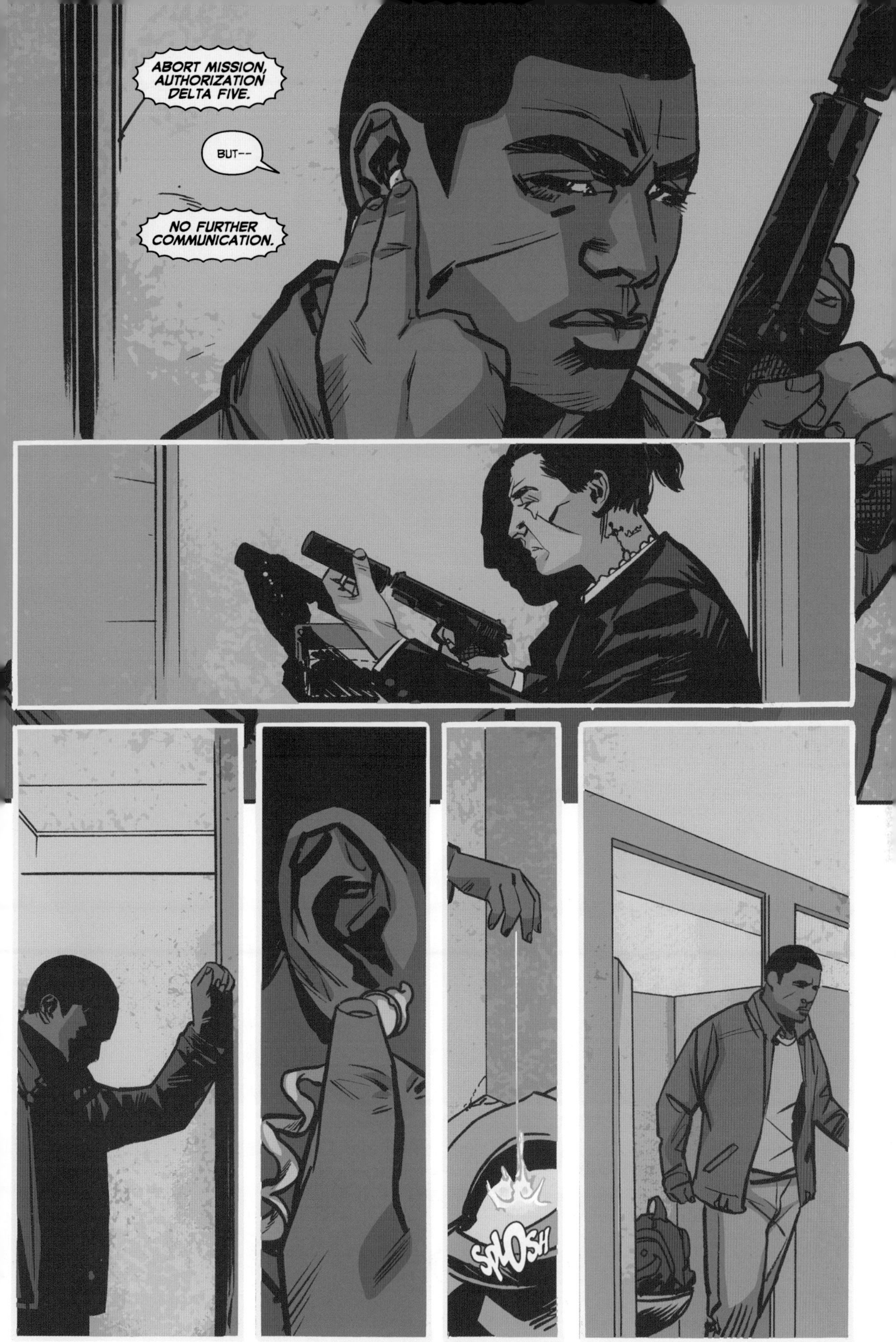
ABORT MISSION, AUTHORIZATION DELTA FIVE.
BUT--
NO FURTHER COMMUNICATION.
SPLOSH

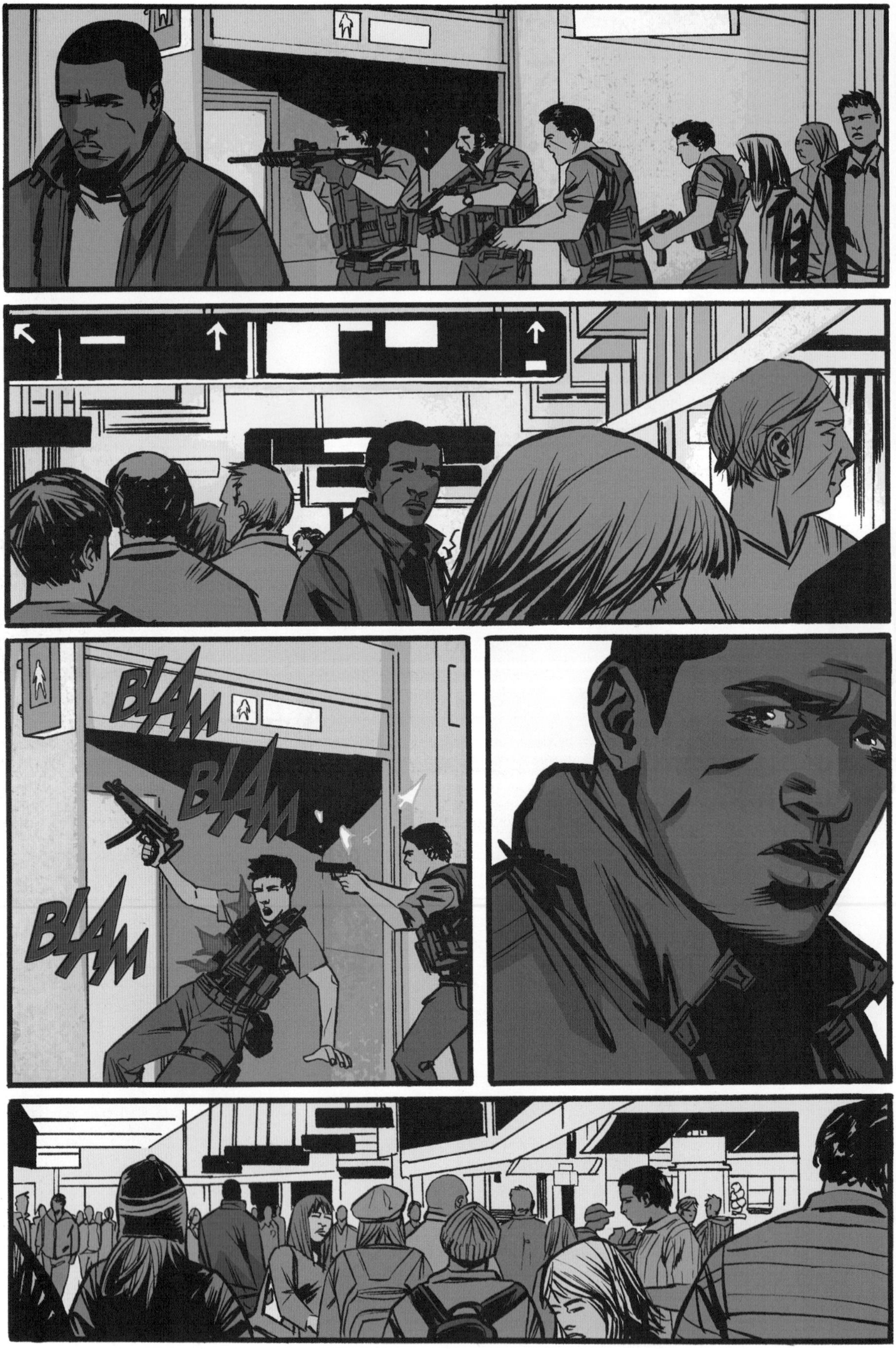
BLAM
BLAM
BLAM

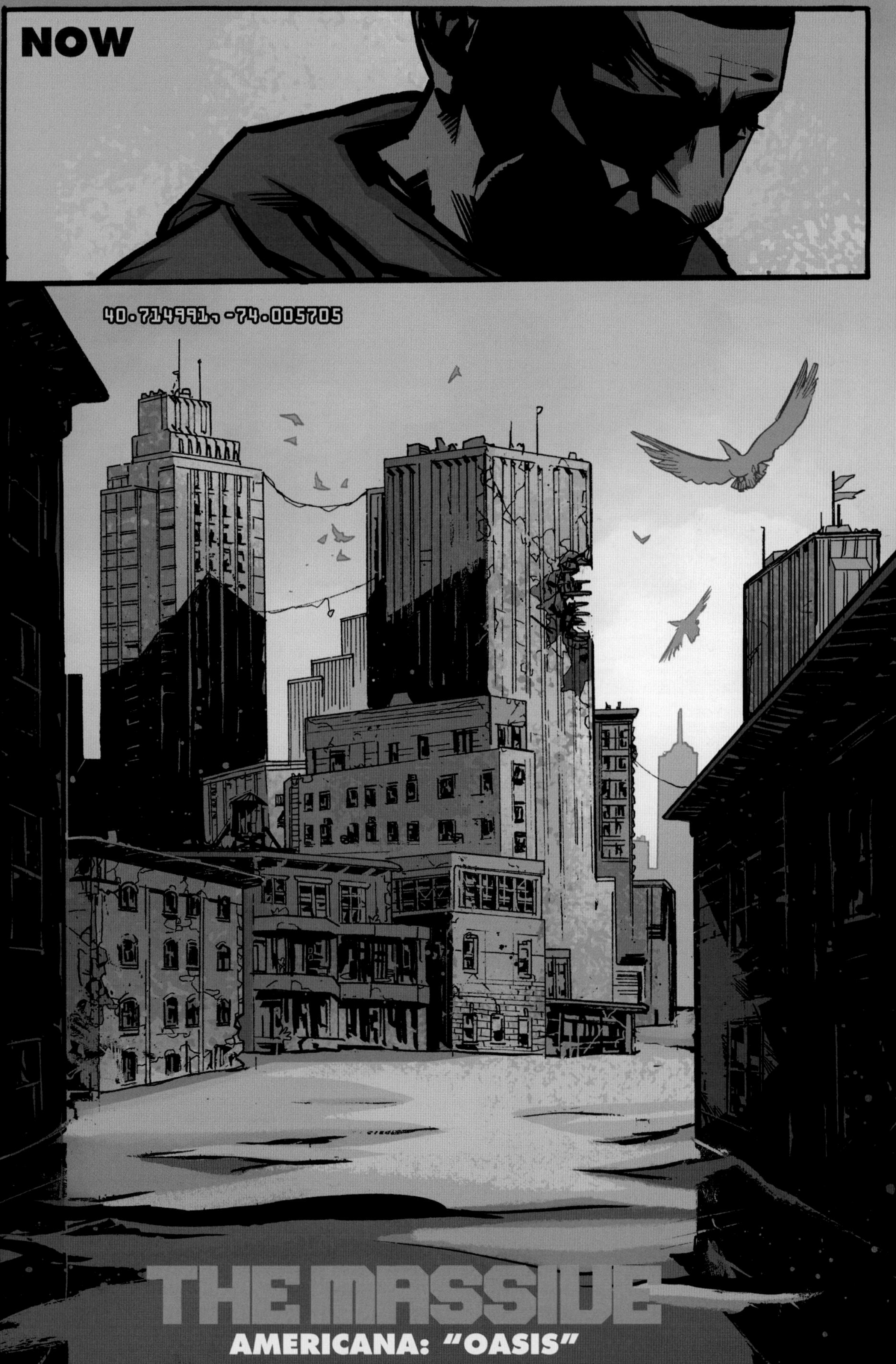
NOW
40.714991, -74.005705
THE MASSIVE
AMERICANA: "OASIS"

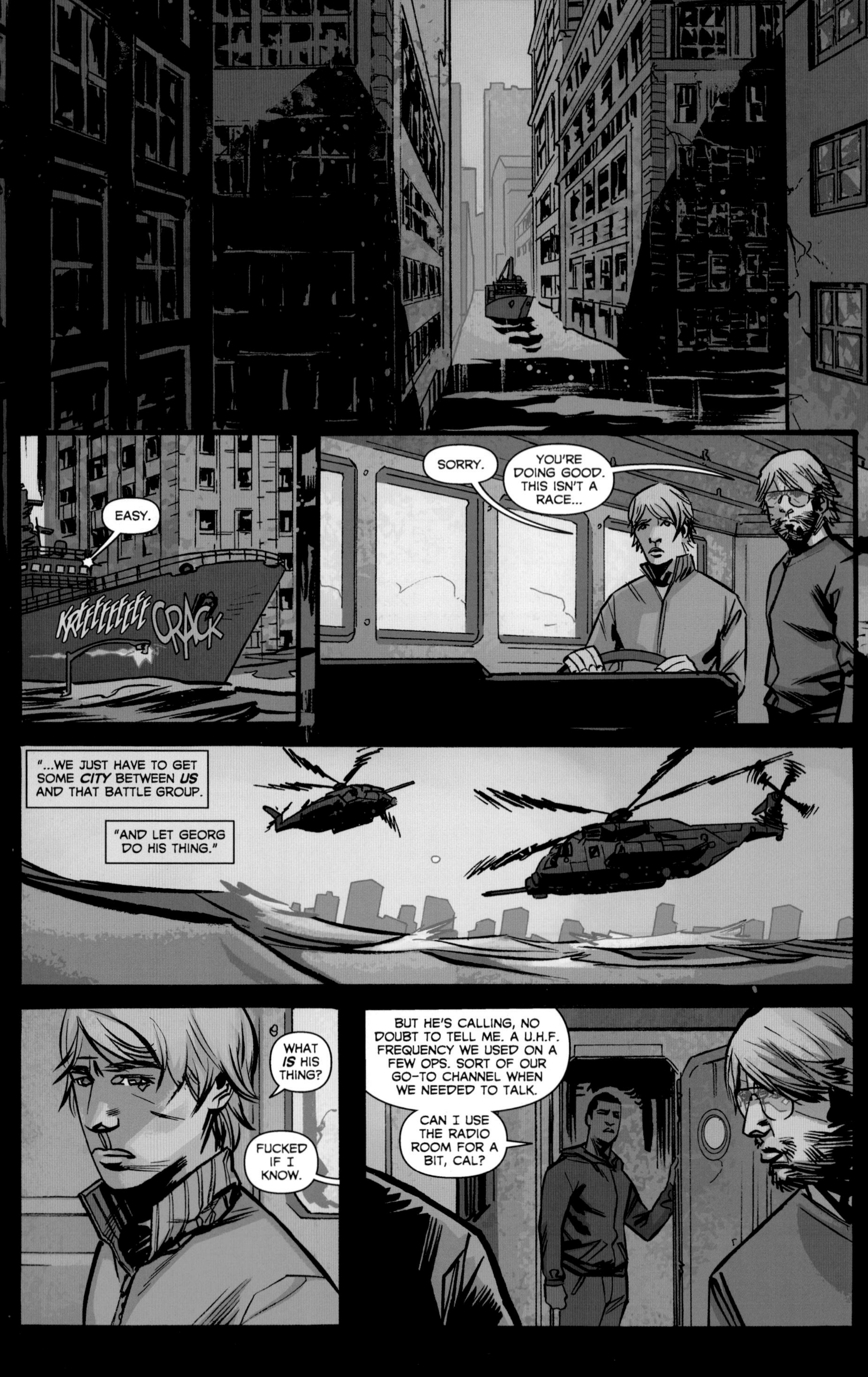
EASY.
KREEEEEEEEE CRACK
SORRY.
YOU'RE DOING GOOD. THIS ISN'T A RACE...
"...WE JUST HAVE TO GET SOME *CITY* BETWEEN *US* AND THAT BATTLE GROUP.
"AND LET GEORG DO HIS THING."
WHAT *IS* HIS THING?
FUCKED IF I KNOW.
BUT HE'S CALLING, NO DOUBT TO TELL ME. A U.H.F. FREQUENCY WE USED ON A FEW OPS. SORT OF OUR GO-TO CHANNEL WHEN WE NEEDED TO TALK.
CAN I USE THE RADIO ROOM FOR A BIT, CAL?

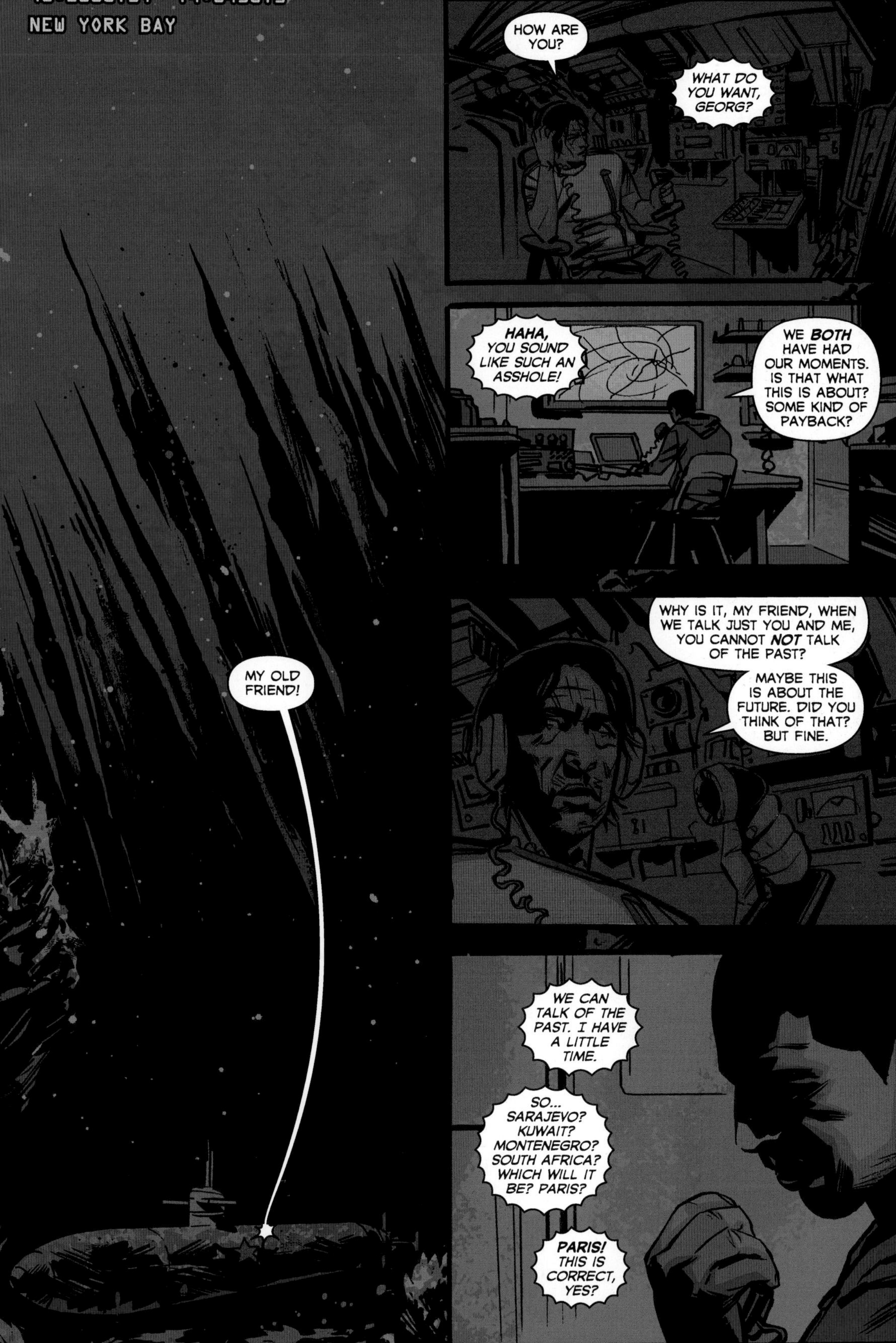
NEW YORK BAY
MY OLD FRIEND!
HOW ARE YOU?
WHAT DO YOU WANT, GEORG?
HAHA, YOU SOUND LIKE SUCH AN ASSHOLE!
WE BOTH HAVE HAD OUR MOMENTS. IS THAT WHAT THIS IS ABOUT? SOME KIND OF PAYBACK?
WHY IS IT, MY FRIEND, WHEN WE TALK JUST YOU AND ME, YOU CANNOT NOT TALK OF THE PAST?
MAYBE THIS IS ABOUT THE FUTURE. DID YOU THINK OF THAT? BUT FINE.
WE CAN TALK OF THE PAST. I HAVE A LITTLE TIME.
SO... SARAJEVO? KUWAIT? MONTENEGRO? SOUTH AFRICA? WHICH WILL IT BE? PARIS?
PARIS! THIS IS CORRECT, YES?

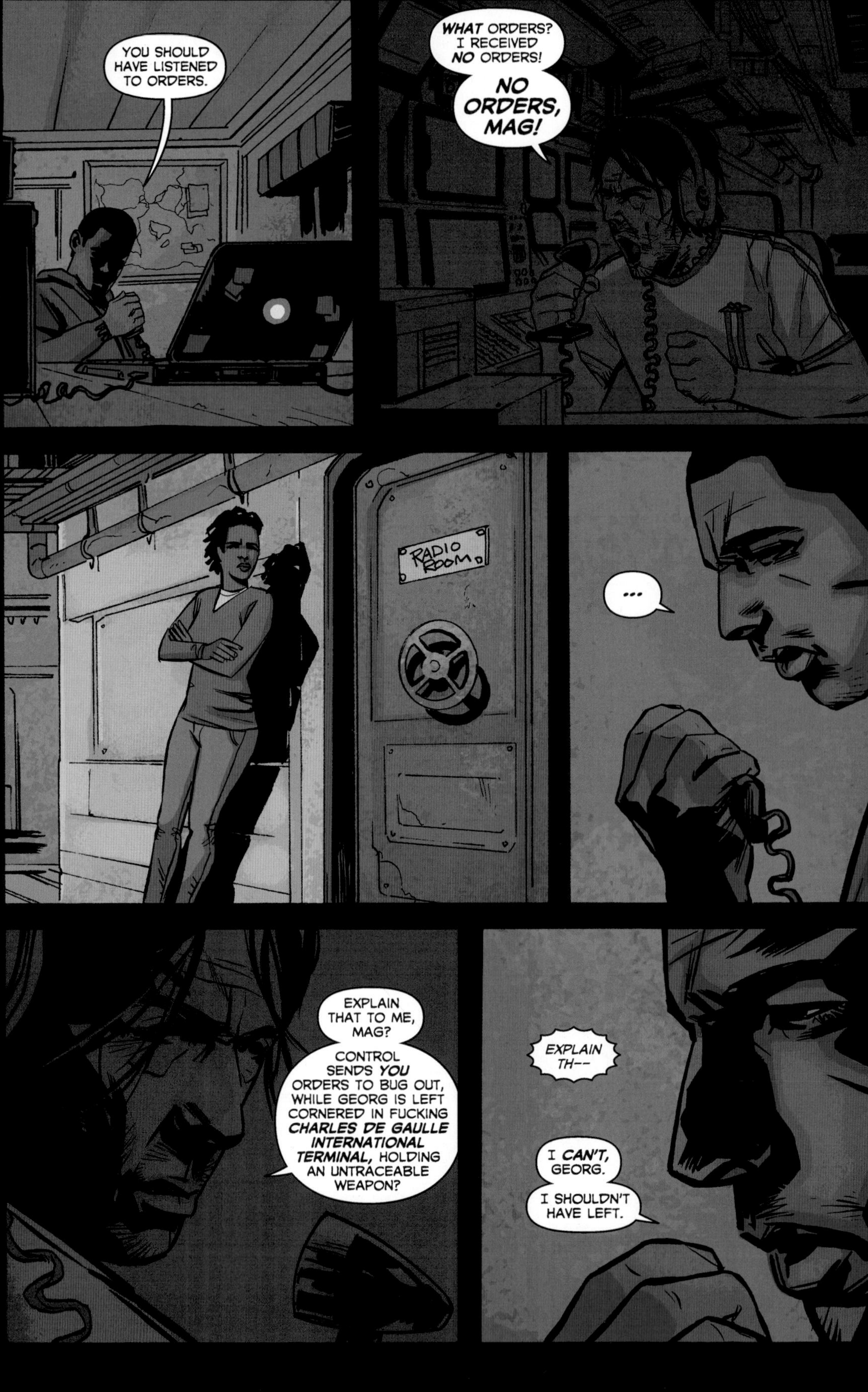

YOU SHOULD HAVE LISTENED TO ORDERS.
WHAT ORDERS? I RECEIVED NO ORDERS!
NO ORDERS, MAG!
RADIO ROOM
...
EXPLAIN THAT TO ME, MAG?
CONTROL SENDS YOU ORDERS TO BUG OUT, WHILE GEORG IS LEFT CORNERED IN FUCKING CHARLES DE GAULLE INTERNATIONAL TERMINAL, HOLDING AN UNTRACEABLE WEAPON?
EXPLAIN TH--
I CAN'T, GEORG.
I SHOULDN'T HAVE LEFT.

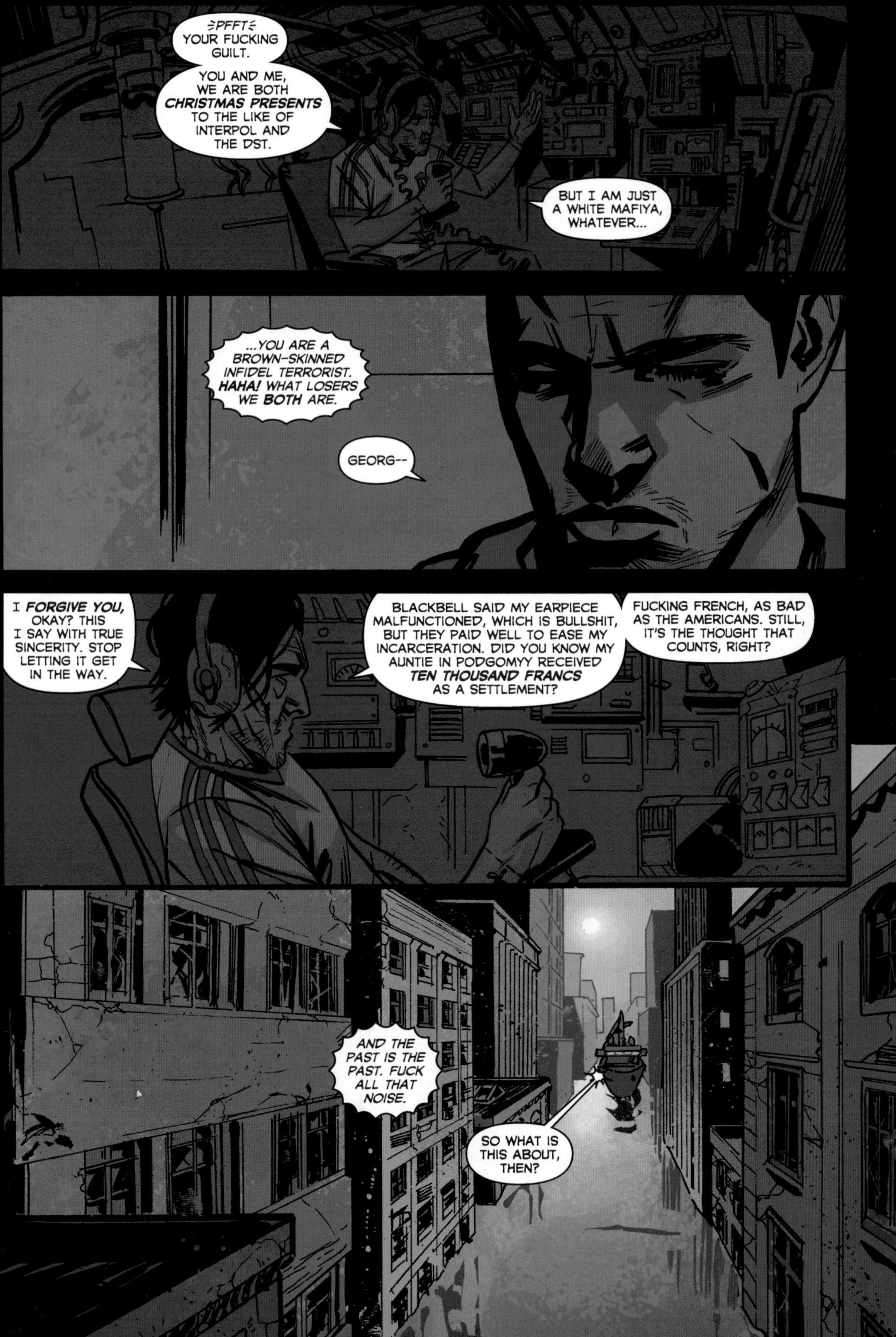

≠PFFT≠ YOUR FUCKING GUILT.
YOU AND ME, WE ARE BOTH CHRISTMAS PRESENTS TO THE LIKE OF INTERPOL AND THE DST.
BUT I AM JUST A WHITE MAFIYA, WHATEVER...
...YOU ARE A BROWN-SKINNED INFIDEL TERRORIST. HAHA! WHAT LOSERS WE BOTH ARE.
GEORG--
I FORGIVE YOU, OKAY? THIS I SAY WITH TRUE SINCERITY. STOP LETTING IT GET IN THE WAY.
BLACKBELL SAID MY EARPIECE MALFUNCTIONED, WHICH IS BULLSHIT, BUT THEY PAID WELL TO EASE MY INCARCERATION. DID YOU KNOW MY AUNTIE IN PODGOMYY RECEIVED TEN THOUSAND FRANCS AS A SETTLEMENT?
FUCKING FRENCH, AS BAD AS THE AMERICANS. STILL, IT'S THE THOUGHT THAT COUNTS, RIGHT?
AND THE PAST IS THE PAST. FUCK ALL THAT NOISE.
SO WHAT IS THIS ABOUT, THEN?

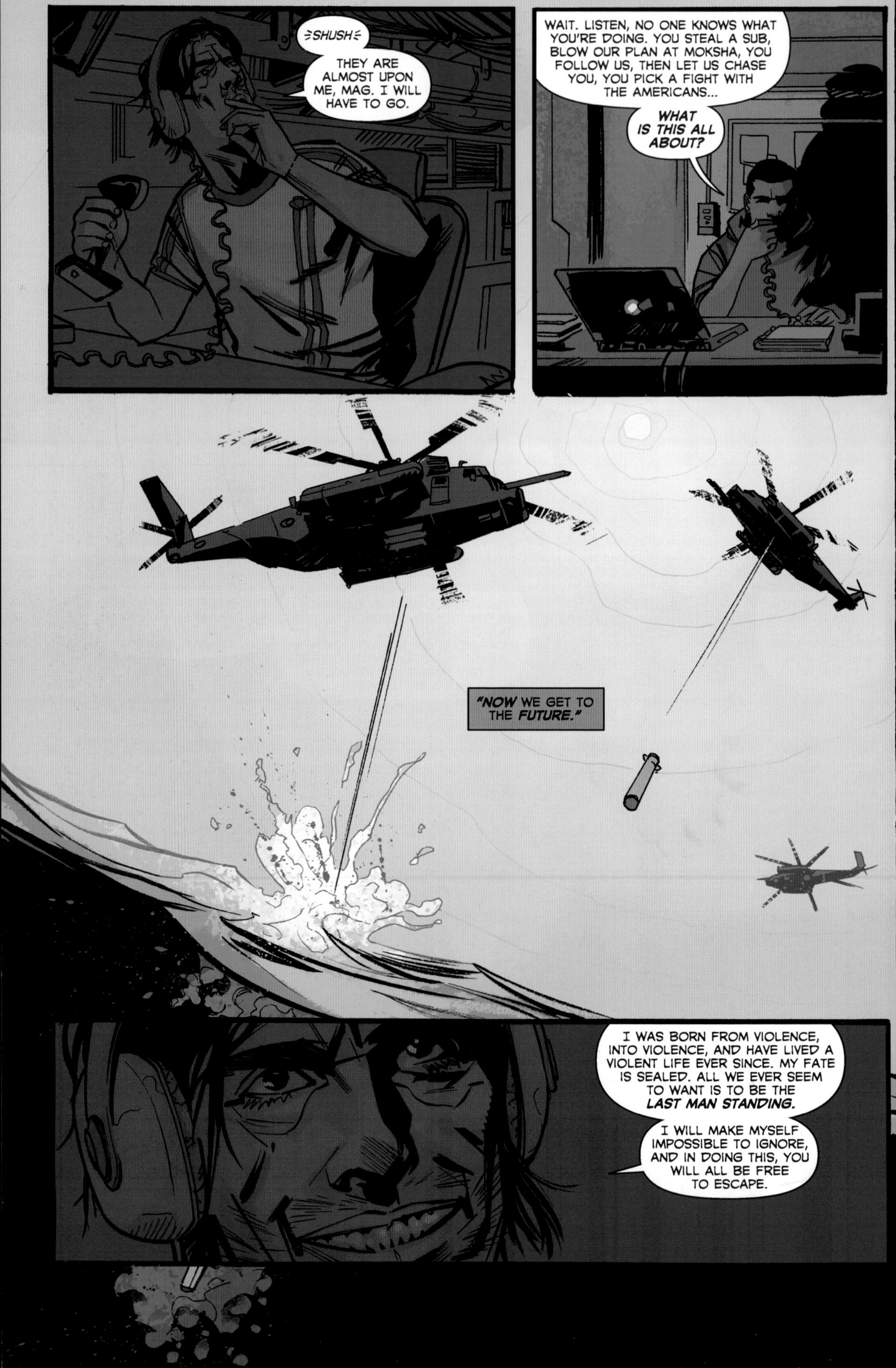
SHUSH
THEY ARE ALMOST UPON ME, MAG. I WILL HAVE TO GO.
WAIT. LISTEN, NO ONE KNOWS WHAT YOU'RE DOING. YOU STEAL A SUB, BLOW OUR PLAN AT MOKSHA, YOU FOLLOW US, THEN LET US CHASE YOU, YOU PICK A FIGHT WITH THE AMERICANS...
WHAT IS THIS ALL ABOUT?
"NOW WE GET TO THE FUTURE."
I WAS BORN FROM VIOLENCE, INTO VIOLENCE, AND HAVE LIVED A VIOLENT LIFE EVER SINCE. MY FATE IS SEALED. ALL WE EVER SEEM TO WANT IS TO BE THE LAST MAN STANDING.
I WILL MAKE MYSELF IMPOSSIBLE TO IGNORE, AND IN DOING THIS, YOU WILL ALL BE FREE TO ESCAPE.

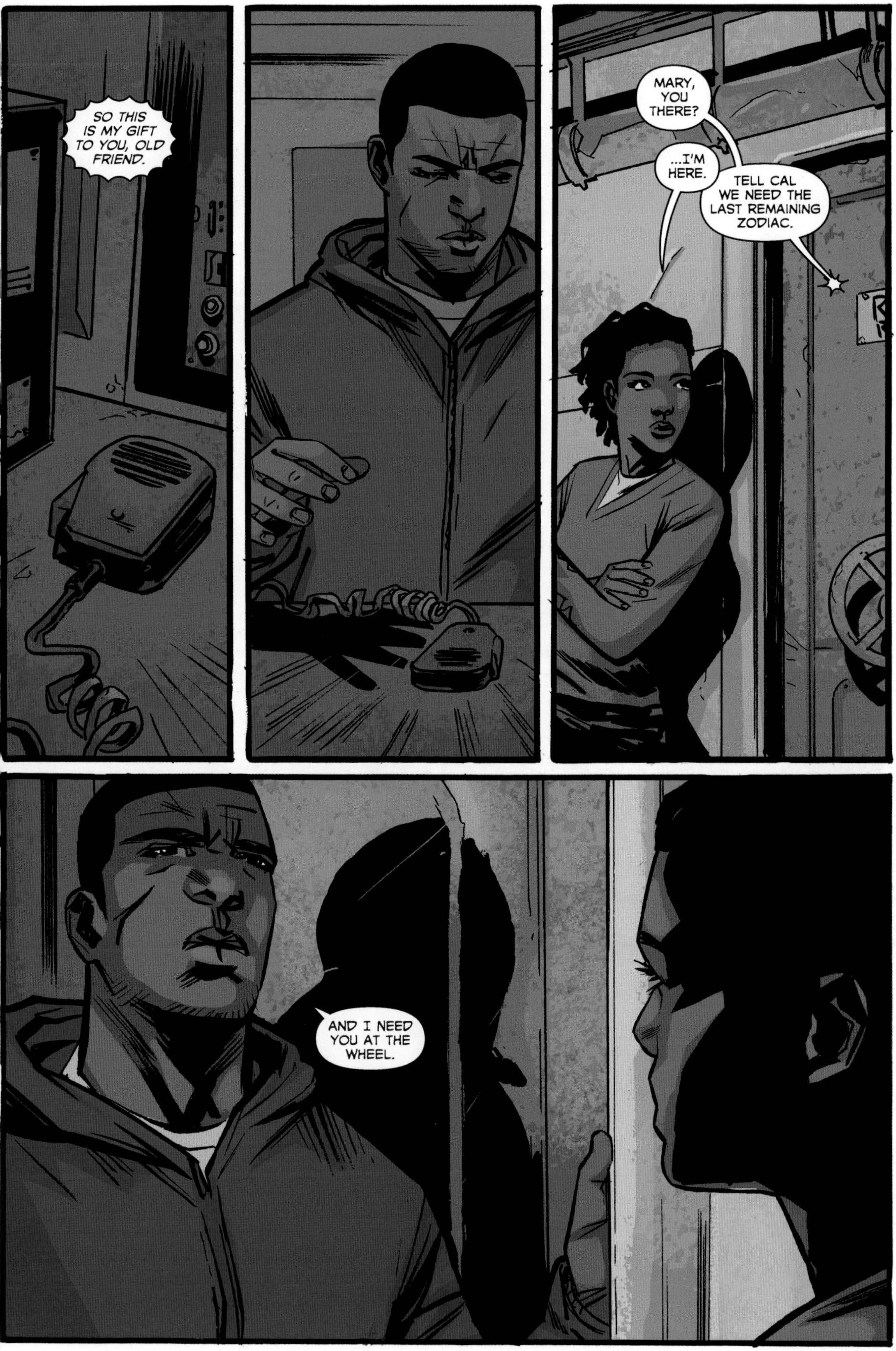
SO THIS IS MY GIFT TO YOU, OLD FRIEND.
MARY, YOU THERE?
...I'M HERE.
TELL CAL WE NEED THE LAST REMAINING ZODIAC.
AND I NEED YOU AT THE WHEEL.

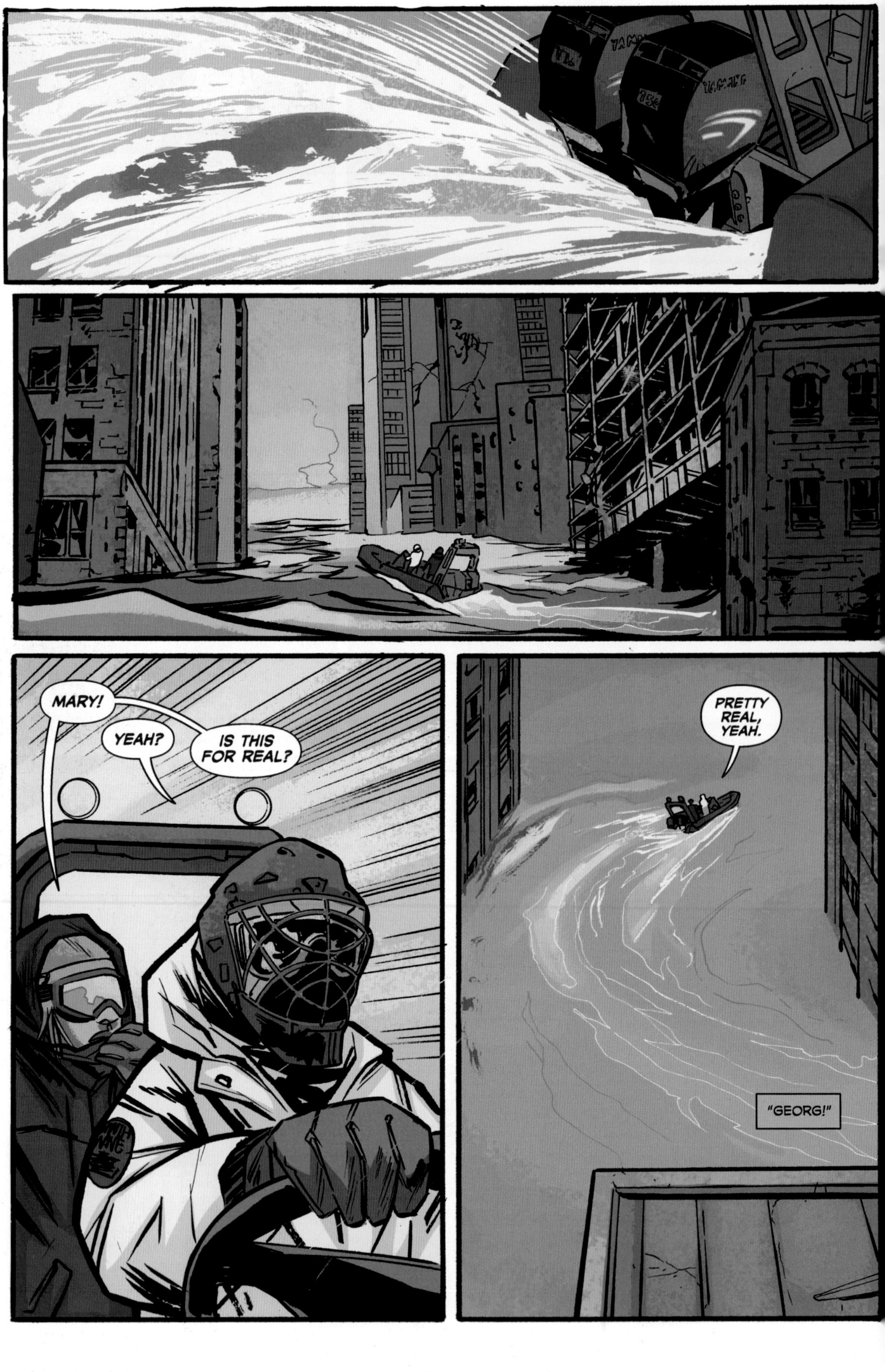
MARY!
YEAH?
IS THIS FOR REAL?
PRETTY REAL, YEAH.
"GEORG!"

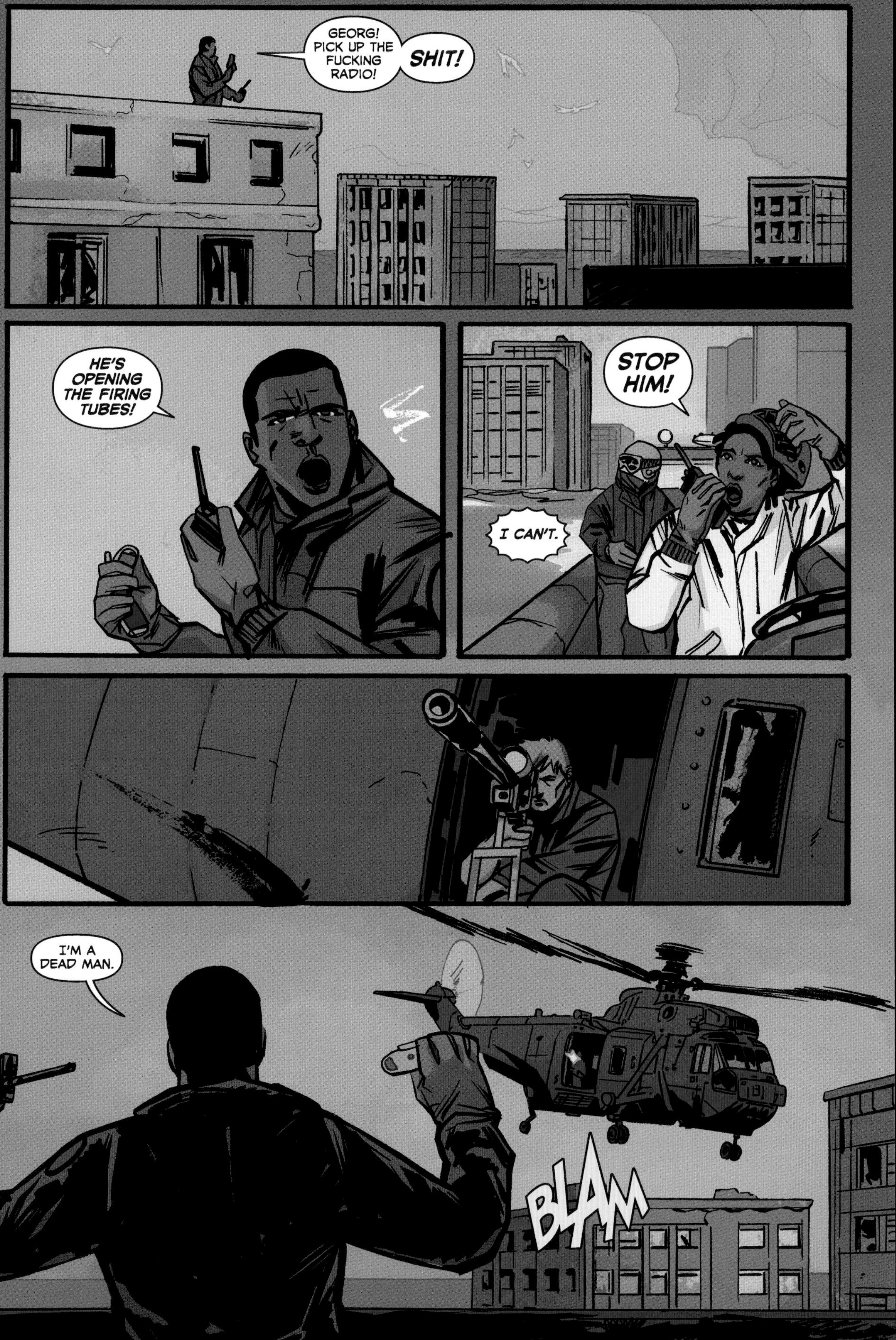
GEORG! PICK UP THE FUCKING RADIO!
SHIT!
HE'S OPENING THE FIRING TUBES!
STOP HIM!
I CAN'T.
I'M A DEAD MAN.
BLAM

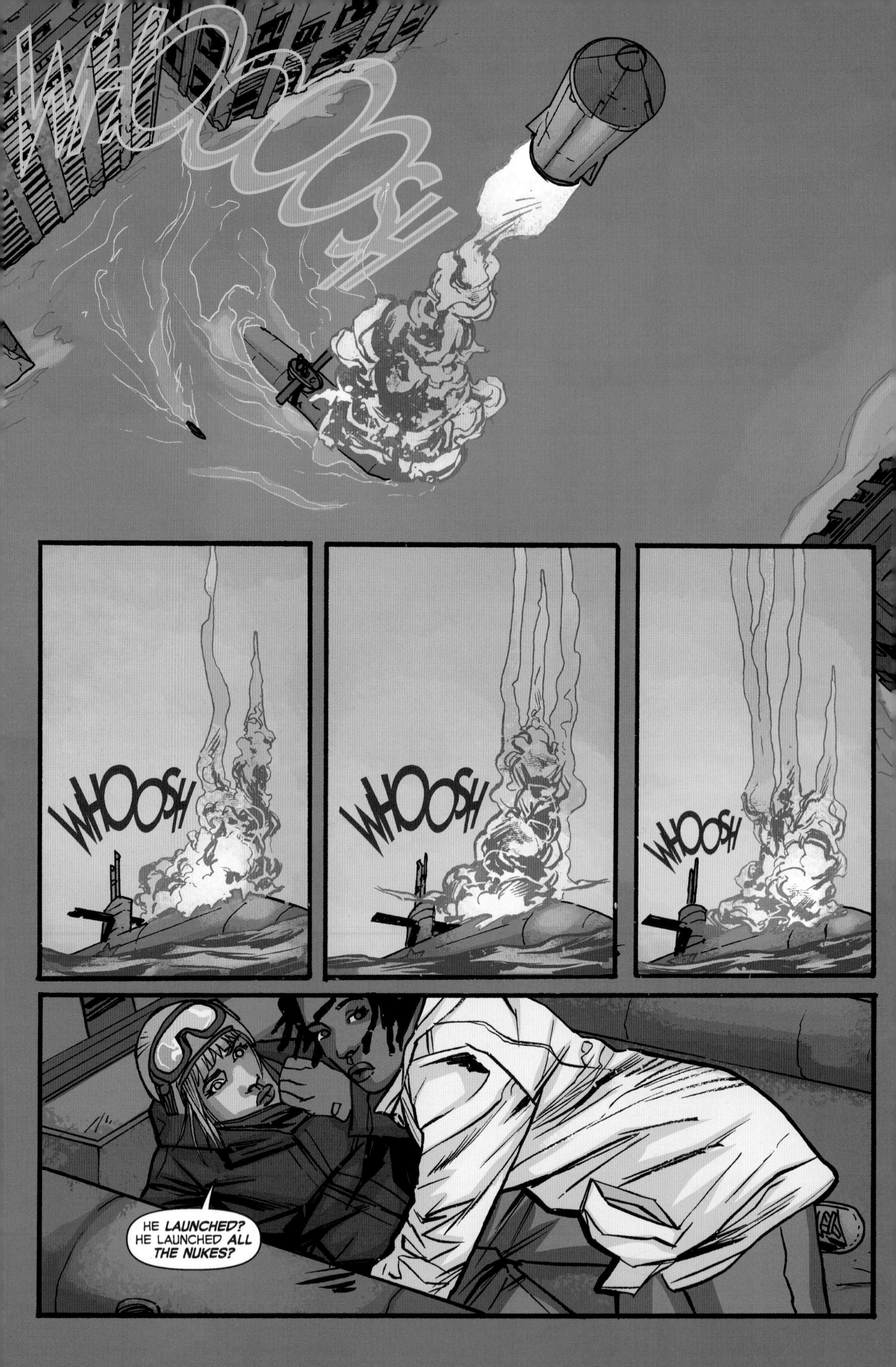
WHOOSH
WHOOSH
WHOOSH
WHOOSH
HE LAUNCHED? HE LAUNCHED ALL THE NUKES?

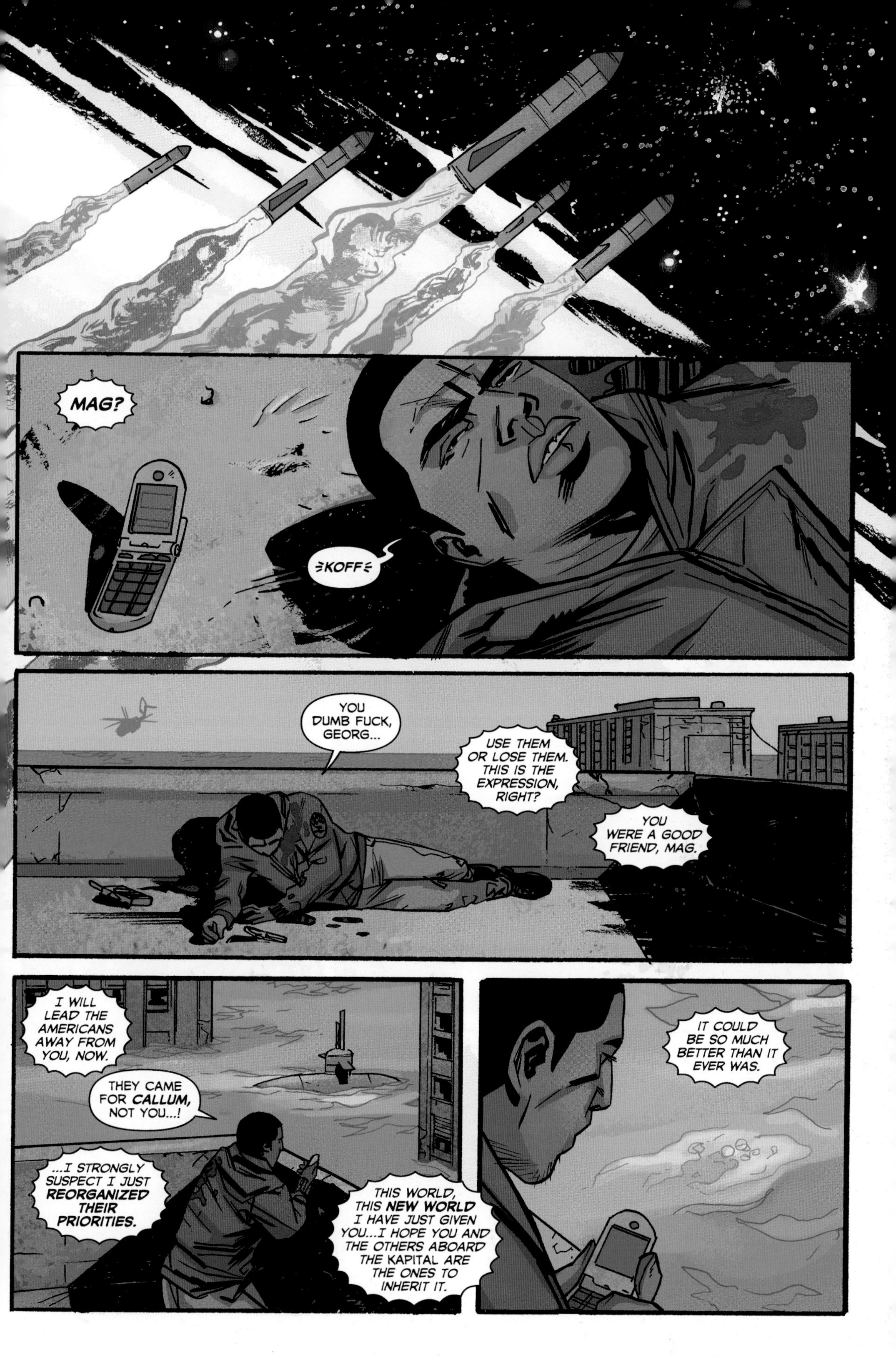
MAG?
KOFF
YOU DUMB FUCK, GEORG...
USE THEM OR LOSE THEM. THIS IS THE EXPRESSION, RIGHT?
YOU WERE A GOOD FRIEND, MAG.
I WILL LEAD THE AMERICANS AWAY FROM YOU, NOW.
THEY CAME FOR CALLUM, NOT YOU...!
...I STRONGLY SUSPECT I JUST REORGANIZED THEIR PRIORITIES.
THIS WORLD, THIS NEW WORLD I HAVE JUST GIVEN YOU...I HOPE YOU AND THE OTHERS ABOARD THE KAPITAL ARE THE ONES TO INHERIT IT.
IT COULD BE SO MUCH BETTER THAN IT EVER WAS.

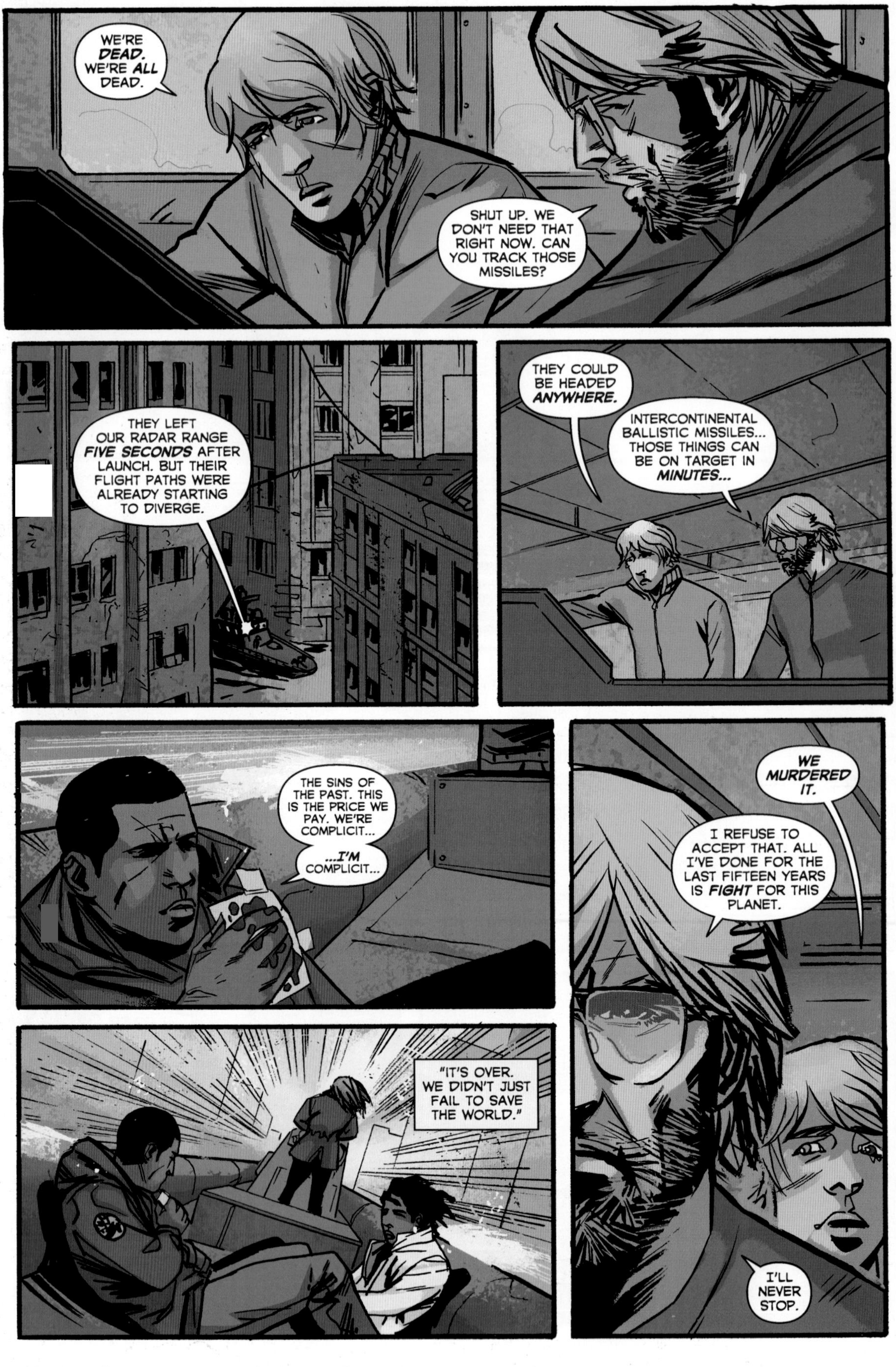
WE'RE DEAD. WE'RE ALL DEAD.
SHUT UP. WE DON'T NEED THAT RIGHT NOW. CAN YOU TRACK THOSE MISSILES?
THEY LEFT OUR RADAR RANGE FIVE SECONDS AFTER LAUNCH. BUT THEIR FLIGHT PATHS WERE ALREADY STARTING TO DIVERGE.
THEY COULD BE HEADED ANYWHERE.
INTERCONTINENTAL BALLISTIC MISSILES... THOSE THINGS CAN BE ON TARGET IN MINUTES...
THE SINS OF THE PAST. THIS IS THE PRICE WE PAY. WE'RE COMPLICIT...
...I'M COMPLICIT...
"IT'S OVER. WE DIDN'T JUST FAIL TO SAVE THE WORLD."
WE MURDERED IT.
I REFUSE TO ACCEPT THAT. ALL I'VE DONE FOR THE LAST FIFTEEN YEARS IS FIGHT FOR THIS PLANET.
I'LL NEVER STOP.

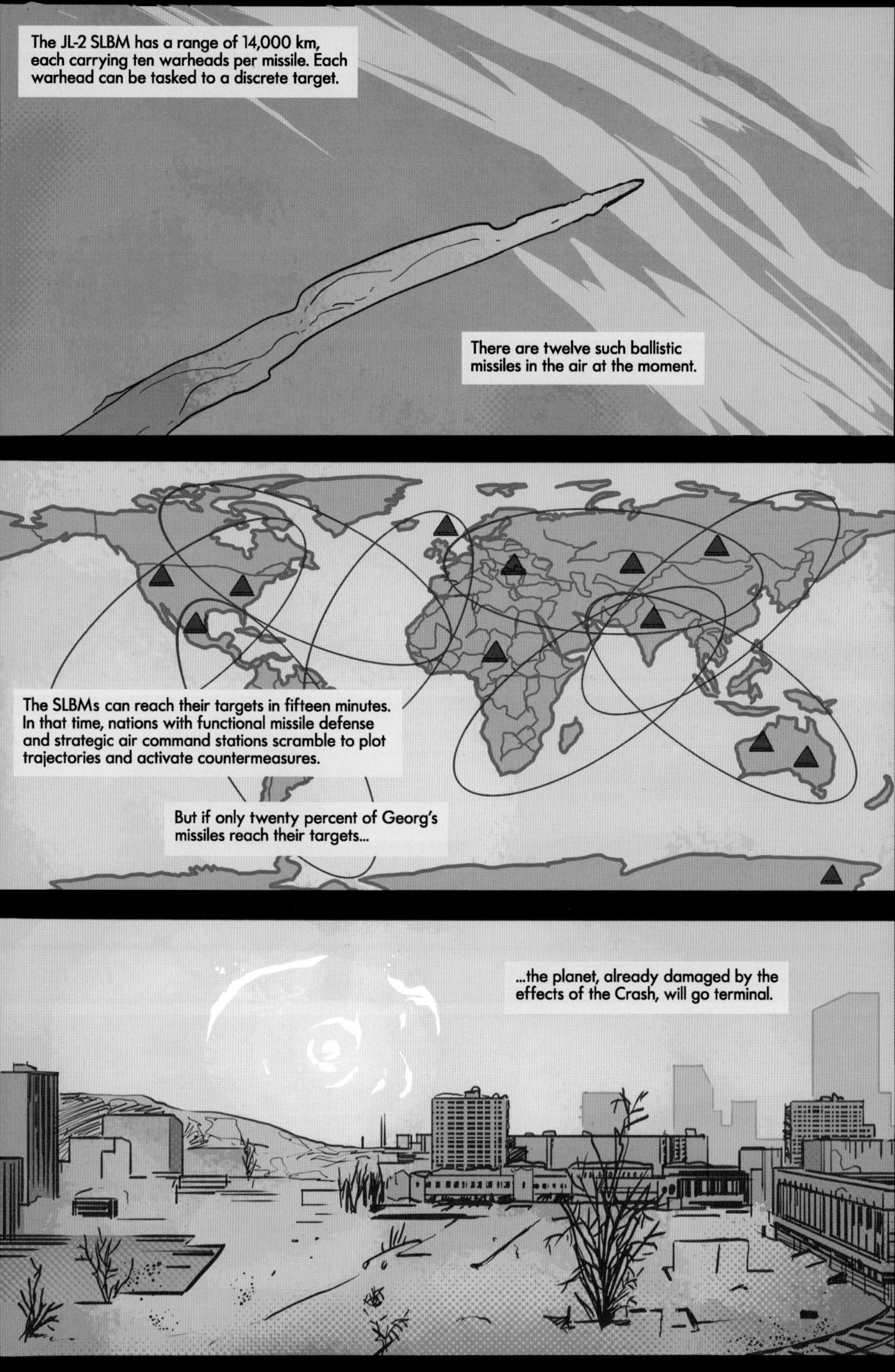
The JL-2 SLBM has a range of 14,000 km, each carrying ten warheads per missile. Each warhead can be tasked to a discrete target.
There are twelve such ballistic missiles in the air at the moment.
The SLBMs can reach their targets in fifteen minutes. In that time, nations with functional missile defense and strategic air command stations scramble to plot trajectories and activate countermeasures.
But if only twenty percent of Georg's missiles reach their targets...
...the planet, already damaged by the effects of the Crash, will go terminal.

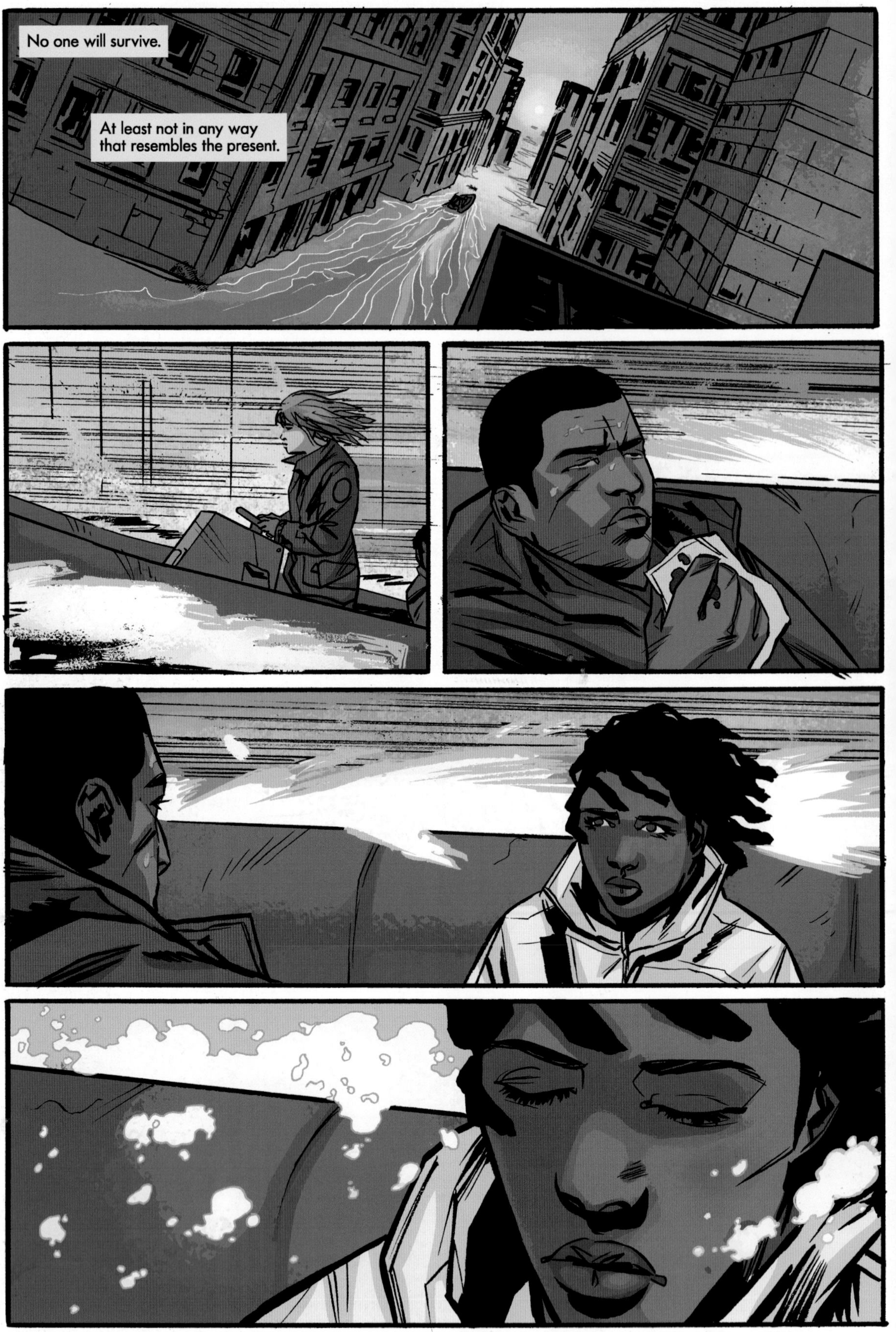
No one will survive.
At least not in any way that resembles the present.

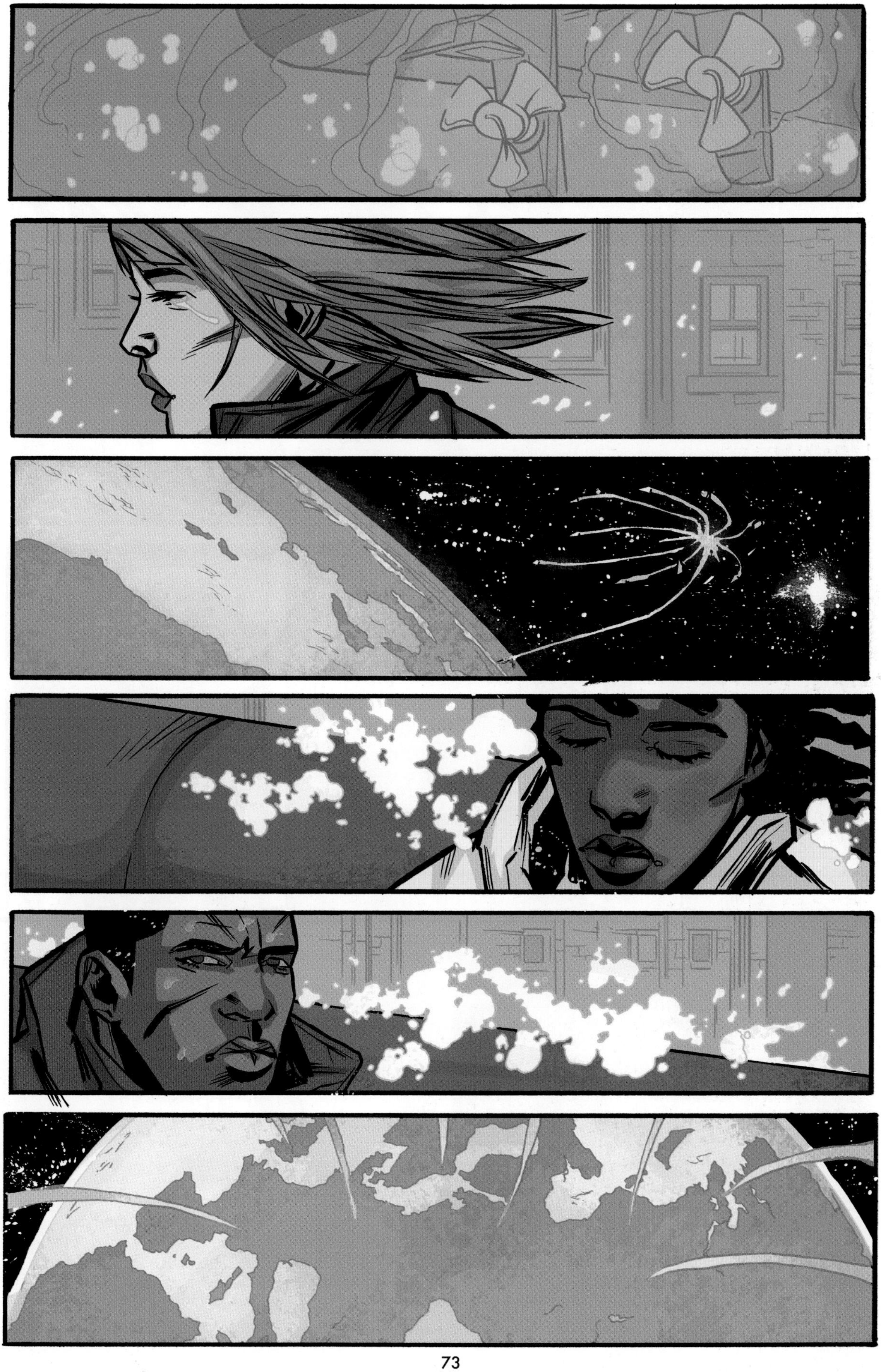

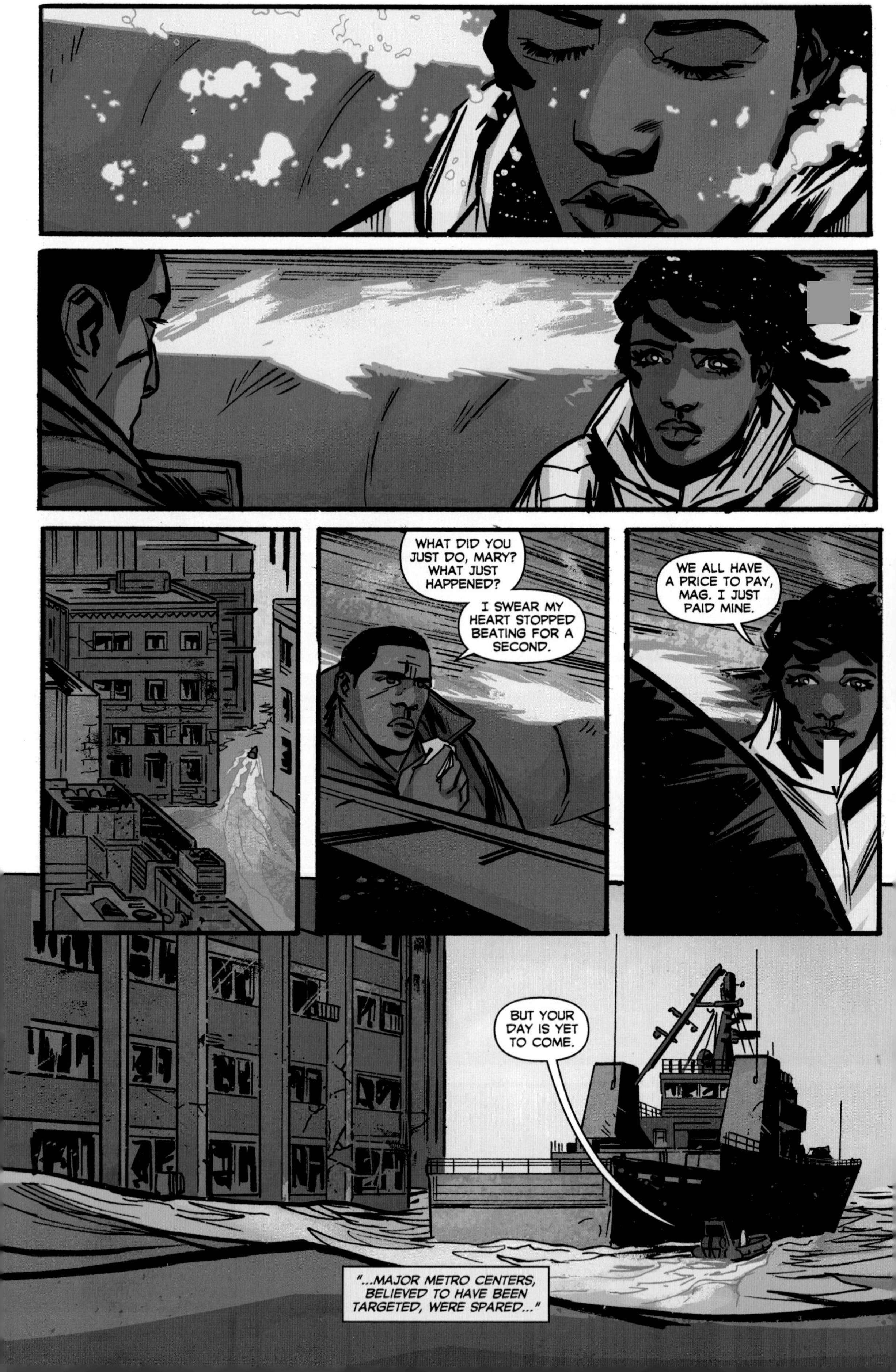
WHAT DID YOU JUST DO, MARY? WHAT JUST HAPPENED?
I SWEAR MY HEART STOPPED BEATING FOR A SECOND.
WE ALL HAVE A PRICE TO PAY, MAG. I JUST PAID MINE.
BUT YOUR DAY IS YET TO COME.
"...MAJOR METRO CENTERS, BELIEVED TO HAVE BEEN TARGETED, WERE SPARED..."

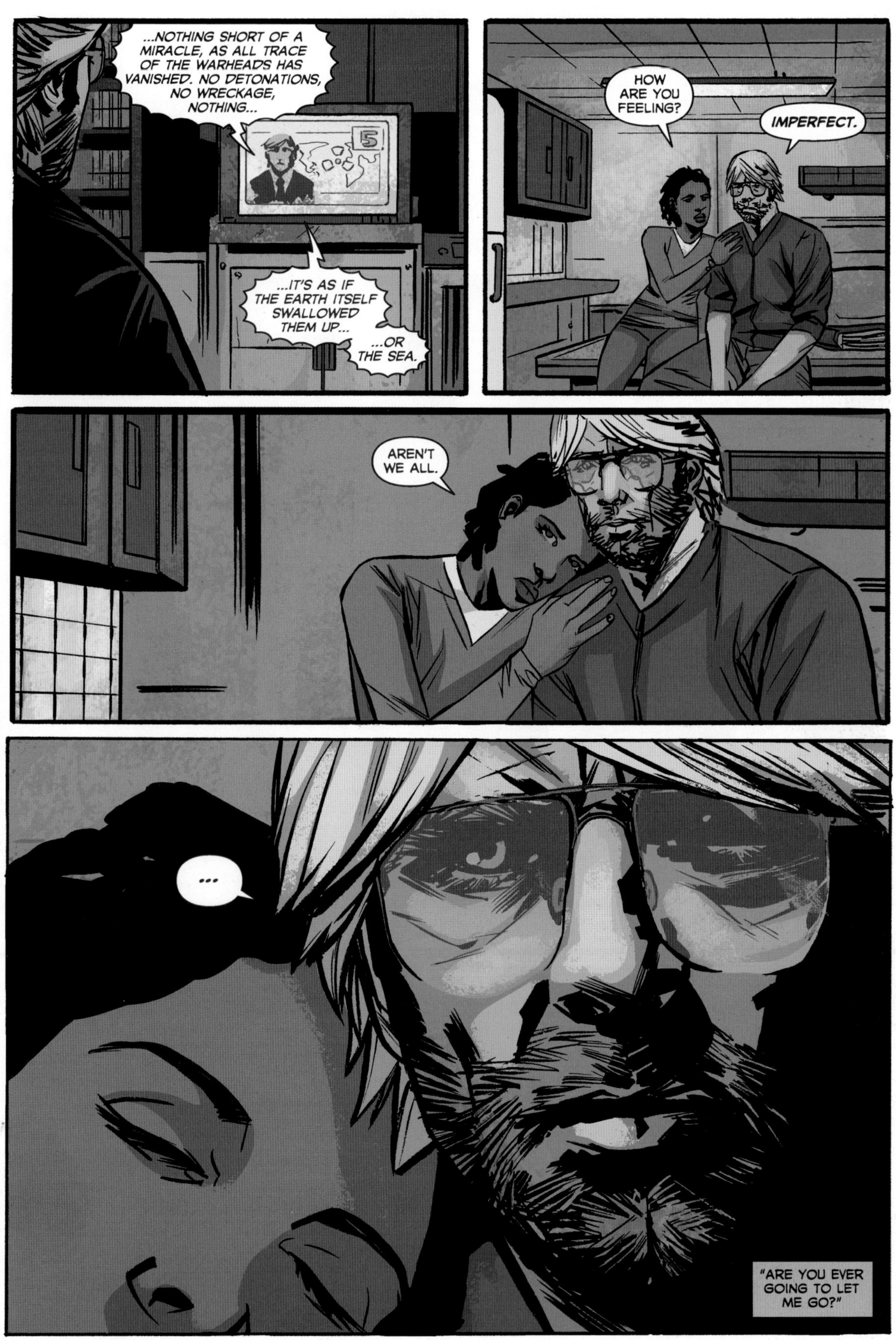
...NOTHING SHORT OF A MIRACLE, AS ALL TRACE OF THE WARHEADS HAS VANISHED. NO DETONATIONS, NO WRECKAGE, NOTHING...
...IT'S AS IF THE EARTH ITSELF SWALLOWED THEM UP...
...OR THE SEA.
HOW ARE YOU FEELING?
IMPERFECT.
AREN'T WE ALL.
...
"ARE YOU EVER GOING TO LET ME GO?"

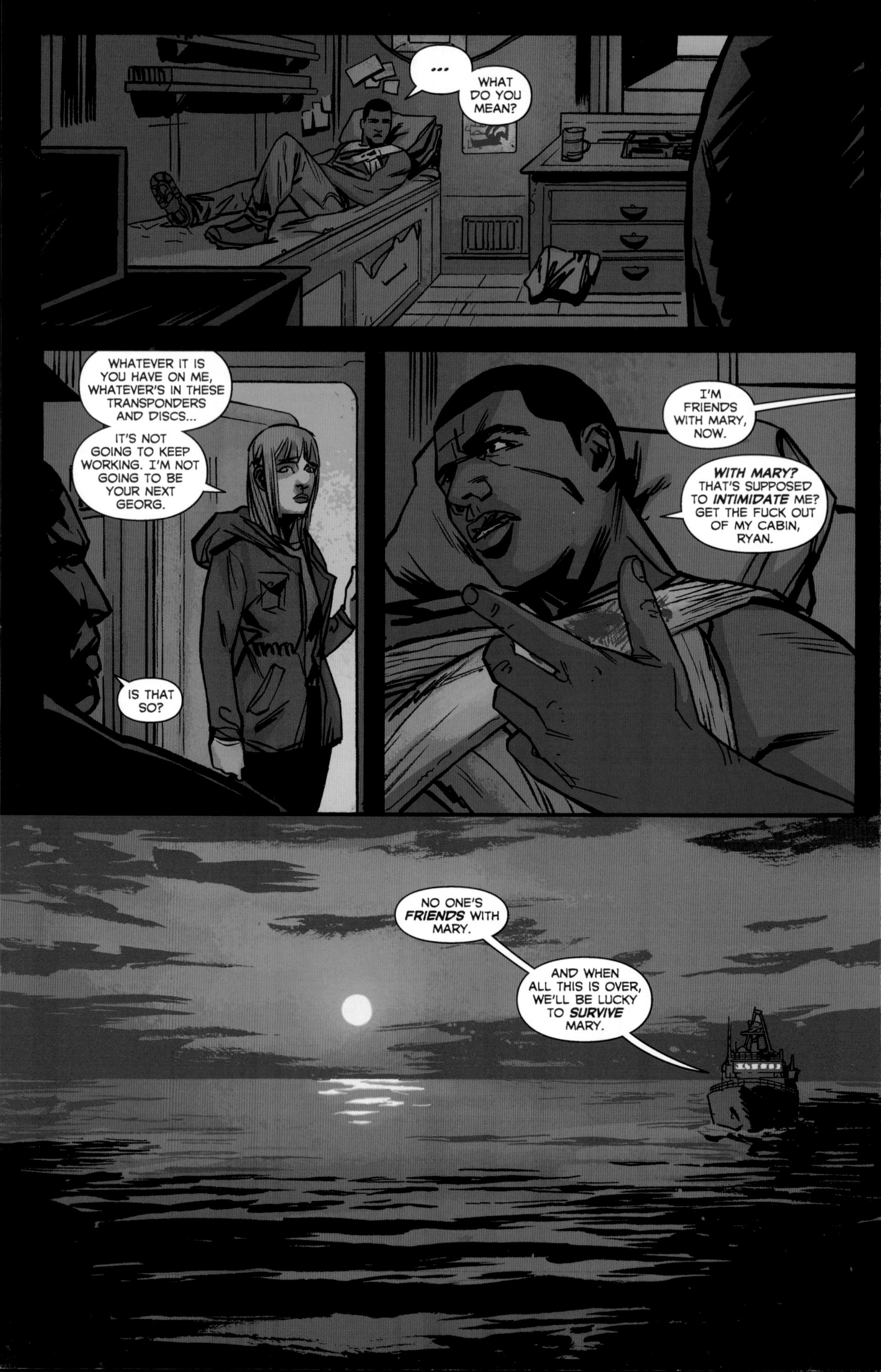
...
WHAT DO YOU MEAN?
WHATEVER IT IS YOU HAVE ON ME, WHATEVER'S IN THESE TRANSPONDERS AND DISCS...
IT'S NOT GOING TO KEEP WORKING. I'M NOT GOING TO BE YOUR NEXT GEORG.
IS THAT SO?
I'M FRIENDS WITH MARY, NOW.
WITH MARY? THAT'S SUPPOSED TO INTIMIDATE ME? GET THE FUCK OUT OF MY CABIN, RYAN.
NO ONE'S FRIENDS WITH MARY.
AND WHEN ALL THIS IS OVER, WE'LL BE LUCKY TO SURVIVE MARY.

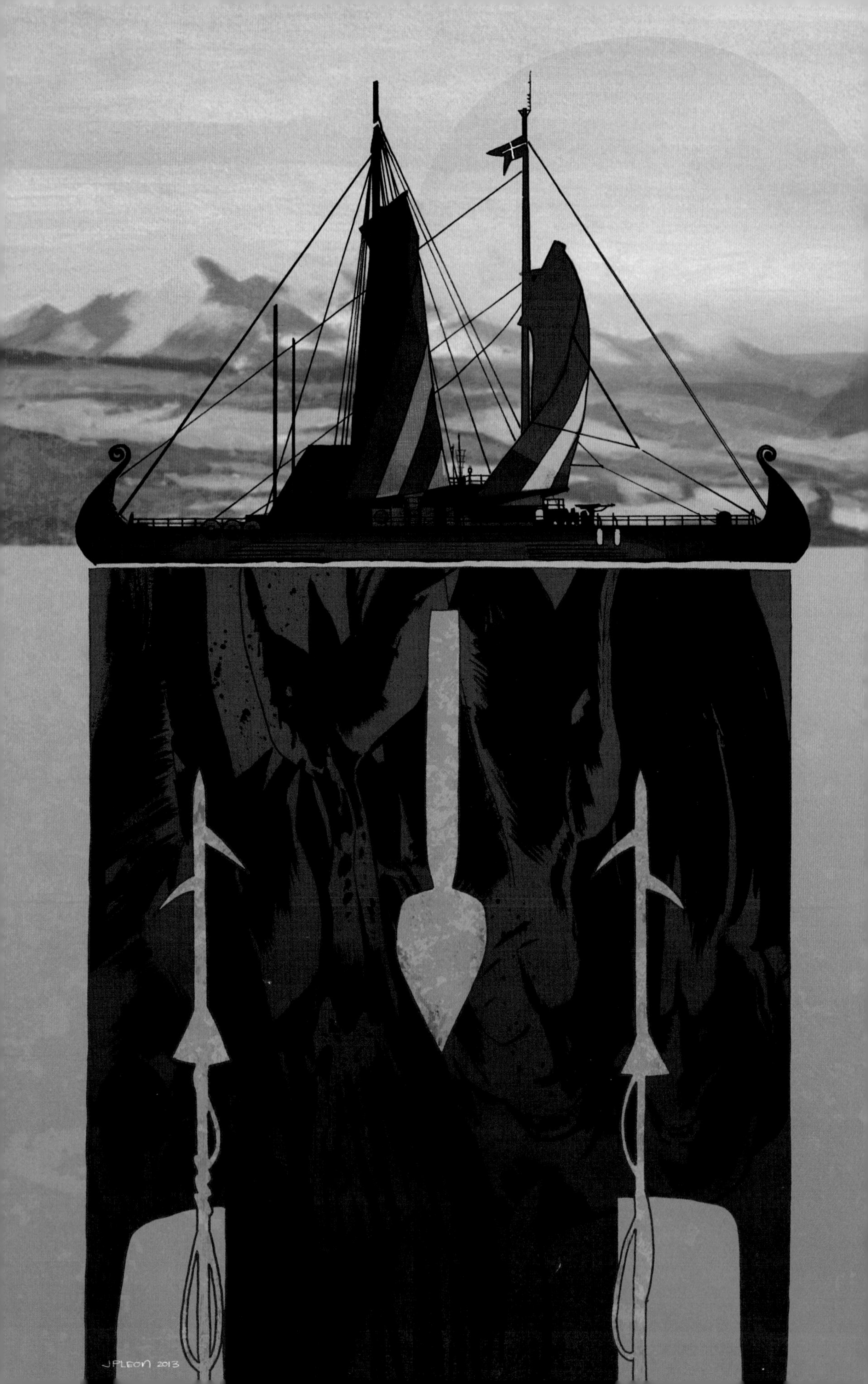
JPLEON 2013

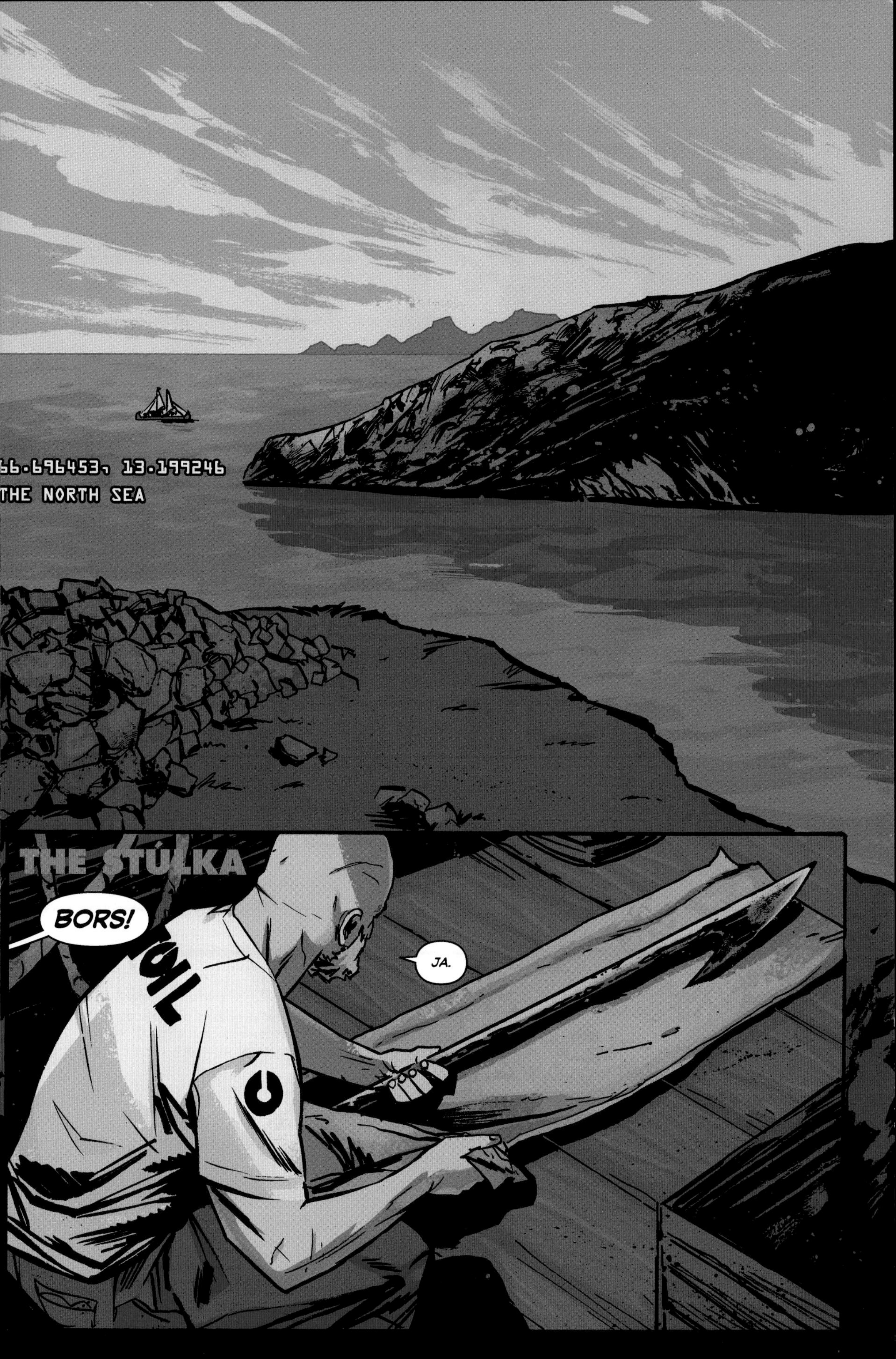
66.696453, 13.199246
THE NORTH SEA
THE STÚLKA
BORS!
JA.

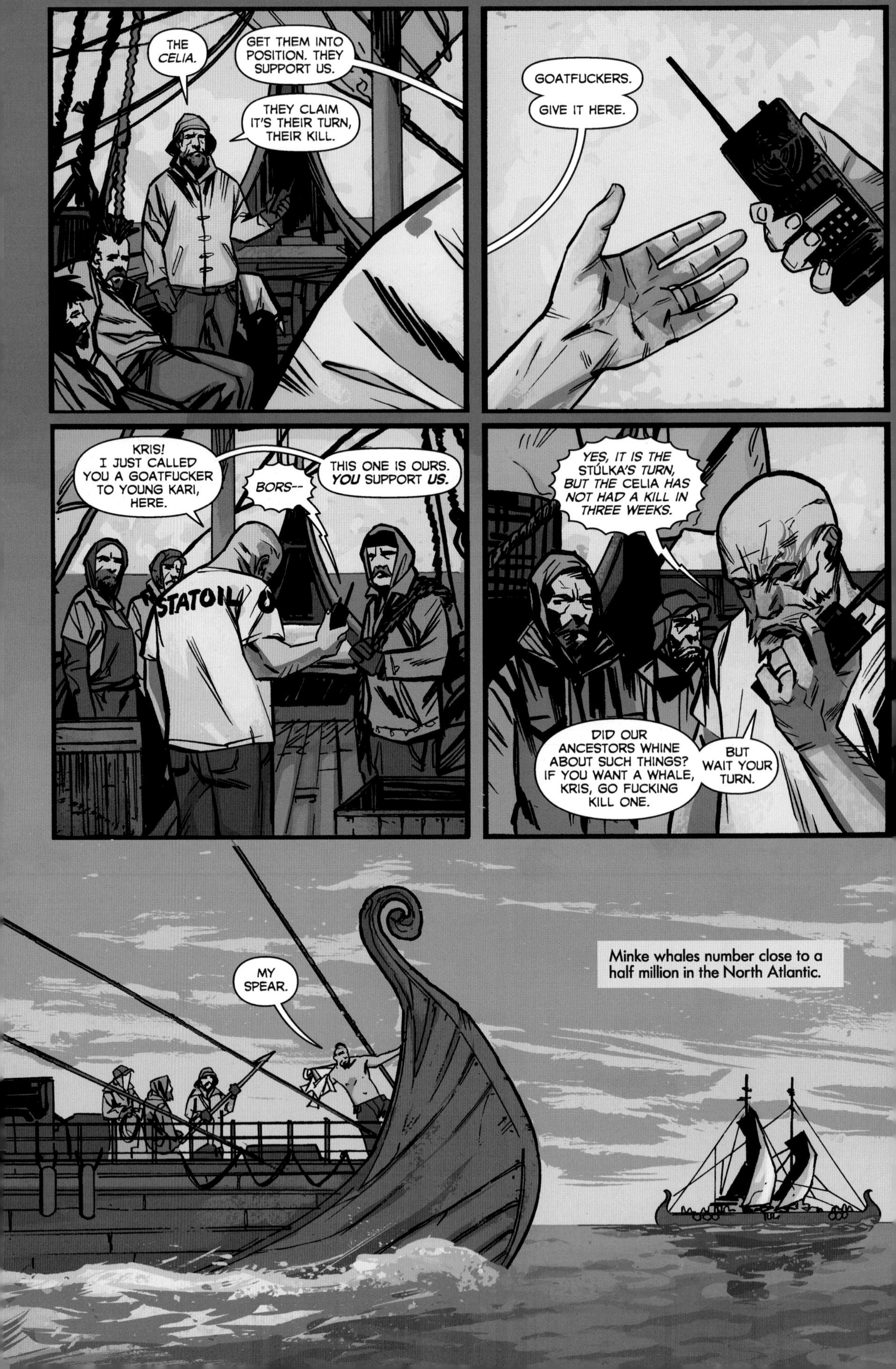
THE CELIA.
GET THEM INTO POSITION. THEY SUPPORT US.
THEY CLAIM IT'S THEIR TURN, THEIR KILL.
GOATFUCKERS.
GIVE IT HERE.
KRIS! I JUST CALLED YOU A GOATFUCKER TO YOUNG KARI, HERE.
BORS--
THIS ONE IS OURS. YOU SUPPORT US.
STATOIL
YES, IT IS THE STÚLKA'S TURN, BUT THE CELIA HAS NOT HAD A KILL IN THREE WEEKS.
DID OUR ANCESTORS WHINE ABOUT SUCH THINGS? IF YOU WANT A WHALE, KRIS, GO FUCKING KILL ONE.
BUT WAIT YOUR TURN.
MY SPEAR.
Minke whales number close to a half million in the North Atlantic.

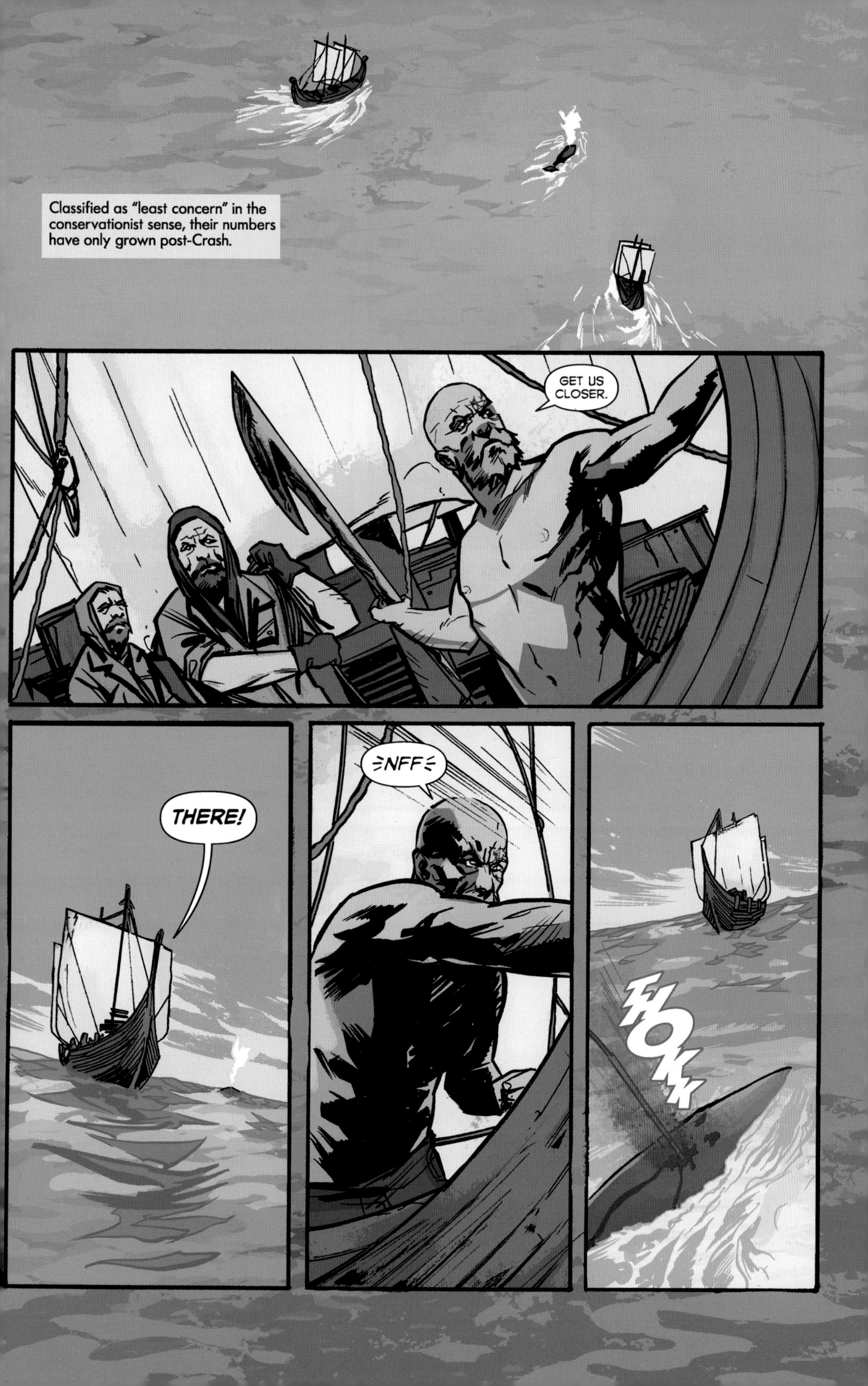
Classified as "least concern" in the conservationist sense, their numbers have only grown post-Crash.
GET US CLOSER.
THERE!
NFF
THOKK

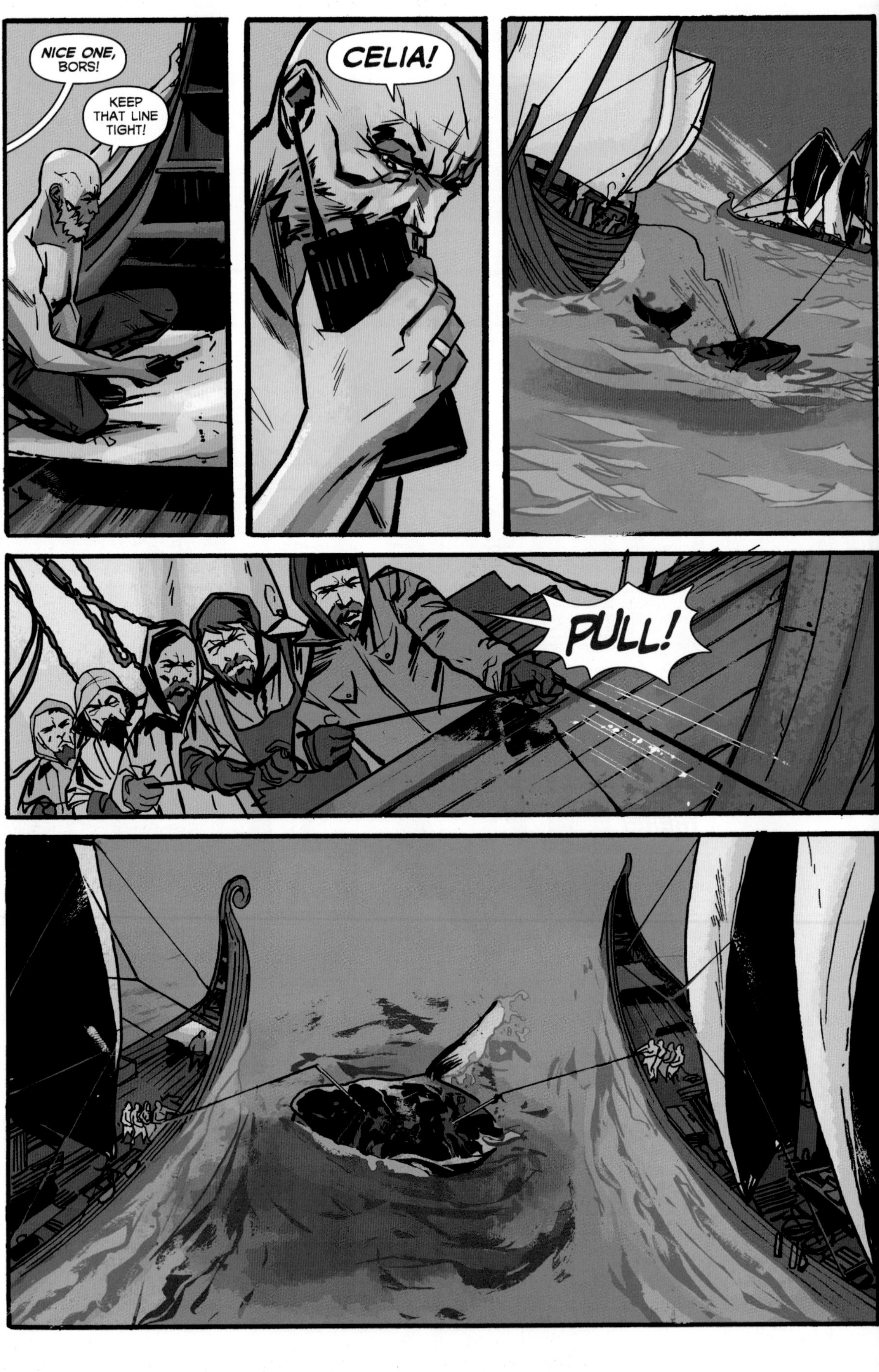
NICE ONE, BORS!
KEEP THAT LINE TIGHT!
CELIA!
PULL!

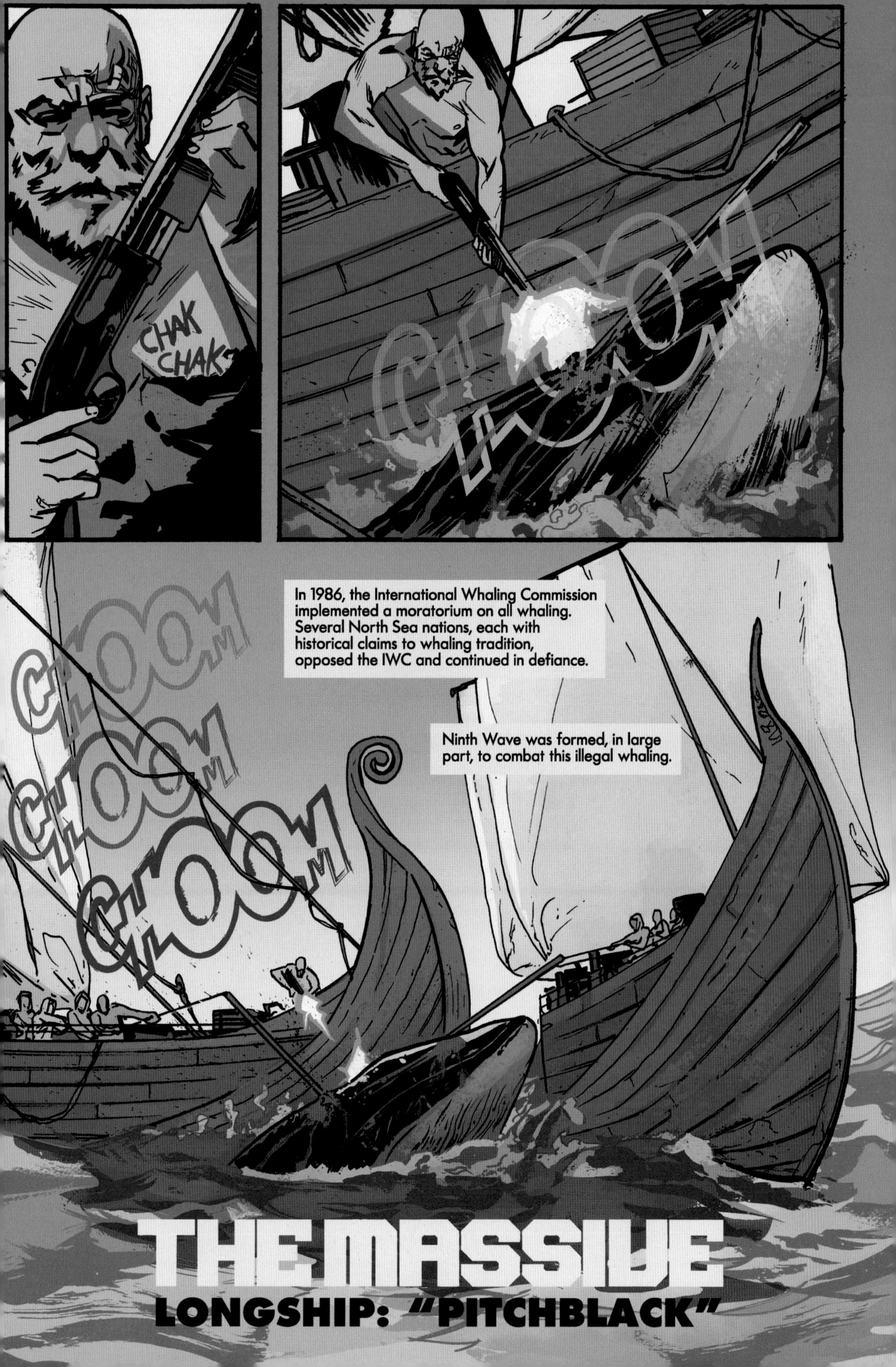
CHAK CHAK
CHOOOM
In 1986, the International Whaling Commission implemented a moratorium on all whaling. Several North Sea nations, each with historical claims to whaling tradition, opposed the IWC and continued in defiance.
Ninth Wave was formed, in large part, to combat this illegal whaling.
CHOOOM
CHOOOM
CHOOOM
CHOOOM
THE MASSIVE
LONGSHIP: "PITCHBLACK"

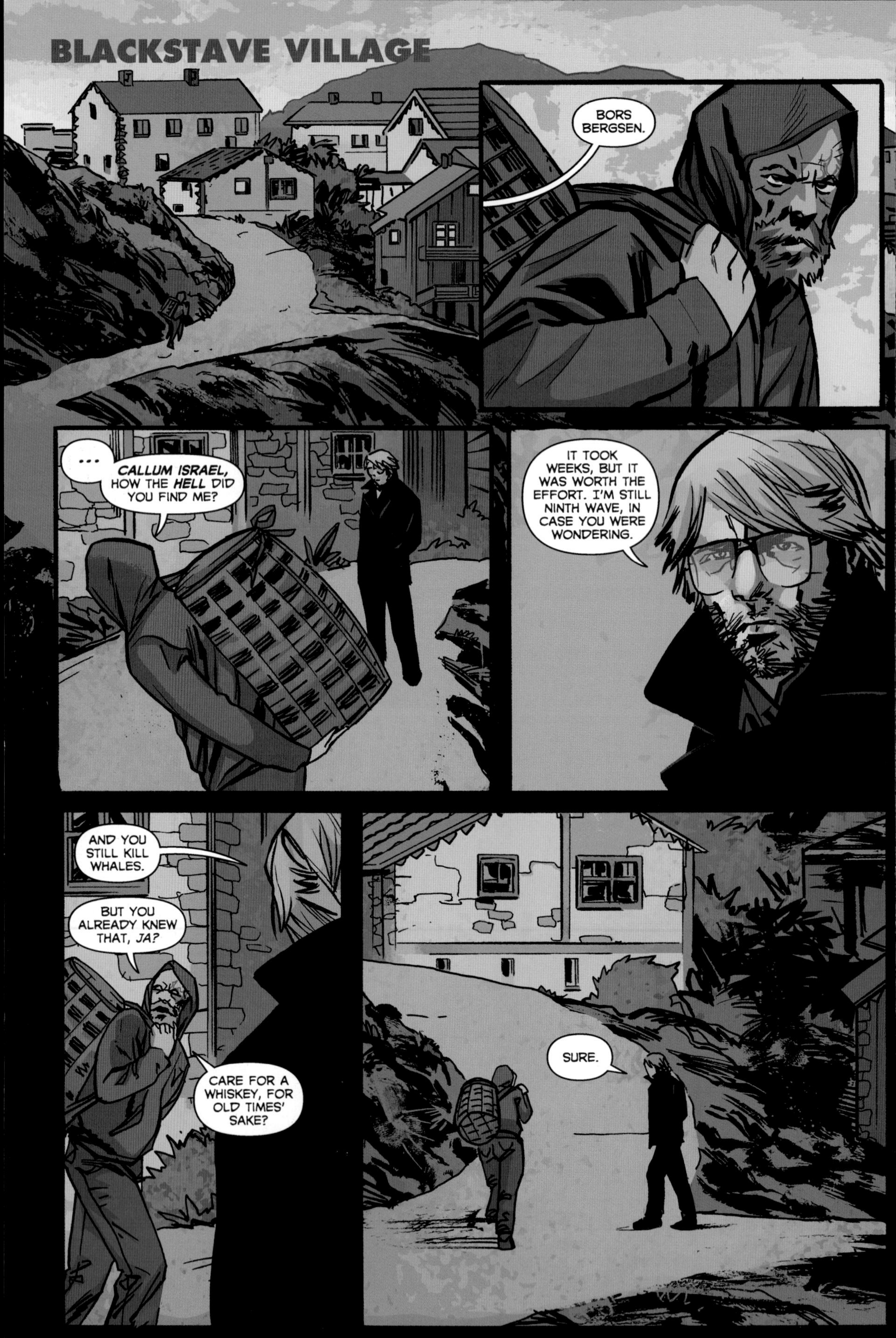
BLACKSTAVE VILLAGE
BORS BERGSEN.
... CALLUM ISRAEL, HOW THE HELL DID YOU FIND ME?
IT TOOK WEEKS, BUT IT WAS WORTH THE EFFORT. I'M STILL NINTH WAVE, IN CASE YOU WERE WONDERING.
AND YOU STILL KILL WHALES.
BUT YOU ALREADY KNEW THAT, JA?
CARE FOR A WHISKEY, FOR OLD TIMES' SAKE?
SURE.

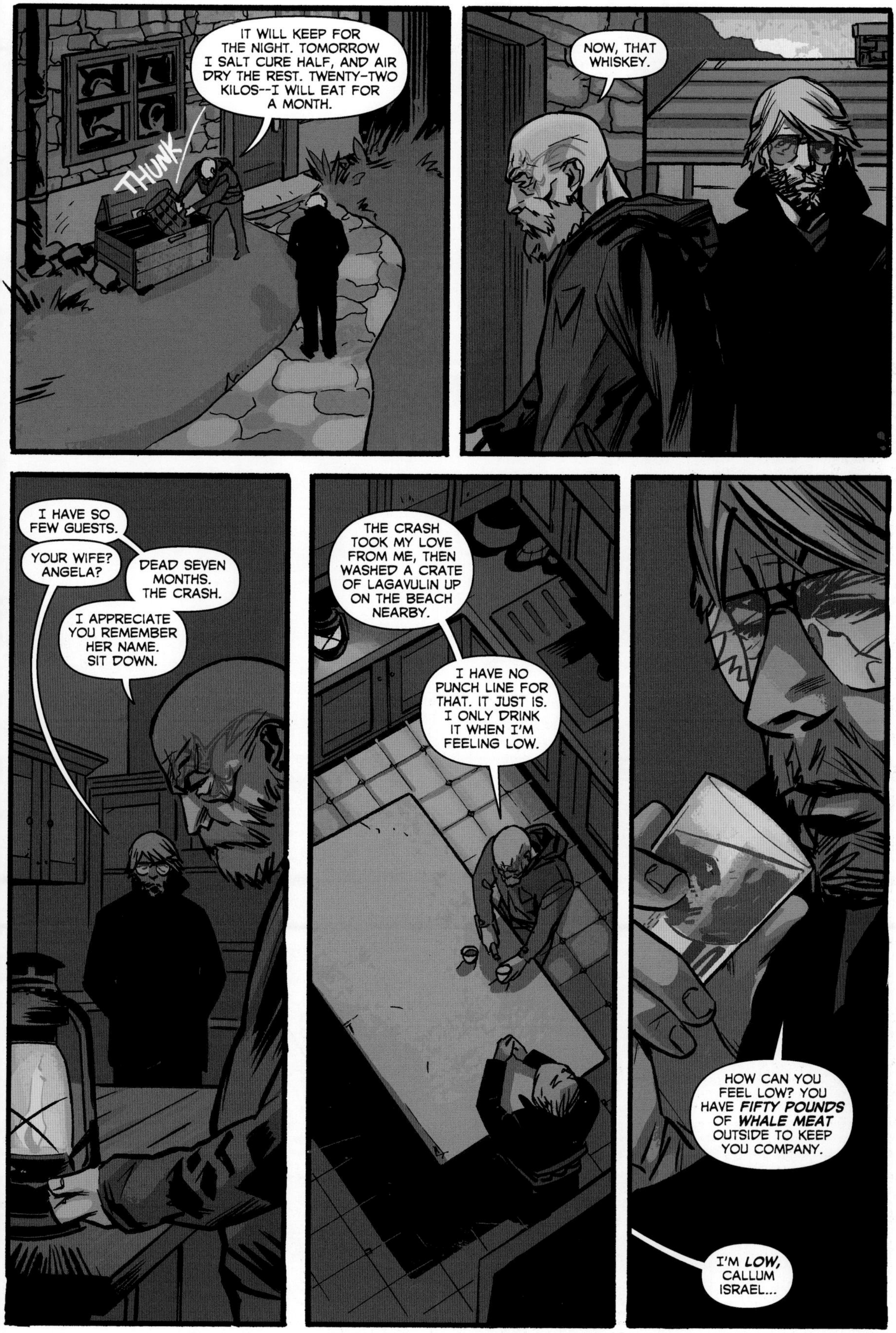
IT WILL KEEP FOR THE NIGHT. TOMORROW I SALT CURE HALF, AND AIR DRY THE REST. TWENTY-TWO KILOS--I WILL EAT FOR A MONTH.
THUNK
NOW, THAT WHISKEY.
I HAVE SO FEW GUESTS.
YOUR WIFE? ANGELA?
DEAD SEVEN MONTHS. THE CRASH.
I APPRECIATE YOU REMEMBER HER NAME. SIT DOWN.
THE CRASH TOOK MY LOVE FROM ME, THEN WASHED A CRATE OF LAGAVULIN UP ON THE BEACH NEARBY.
I HAVE NO PUNCH LINE FOR THAT. IT JUST IS. I ONLY DRINK IT WHEN I'M FEELING LOW.
HOW CAN YOU FEEL LOW? YOU HAVE ***FIFTY POUNDS*** OF ***WHALE MEAT*** OUTSIDE TO KEEP YOU COMPANY.
I'M ***LOW,*** CALLUM ISRAEL...

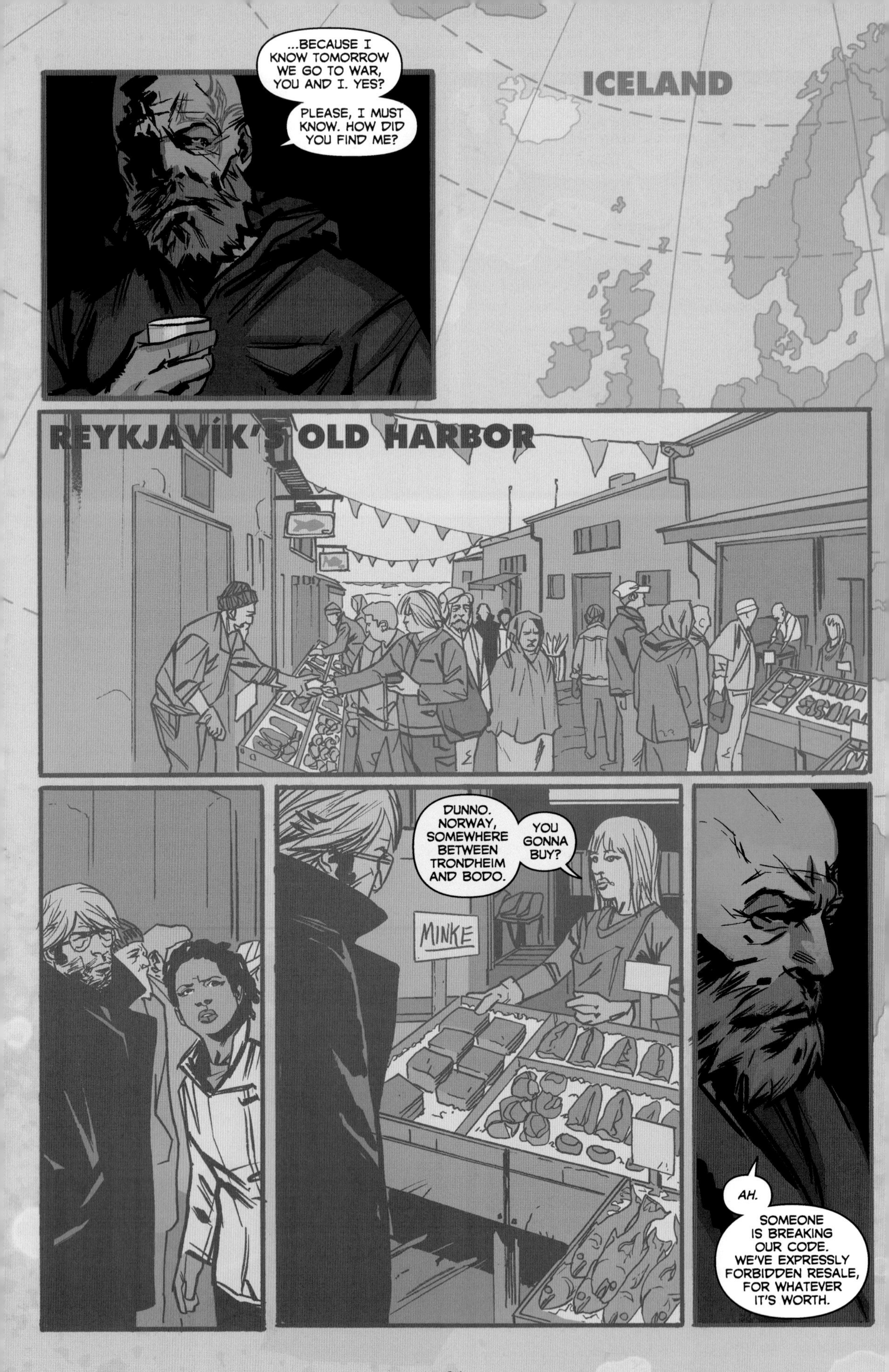
...BECAUSE I KNOW TOMORROW WE GO TO WAR, YOU AND I. YES?
PLEASE, I MUST KNOW. HOW DID YOU FIND ME?
ICELAND
REYKJAVÍK'S OLD HARBOR
DUNNO. NORWAY, SOMEWHERE BETWEEN TRONDHEIM AND BODO.
YOU GONNA BUY?
MINKE
AH.
SOMEONE IS BREAKING OUR CODE. WE'VE EXPRESSLY FORBIDDEN RESALE, FOR WHATEVER IT'S WORTH.

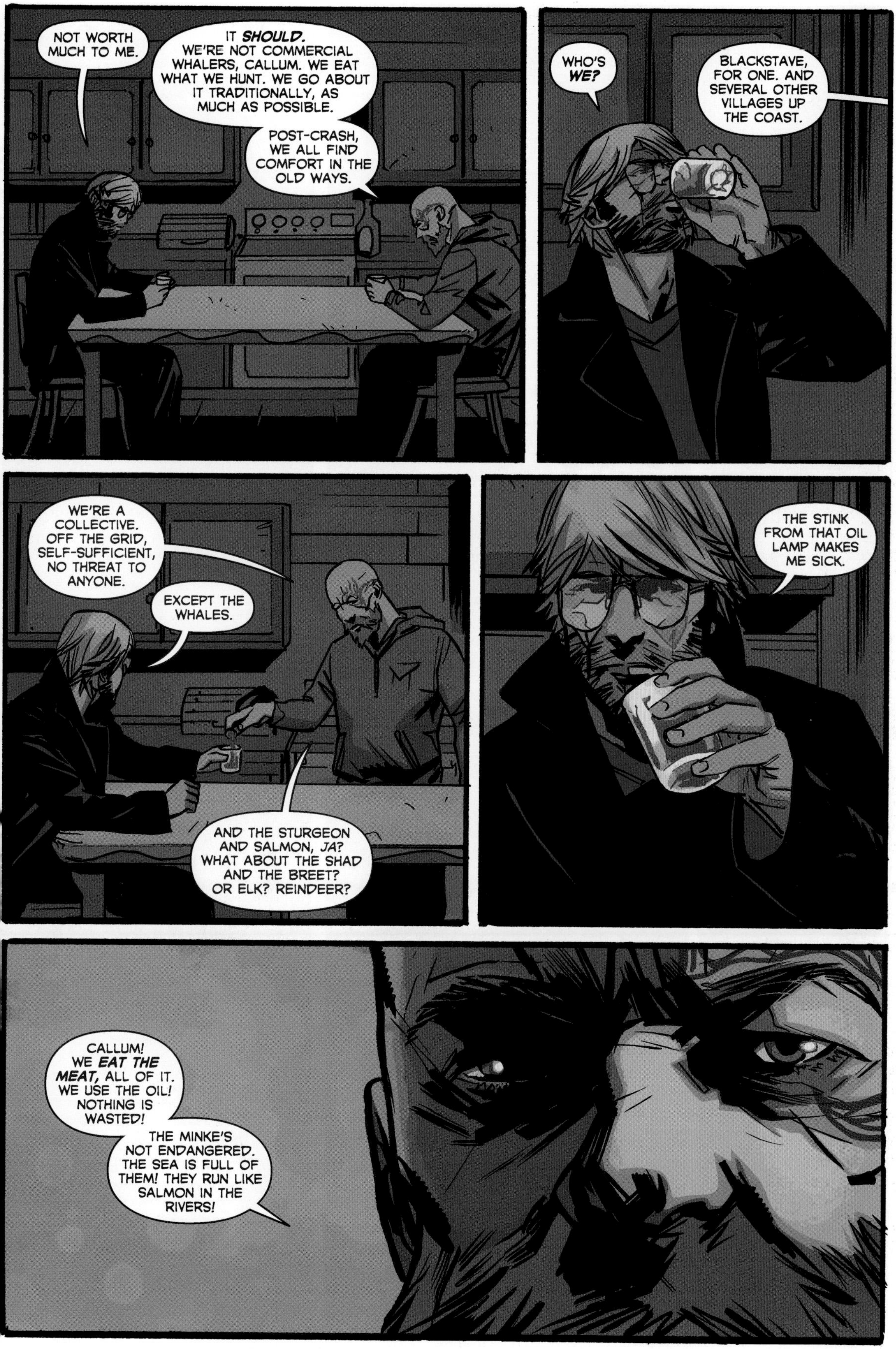
NOT WORTH MUCH TO ME.
IT **SHOULD.** WE'RE NOT COMMERCIAL WHALERS, CALLUM. WE EAT WHAT WE HUNT. WE GO ABOUT IT TRADITIONALLY, AS MUCH AS POSSIBLE.
POST-CRASH, WE ALL FIND COMFORT IN THE OLD WAYS.
WHO'S **WE?**
BLACKSTAVE, FOR ONE. AND SEVERAL OTHER VILLAGES UP THE COAST.
WE'RE A COLLECTIVE. OFF THE GRID, SELF-SUFFICIENT, NO THREAT TO ANYONE.
EXCEPT THE WHALES.
AND THE STURGEON AND SALMON, *JA?* WHAT ABOUT THE SHAD AND THE BREET? OR ELK? REINDEER?
THE STINK FROM THAT OIL LAMP MAKES ME SICK.
CALLUM! WE **EAT THE MEAT,** ALL OF IT. WE USE THE OIL! NOTHING IS WASTED!
THE MINKE'S NOT ENDANGERED. THE SEA IS FULL OF THEM! THEY RUN LIKE SALMON IN THE RIVERS!

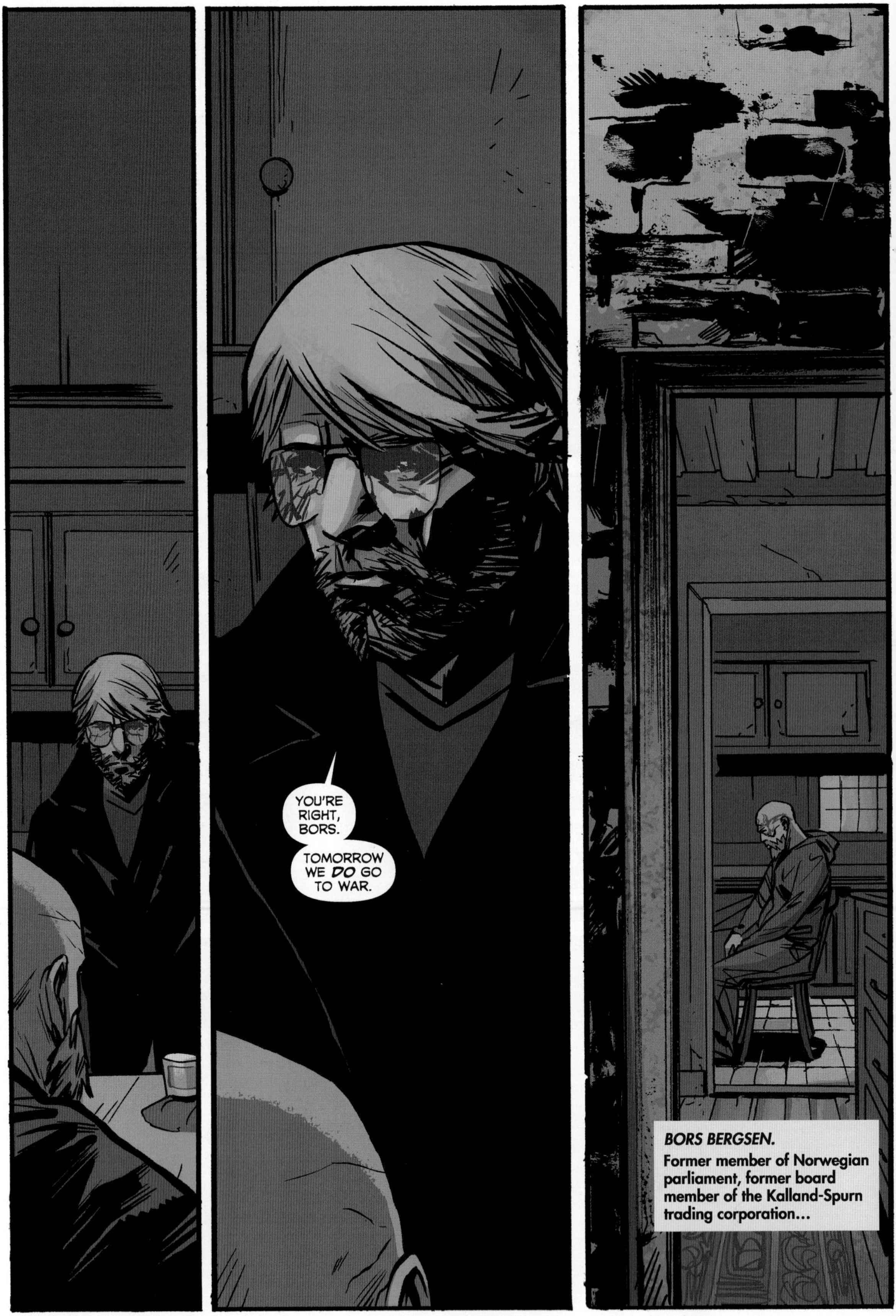

YOU'RE RIGHT, BORS.
TOMORROW WE *DO* GO TO WAR.
BORS BERGSEN.
Former member of Norwegian parliament, former board member of the Kalland-Spurn trading corporation...

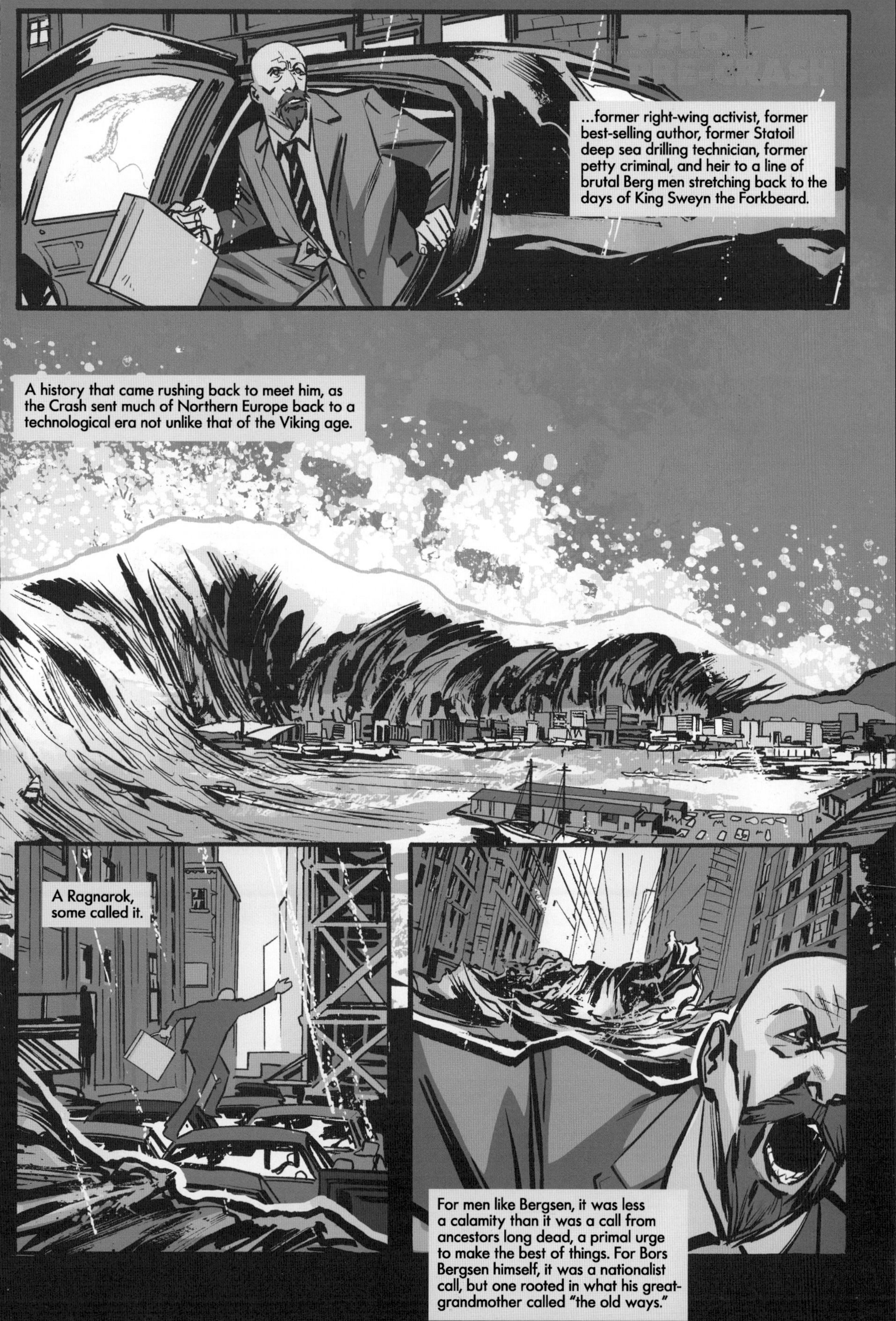
...former right-wing activist, former best-selling author, former Statoil deep sea drilling technician, former petty criminal, and heir to a line of brutal Berg men stretching back to the days of King Sweyn the Forkbeard.
A history that came rushing back to meet him, as the Crash sent much of Northern Europe back to a technological era not unlike that of the Viking age.
A Ragnarok, some called it.
For men like Bergsen, it was less a calamity than it was a call from ancestors long dead, a primal urge to make the best of things. For Bors Bergsen himself, it was a nationalist call, but one rooted in what his great-grandmother called "the old ways."

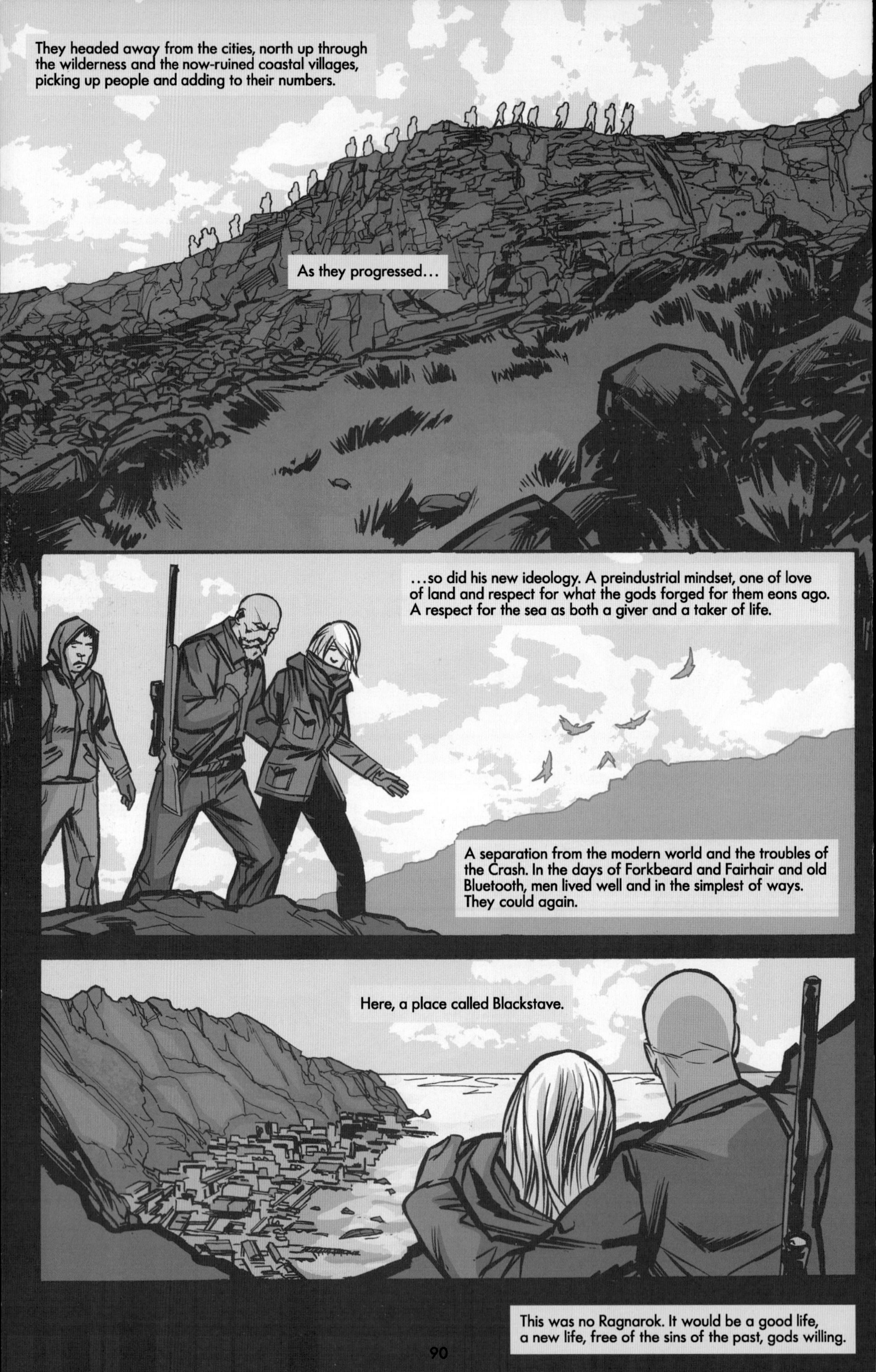
They headed away from the cities, north up through the wilderness and the now-ruined coastal villages, picking up people and adding to their numbers.
As they progressed...
...so did his new ideology. A preindustrial mindset, one of love of land and respect for what the gods forged for them eons ago. A respect for the sea as both a giver and a taker of life.
A separation from the modern world and the troubles of the Crash. In the days of Forkbeard and Fairhair and old Bluetooth, men lived well and in the simplest of ways. They could again.
Here, a place called Blackstave.
This was no Ragnarok. It would be a good life, a new life, free of the sins of the past, gods willing.

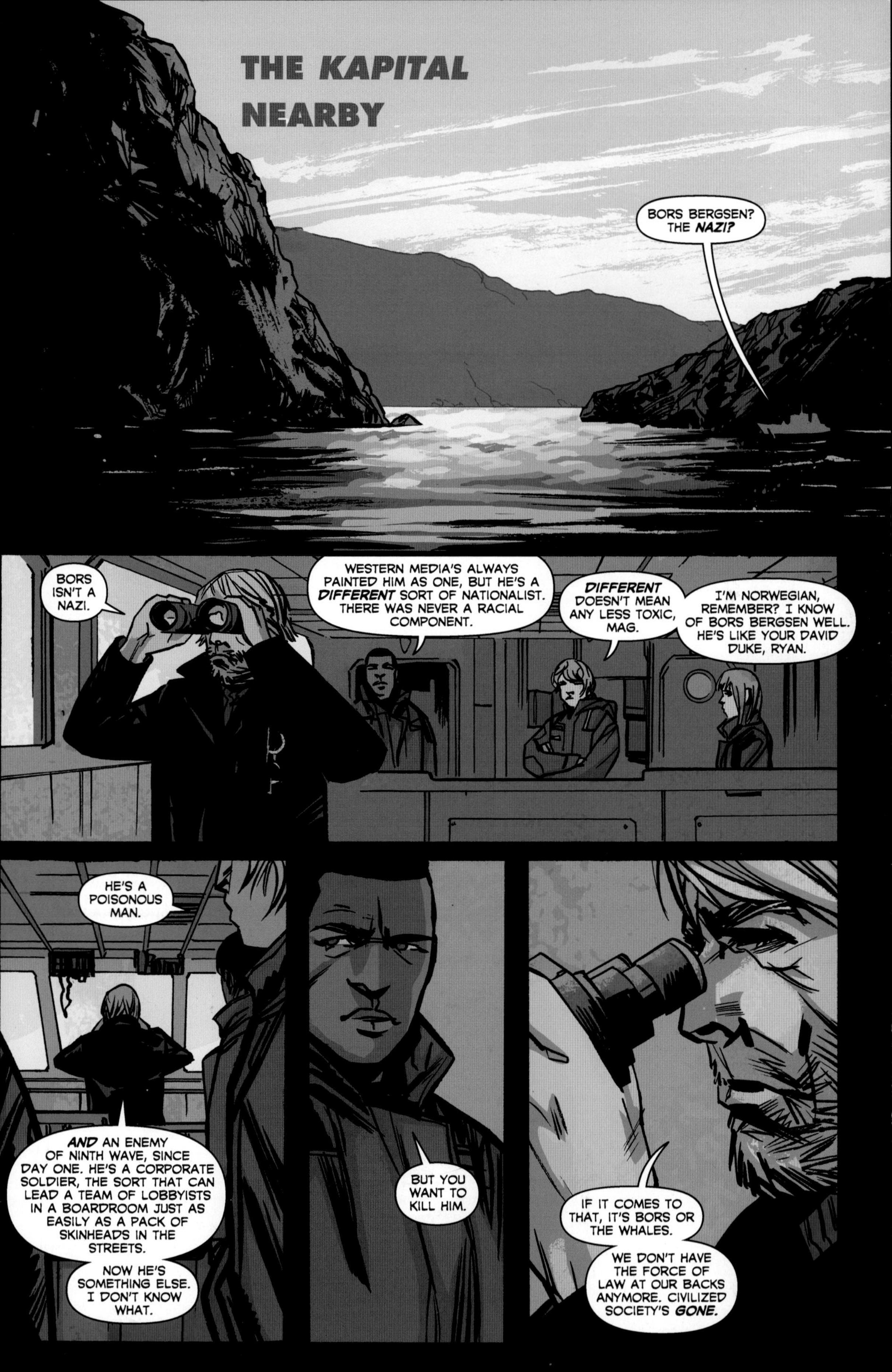
THE KAPITAL NEARBY
BORS BERGSEN? THE NAZI?
BORS ISN'T A NAZI.
WESTERN MEDIA'S ALWAYS PAINTED HIM AS ONE, BUT HE'S A DIFFERENT SORT OF NATIONALIST. THERE WAS NEVER A RACIAL COMPONENT.
DIFFERENT DOESN'T MEAN ANY LESS TOXIC, MAG.
I'M NORWEGIAN, REMEMBER? I KNOW OF BORS BERGSEN WELL. HE'S LIKE YOUR DAVID DUKE, RYAN.
HE'S A POISONOUS MAN.
AND AN ENEMY OF NINTH WAVE, SINCE DAY ONE. HE'S A CORPORATE SOLDIER, THE SORT THAT CAN LEAD A TEAM OF LOBBYISTS IN A BOARDROOM JUST AS EASILY AS A PACK OF SKINHEADS IN THE STREETS.
NOW HE'S SOMETHING ELSE. I DON'T KNOW WHAT.
BUT YOU WANT TO KILL HIM.
IF IT COMES TO THAT, IT'S BORS OR THE WHALES.
WE DON'T HAVE THE FORCE OF LAW AT OUR BACKS ANYMORE. CIVILIZED SOCIETY'S GONE.

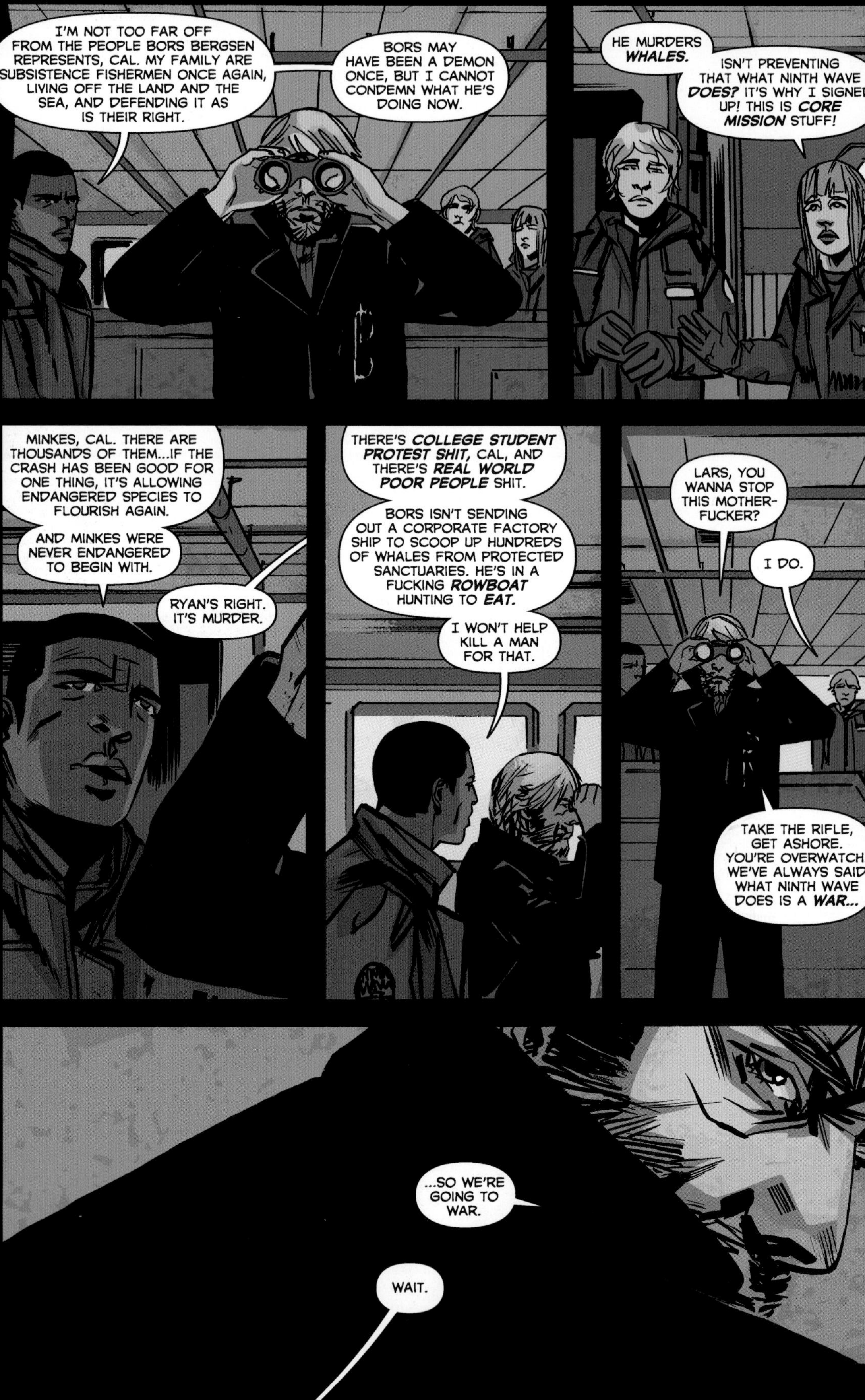
I'M NOT TOO FAR OFF FROM THE PEOPLE BORS BERGSEN REPRESENTS, CAL. MY FAMILY ARE SUBSISTENCE FISHERMEN ONCE AGAIN, LIVING OFF THE LAND AND THE SEA, AND DEFENDING IT AS IS THEIR RIGHT.
BORS MAY HAVE BEEN A DEMON ONCE, BUT I CANNOT CONDEMN WHAT HE'S DOING NOW.
HE MURDERS *WHALES.*
ISN'T PREVENTING THAT WHAT NINTH WAVE *DOES?* IT'S WHY I SIGNED UP! THIS IS *CORE MISSION* STUFF!
MINKES, CAL. THERE ARE THOUSANDS OF THEM...IF THE CRASH HAS BEEN GOOD FOR ONE THING, IT'S ALLOWING ENDANGERED SPECIES TO FLOURISH AGAIN.
AND MINKES WERE NEVER ENDANGERED TO BEGIN WITH.
RYAN'S RIGHT. IT'S MURDER.
THERE'S *COLLEGE STUDENT PROTEST SHIT,* CAL, AND THERE'S *REAL WORLD POOR PEOPLE* SHIT.
BORS ISN'T SENDING OUT A CORPORATE FACTORY SHIP TO SCOOP UP HUNDREDS OF WHALES FROM PROTECTED SANCTUARIES. HE'S IN A FUCKING *ROWBOAT* HUNTING TO *EAT.*
I WON'T HELP KILL A MAN FOR THAT.
LARS, YOU WANNA STOP THIS MOTHER-FUCKER?
I DO.
TAKE THE RIFLE, GET ASHORE. YOU'RE OVERWATCH. WE'VE ALWAYS SAID WHAT NINTH WAVE DOES IS A *WAR...*
...SO WE'RE GOING TO WAR.
WAIT.

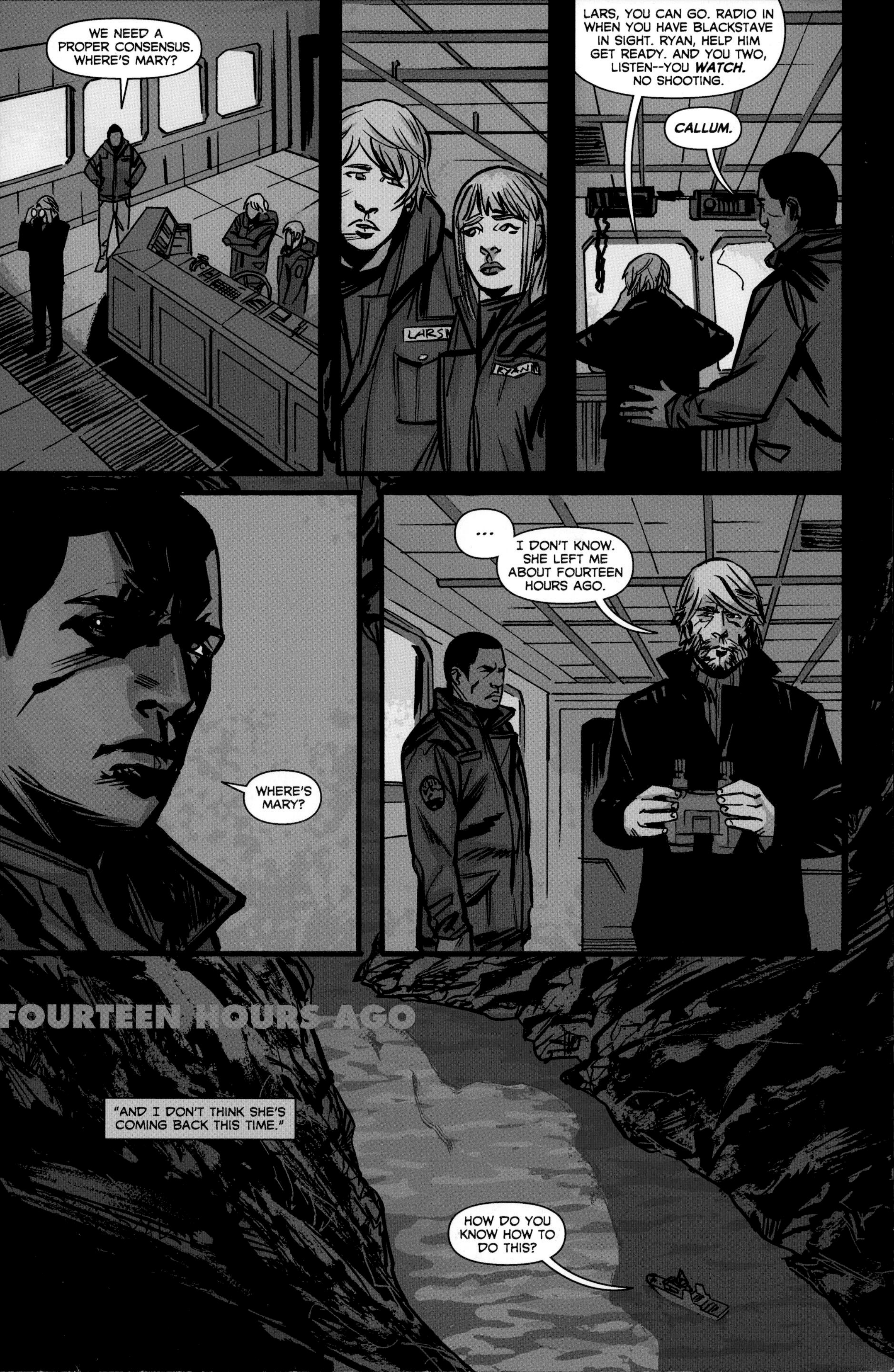
WE NEED A PROPER CONSENSUS. WHERE'S MARY?
LARSW
RYAN
LARS, YOU CAN GO. RADIO IN WHEN YOU HAVE BLACKSTAVE IN SIGHT. RYAN, HELP HIM GET READY. AND YOU TWO, LISTEN--YOU WATCH. NO SHOOTING.
CALLUM.
WHERE'S MARY?
...
I DON'T KNOW. SHE LEFT ME ABOUT FOURTEEN HOURS AGO.
FOURTEEN HOURS AGO
"AND I DON'T THINK SHE'S COMING BACK THIS TIME."
HOW DO YOU KNOW HOW TO DO THIS?

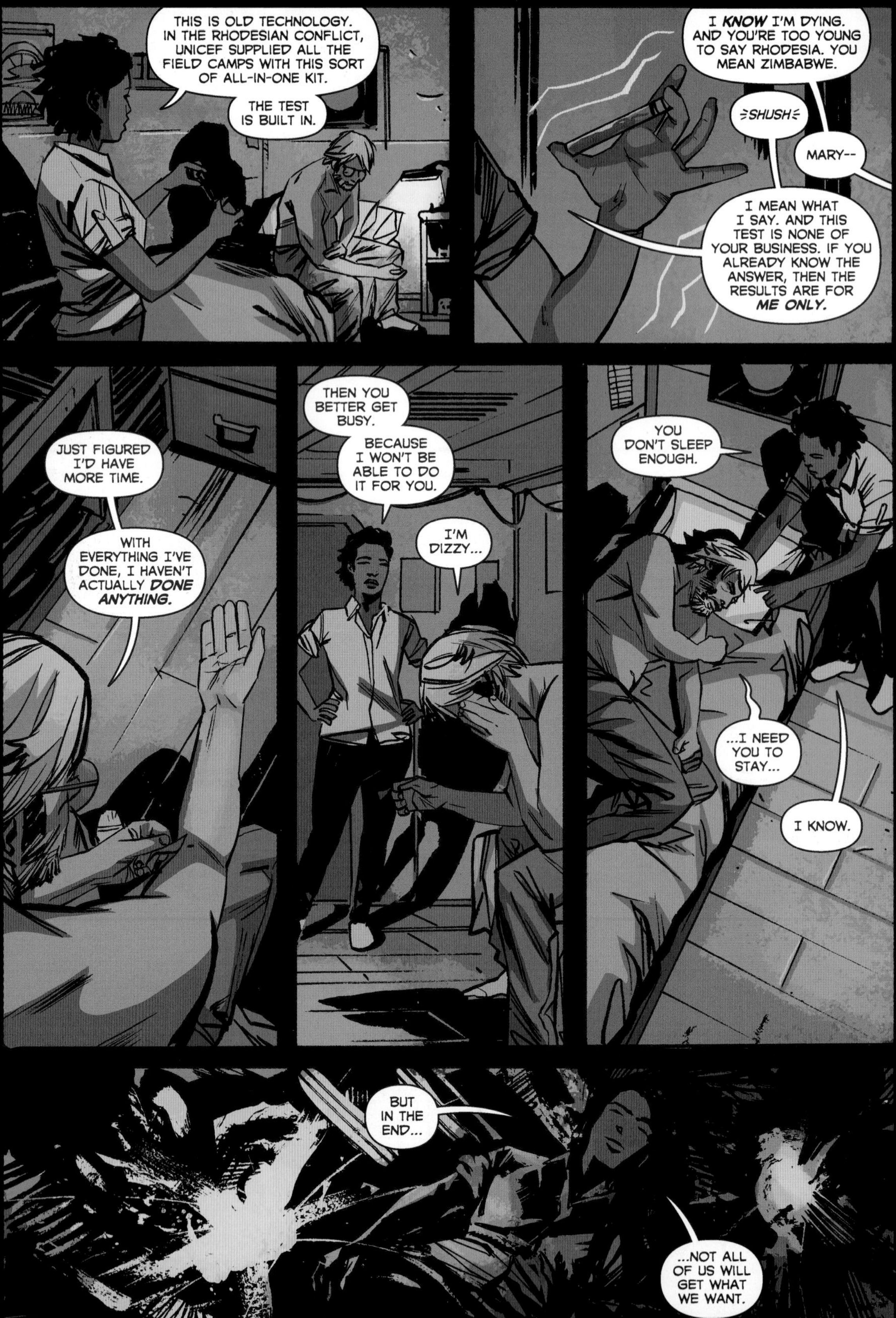
THIS IS OLD TECHNOLOGY. IN THE RHODESIAN CONFLICT, UNICEF SUPPLIED ALL THE FIELD CAMPS WITH THIS SORT OF ALL-IN-ONE KIT.
THE TEST IS BUILT IN.
I **KNOW** I'M DYING. AND YOU'RE TOO YOUNG TO SAY RHODESIA. YOU MEAN ZIMBABWE.
SHUSH
MARY--
I MEAN WHAT I SAY. AND THIS TEST IS NONE OF YOUR BUSINESS. IF YOU ALREADY KNOW THE ANSWER, THEN THE RESULTS ARE FOR ***ME ONLY.***
JUST FIGURED I'D HAVE MORE TIME.
WITH EVERYTHING I'VE DONE, I HAVEN'T ACTUALLY ***DONE ANYTHING.***
THEN YOU BETTER GET BUSY.
BECAUSE I WON'T BE ABLE TO DO IT FOR YOU.
I'M DIZZY...
YOU DON'T SLEEP ENOUGH.
...I NEED YOU TO STAY...
I KNOW.
BUT IN THE END...
...NOT ALL OF US WILL GET WHAT WE WANT.

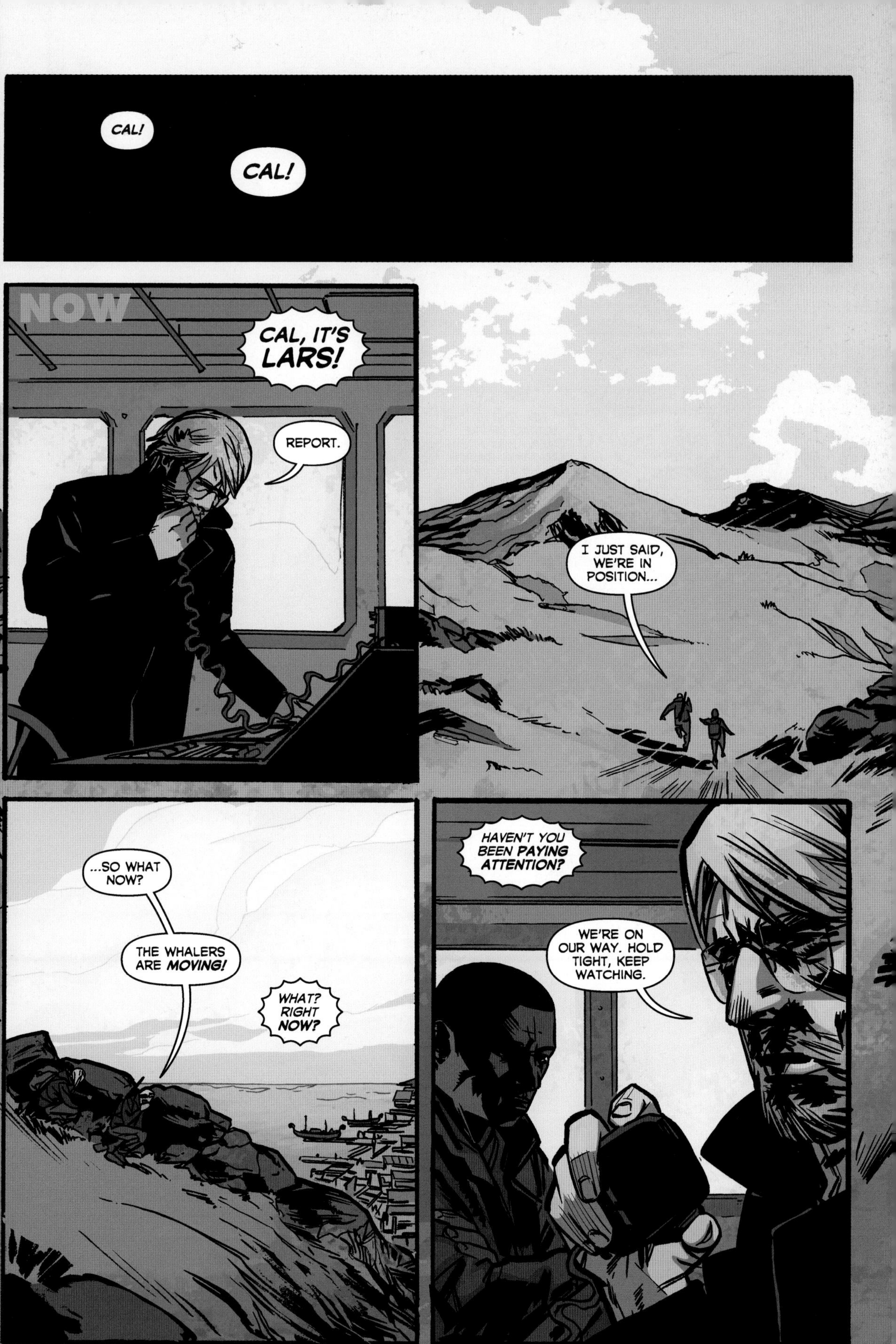
CAL!
CAL!
NOW
CAL, IT'S LARS!
REPORT.
I JUST SAID, WE'RE IN POSITION...
...SO WHAT NOW?
THE WHALERS ARE *MOVING!*
WHAT? RIGHT *NOW?*
HAVEN'T YOU BEEN *PAYING ATTENTION?*
WE'RE ON OUR WAY. HOLD TIGHT, KEEP WATCHING.

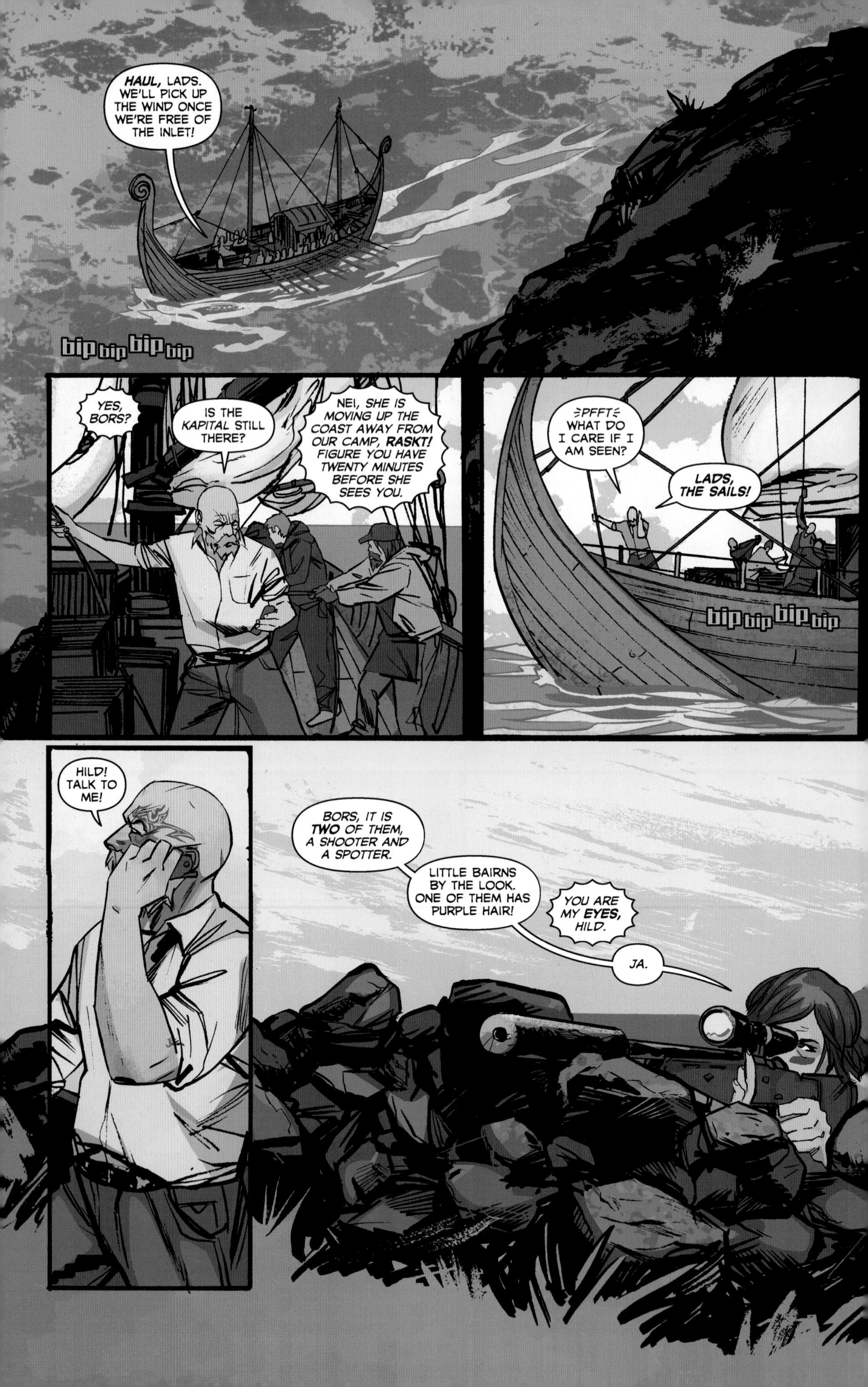

HAUL, LADS. WE'LL PICK UP THE WIND ONCE WE'RE FREE OF THE INLET!
bip bip bip bip
YES, BORS?
IS THE KAPITAL STILL THERE?
NEI, SHE IS MOVING UP THE COAST AWAY FROM OUR CAMP, RASKT! FIGURE YOU HAVE TWENTY MINUTES BEFORE SHE SEES YOU.
PFFT WHAT DO I CARE IF I AM SEEN?
LADS, THE SAILS!
bip bip bip bip
HILD! TALK TO ME!
BORS, IT IS TWO OF THEM, A SHOOTER AND A SPOTTER.
LITTLE BAIRNS BY THE LOOK. ONE OF THEM HAS PURPLE HAIR!
YOU ARE MY EYES, HILD.
JA.

THE STÚLKA

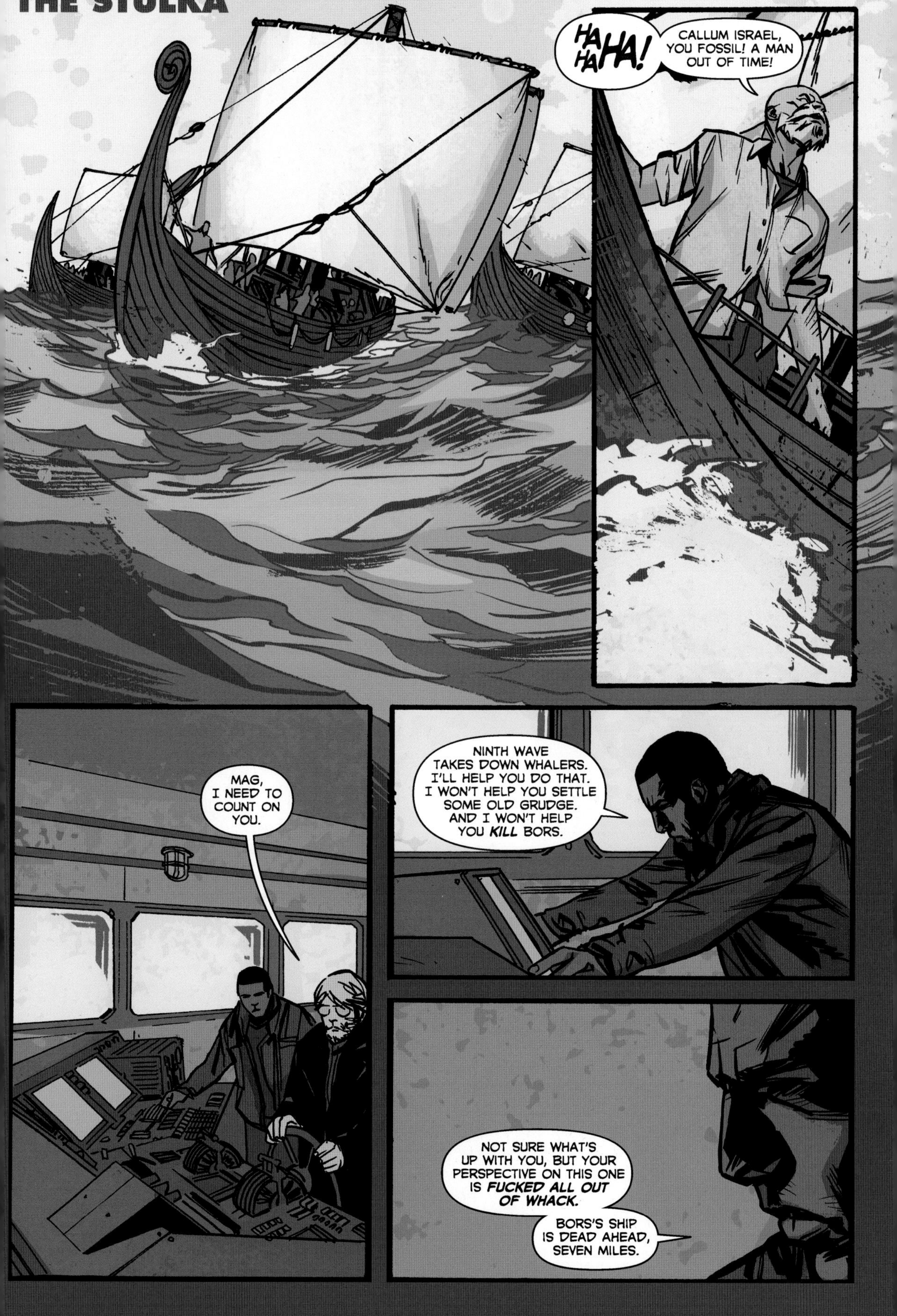

HA HA HA!
CALLUM ISRAEL, YOU FOSSIL! A MAN OUT OF TIME!
MAG, I NEED TO COUNT ON YOU.
NINTH WAVE TAKES DOWN WHALERS. I'LL HELP YOU DO THAT. I WON'T HELP YOU SETTLE SOME OLD GRUDGE. AND I WON'T HELP YOU ***KILL*** BORS.
NOT SURE WHAT'S UP WITH YOU, BUT YOUR PERSPECTIVE ON THIS ONE IS ***FUCKED ALL OUT OF WHACK.***
BORS'S SHIP IS DEAD AHEAD, SEVEN MILES.

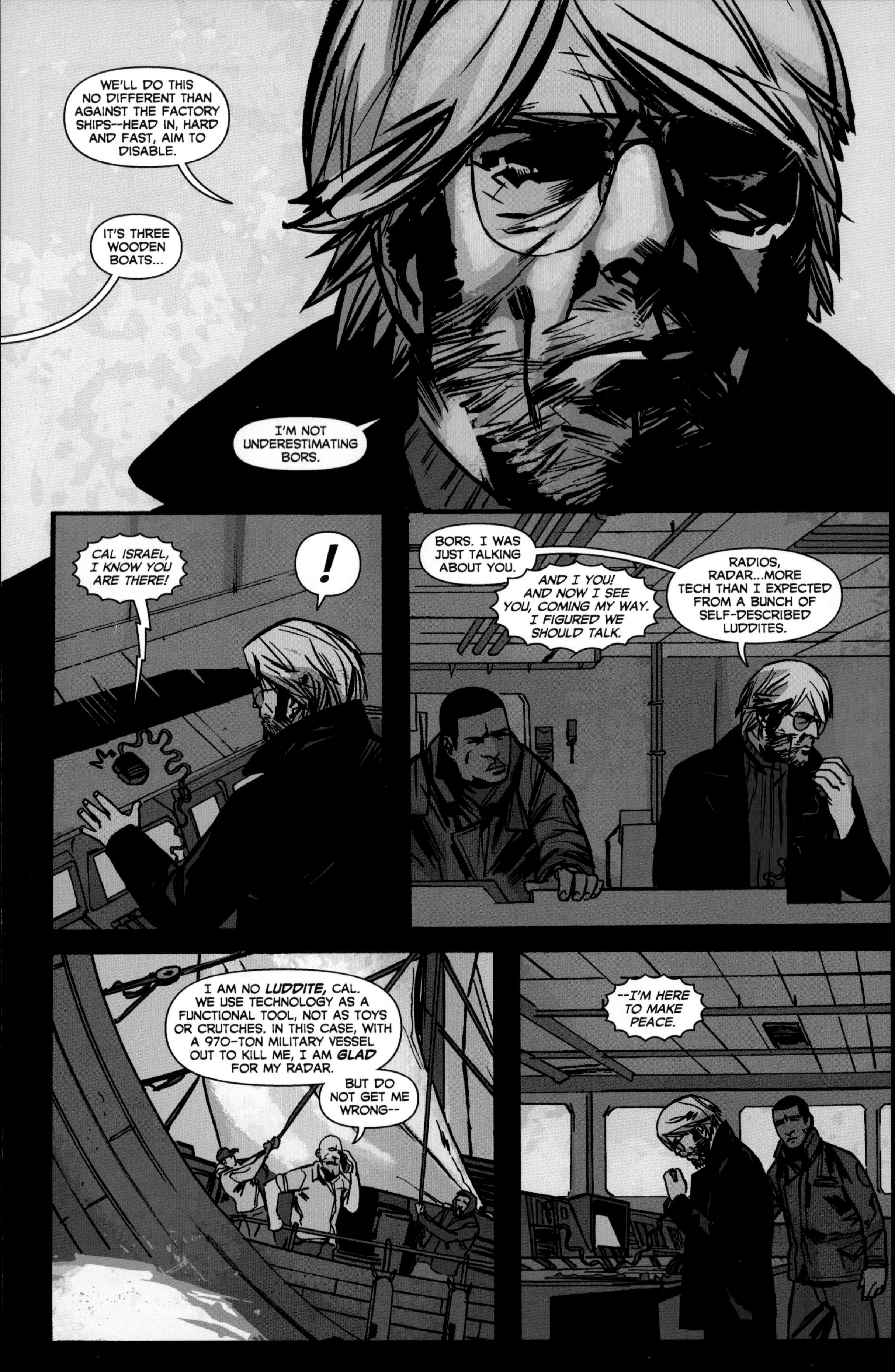
WE'LL DO THIS NO DIFFERENT THAN AGAINST THE FACTORY SHIPS--HEAD IN, HARD AND FAST, AIM TO DISABLE.
IT'S THREE WOODEN BOATS...
I'M NOT UNDERESTIMATING BORS.
CAL ISRAEL, I KNOW YOU ARE THERE!
!
BORS. I WAS JUST TALKING ABOUT YOU.
AND I YOU! AND NOW I SEE YOU, COMING MY WAY. I FIGURED WE SHOULD TALK.
RADIOS, RADAR...MORE TECH THAN I EXPECTED FROM A BUNCH OF SELF-DESCRIBED LUDDITES.
I AM NO *LUDDITE,* CAL. WE USE TECHNOLOGY AS A FUNCTIONAL TOOL, NOT AS TOYS OR CRUTCHES. IN THIS CASE, WITH A 970-TON MILITARY VESSEL OUT TO KILL ME, I AM *GLAD* FOR MY RADAR.
BUT DO NOT GET ME WRONG--
--I'M HERE TO MAKE PEACE.

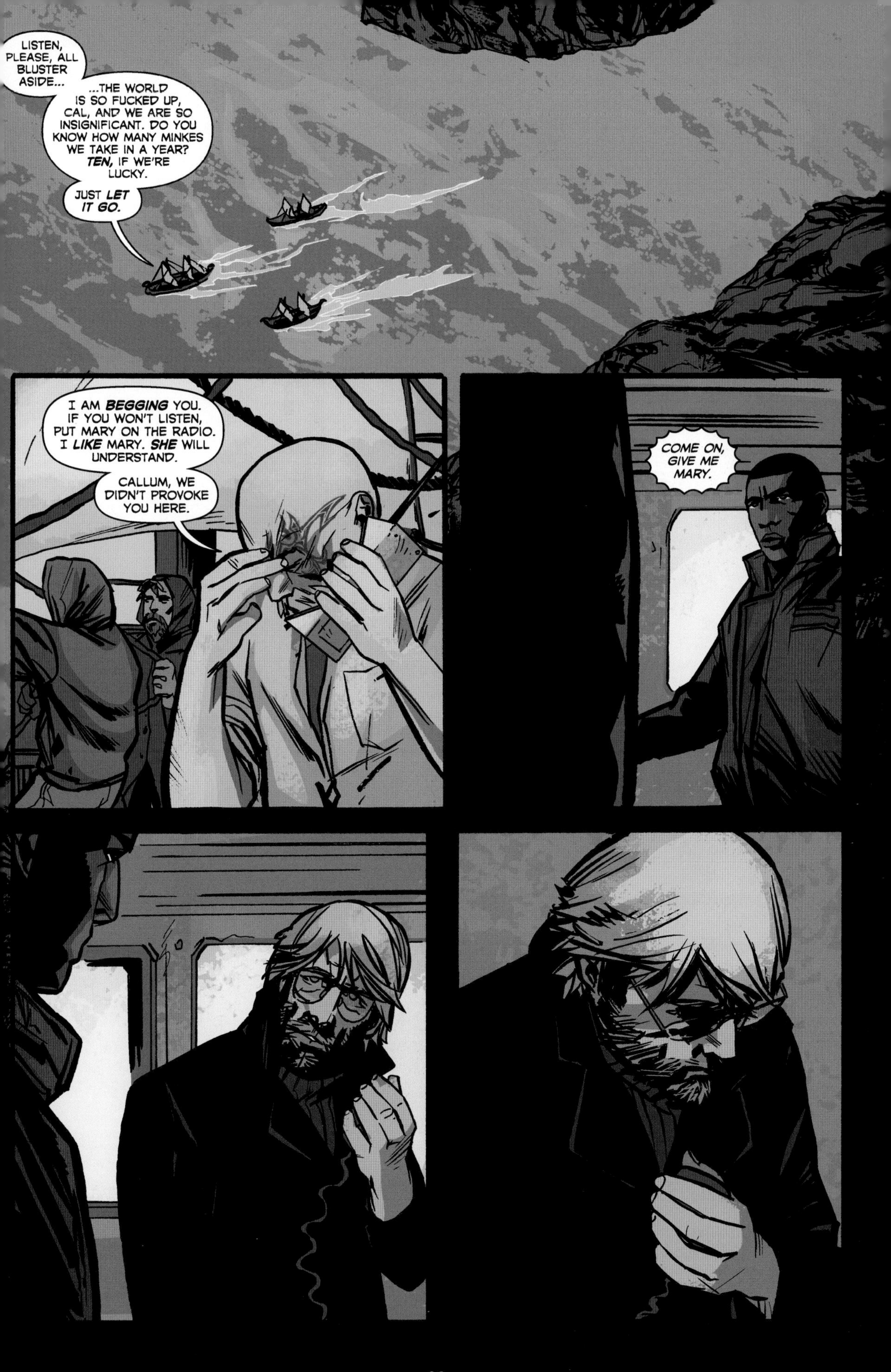
LISTEN, PLEASE, ALL BLUSTER ASIDE...
...THE WORLD IS SO FUCKED UP, CAL, AND WE ARE SO INSIGNIFICANT. DO YOU KNOW HOW MANY MINKES WE TAKE IN A YEAR? TEN, IF WE'RE LUCKY.
JUST LET IT GO.
I AM BEGGING YOU. IF YOU WON'T LISTEN, PUT MARY ON THE RADIO. I LIKE MARY. SHE WILL UNDERSTAND.
CALLUM, WE DIDN'T PROVOKE YOU HERE.
COME ON, GIVE ME MARY.

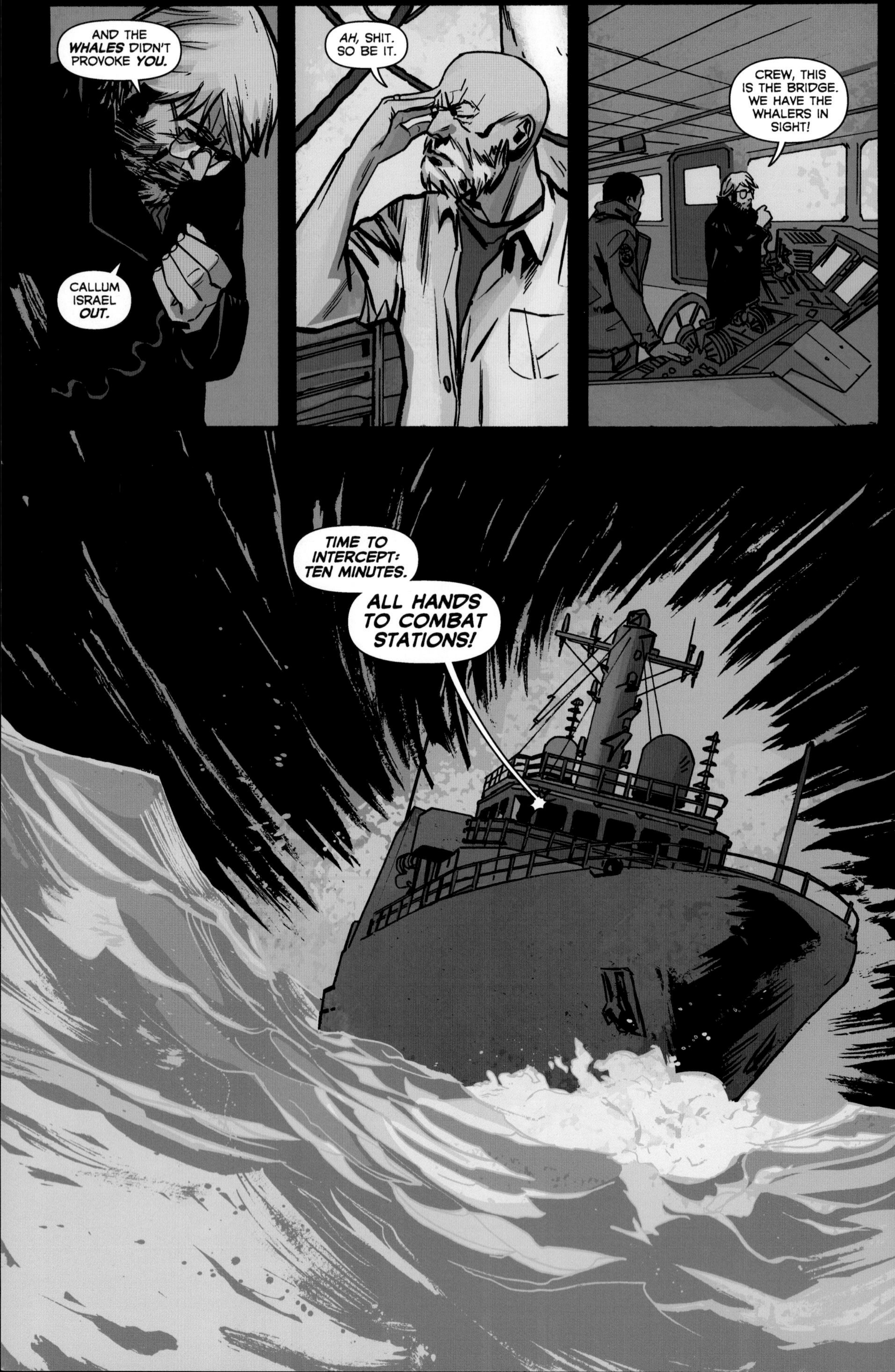
AND THE WHALES DIDN'T PROVOKE YOU.
CALLUM ISRAEL OUT.
AH, SHIT. SO BE IT.
CREW, THIS IS THE BRIDGE. WE HAVE THE WHALERS IN SIGHT!
TIME TO INTERCEPT: TEN MINUTES.
ALL HANDS TO COMBAT STATIONS!

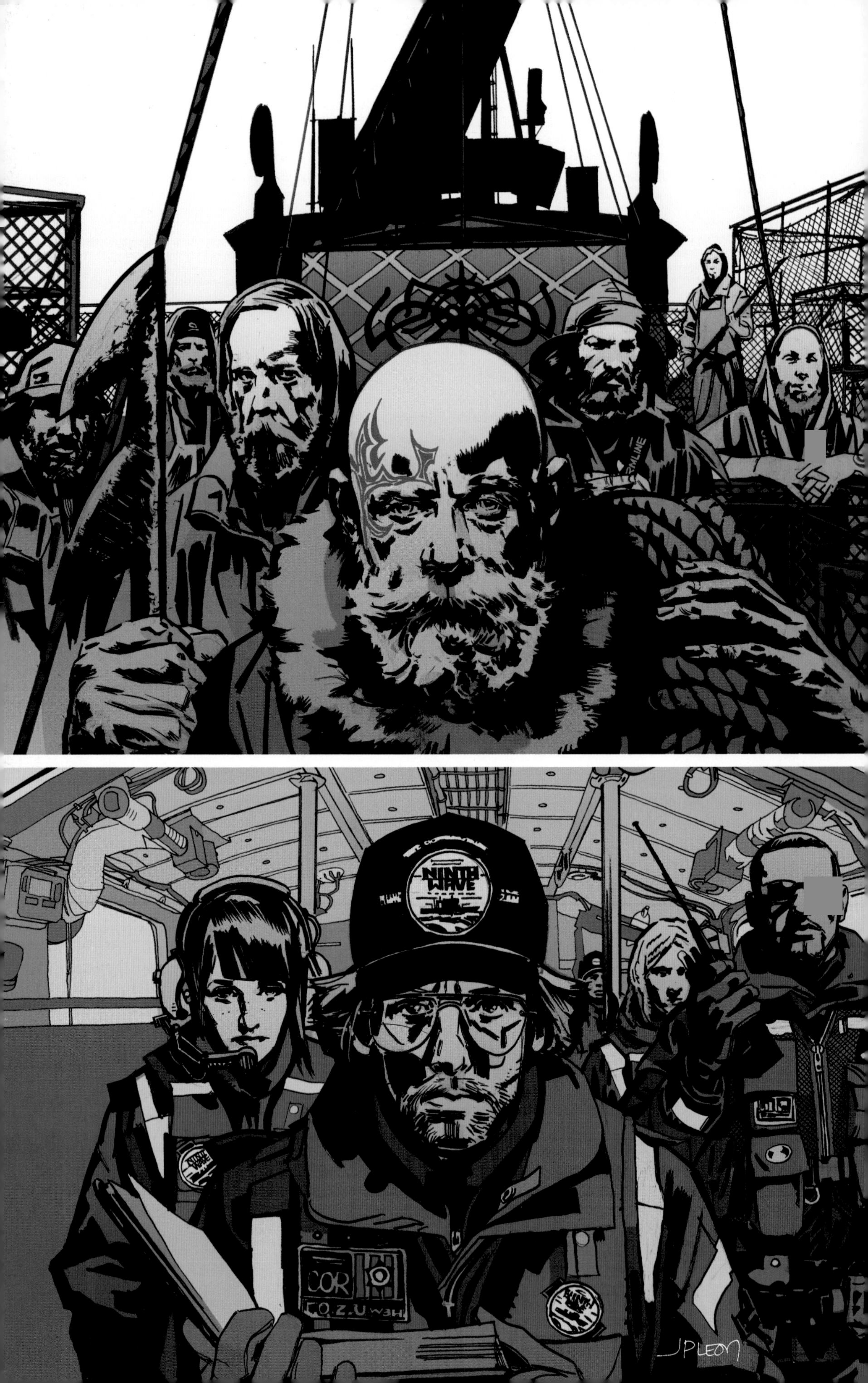
NINTH WAVE
COR
JPLEON

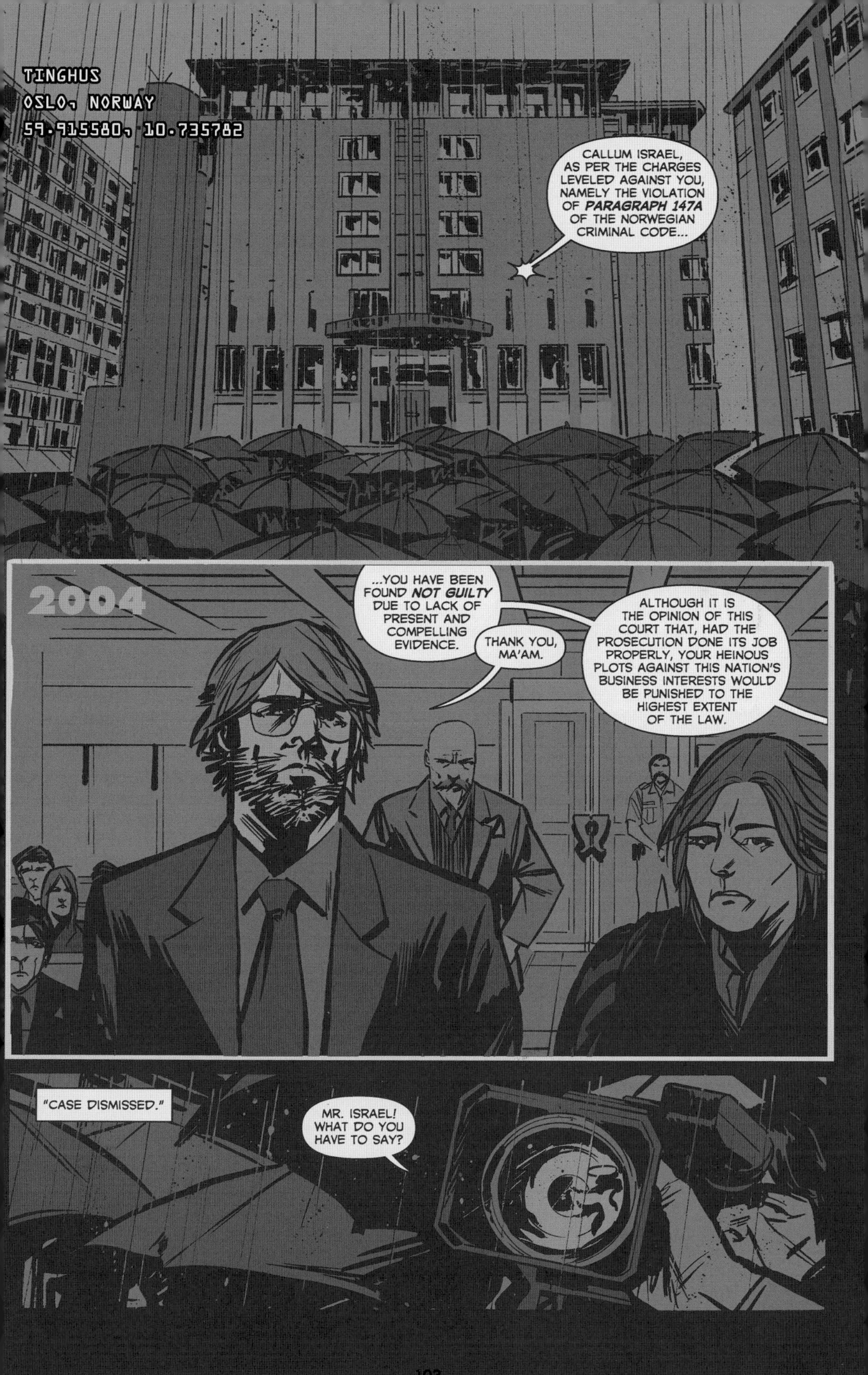
TINGHUS
OSLO, NORWAY
59.915580, 10.735782
CALLUM ISRAEL, AS PER THE CHARGES LEVELED AGAINST YOU, NAMELY THE VIOLATION OF PARAGRAPH 147A OF THE NORWEGIAN CRIMINAL CODE...
2004
...YOU HAVE BEEN FOUND NOT GUILTY DUE TO LACK OF PRESENT AND COMPELLING EVIDENCE.
THANK YOU, MA'AM.
ALTHOUGH IT IS THE OPINION OF THIS COURT THAT, HAD THE PROSECUTION DONE ITS JOB PROPERLY, YOUR HEINOUS PLOTS AGAINST THIS NATION'S BUSINESS INTERESTS WOULD BE PUNISHED TO THE HIGHEST EXTENT OF THE LAW.
"CASE DISMISSED."
MR. ISRAEL! WHAT DO YOU HAVE TO SAY?

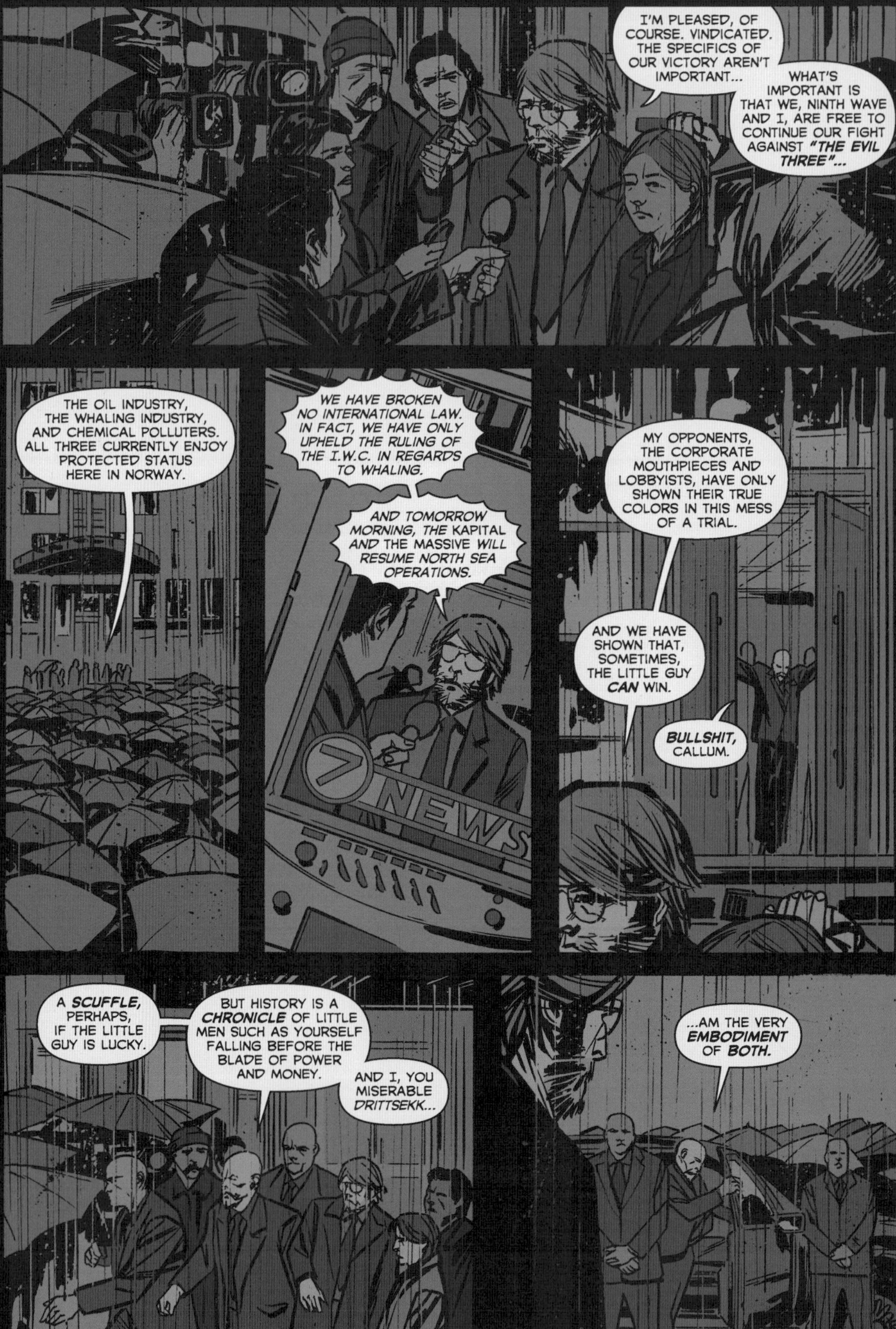
I'M PLEASED, OF COURSE. VINDICATED. THE SPECIFICS OF OUR VICTORY AREN'T IMPORTANT...
WHAT'S IMPORTANT IS THAT WE, NINTH WAVE AND I, ARE FREE TO CONTINUE OUR FIGHT AGAINST *"THE EVIL THREE"*...
THE OIL INDUSTRY, THE WHALING INDUSTRY, AND CHEMICAL POLLUTERS. ALL THREE CURRENTLY ENJOY PROTECTED STATUS HERE IN NORWAY.
WE HAVE BROKEN NO INTERNATIONAL LAW. IN FACT, WE HAVE ONLY UPHELD THE RULING OF THE I.W.C. IN REGARDS TO WHALING.
AND TOMORROW MORNING, THE KAPITAL *AND THE* MASSIVE *WILL RESUME NORTH SEA OPERATIONS.*
7 NEWS
MY OPPONENTS, THE CORPORATE MOUTHPIECES AND LOBBYISTS, HAVE ONLY SHOWN THEIR TRUE COLORS IN THIS MESS OF A TRIAL.
AND WE HAVE SHOWN THAT, SOMETIMES, THE LITTLE GUY **CAN** WIN.
BULLSHIT, CALLUM.
A ***SCUFFLE,*** PERHAPS, IF THE LITTLE GUY IS LUCKY.
BUT HISTORY IS A ***CHRONICLE*** OF LITTLE MEN SUCH AS YOURSELF FALLING BEFORE THE BLADE OF POWER AND MONEY.
AND I, YOU MISERABLE *DRITTSEKK*...
...AM THE VERY ***EMBODIMENT*** OF ***BOTH.***

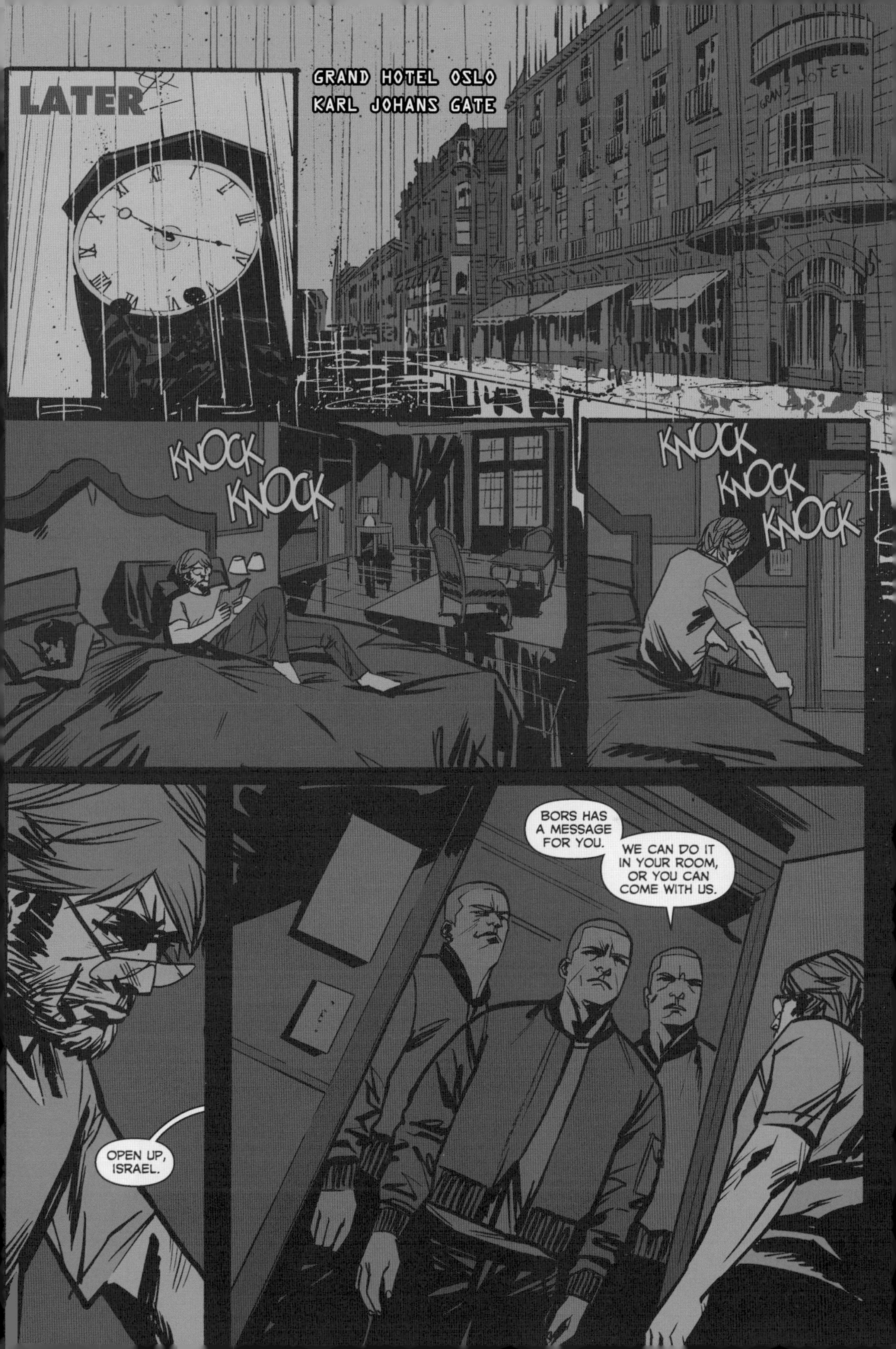
LATER
GRAND HOTEL OSLO
KARL JOHANS GATE
GRAND HOTEL
KNOCK KNOCK
KNOCK KNOCK KNOCK
OPEN UP, ISRAEL.
BORS HAS A MESSAGE FOR YOU.
WE CAN DO IT IN YOUR ROOM, OR YOU CAN COME WITH US.

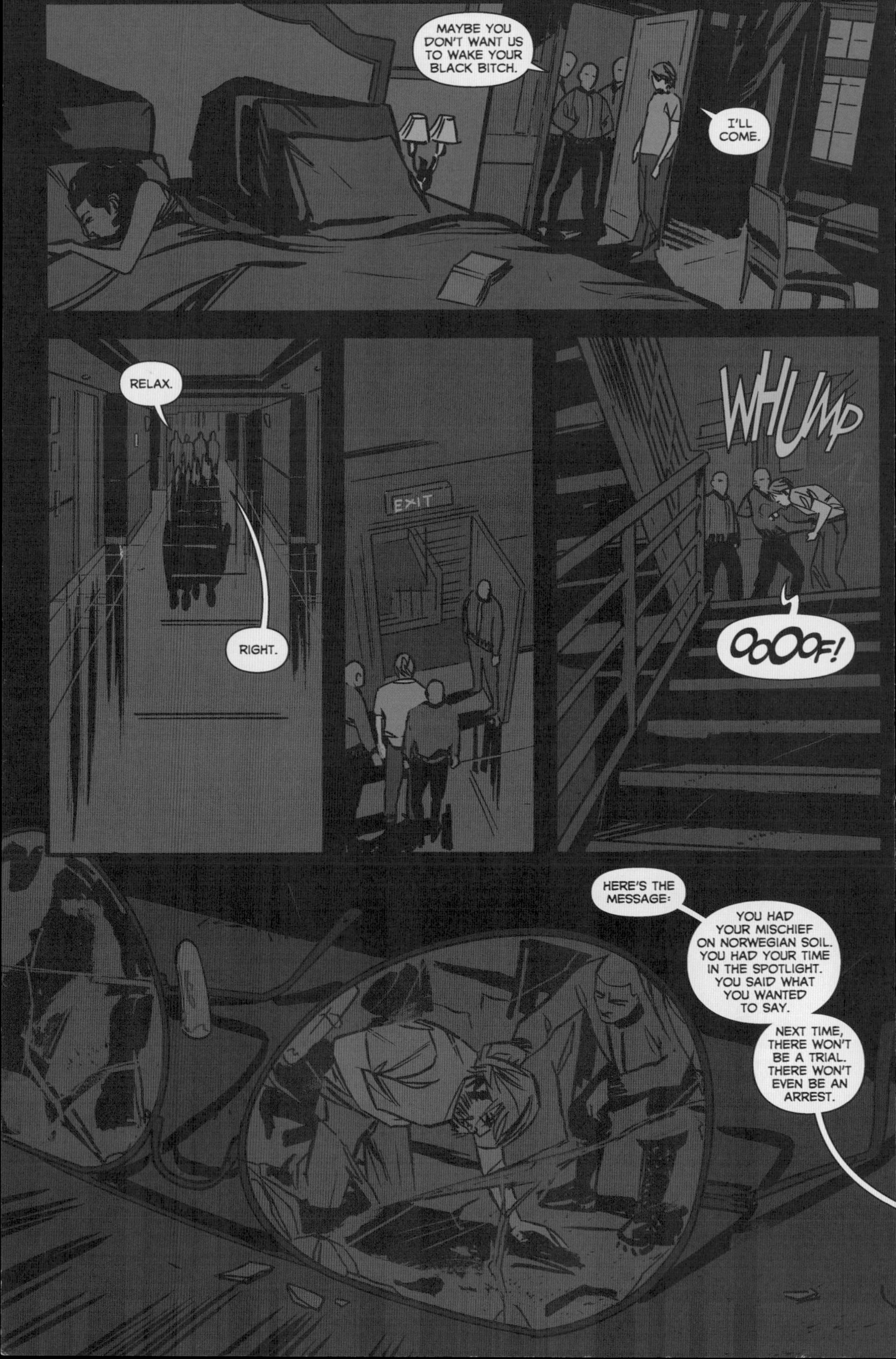
MAYBE YOU DON'T WANT US TO WAKE YOUR BLACK BITCH.
I'LL COME.
RELAX.
RIGHT.
EXIT
WHUMP
OOOOF!
HERE'S THE MESSAGE:
YOU HAD YOUR MISCHIEF ON NORWEGIAN SOIL. YOU HAD YOUR TIME IN THE SPOTLIGHT. YOU SAID WHAT YOU WANTED TO SAY.
NEXT TIME, THERE WON'T BE A TRIAL. THERE WON'T EVEN BE AN ARREST.

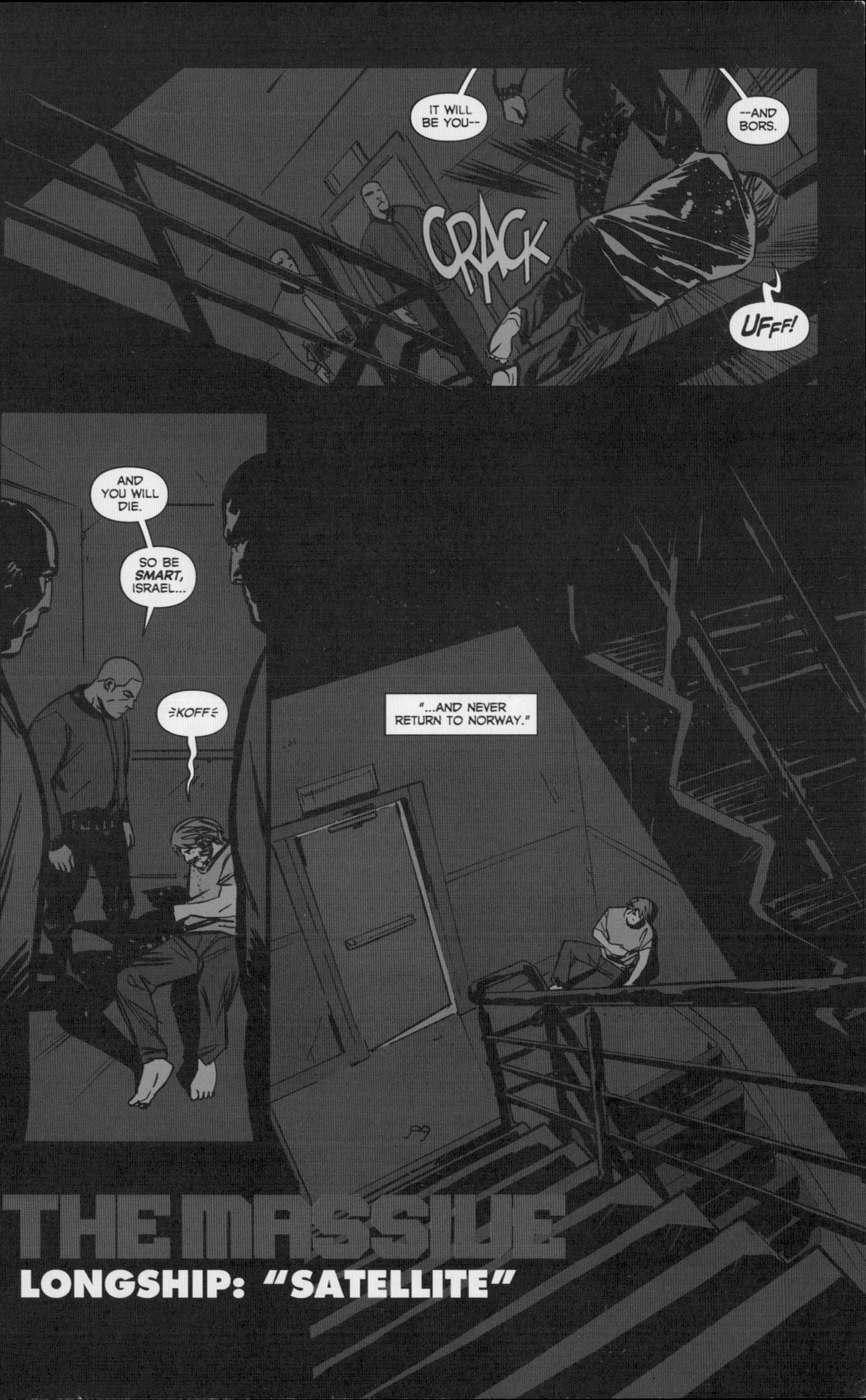
IT WILL BE YOU--
--AND BORS.
CRACK
UFFF!
AND YOU WILL DIE.
SO BE SMART, ISRAEL...
KOFF
"...AND NEVER RETURN TO NORWAY."
THE MASSIVE
LONGSHIP: "SATELLITE"

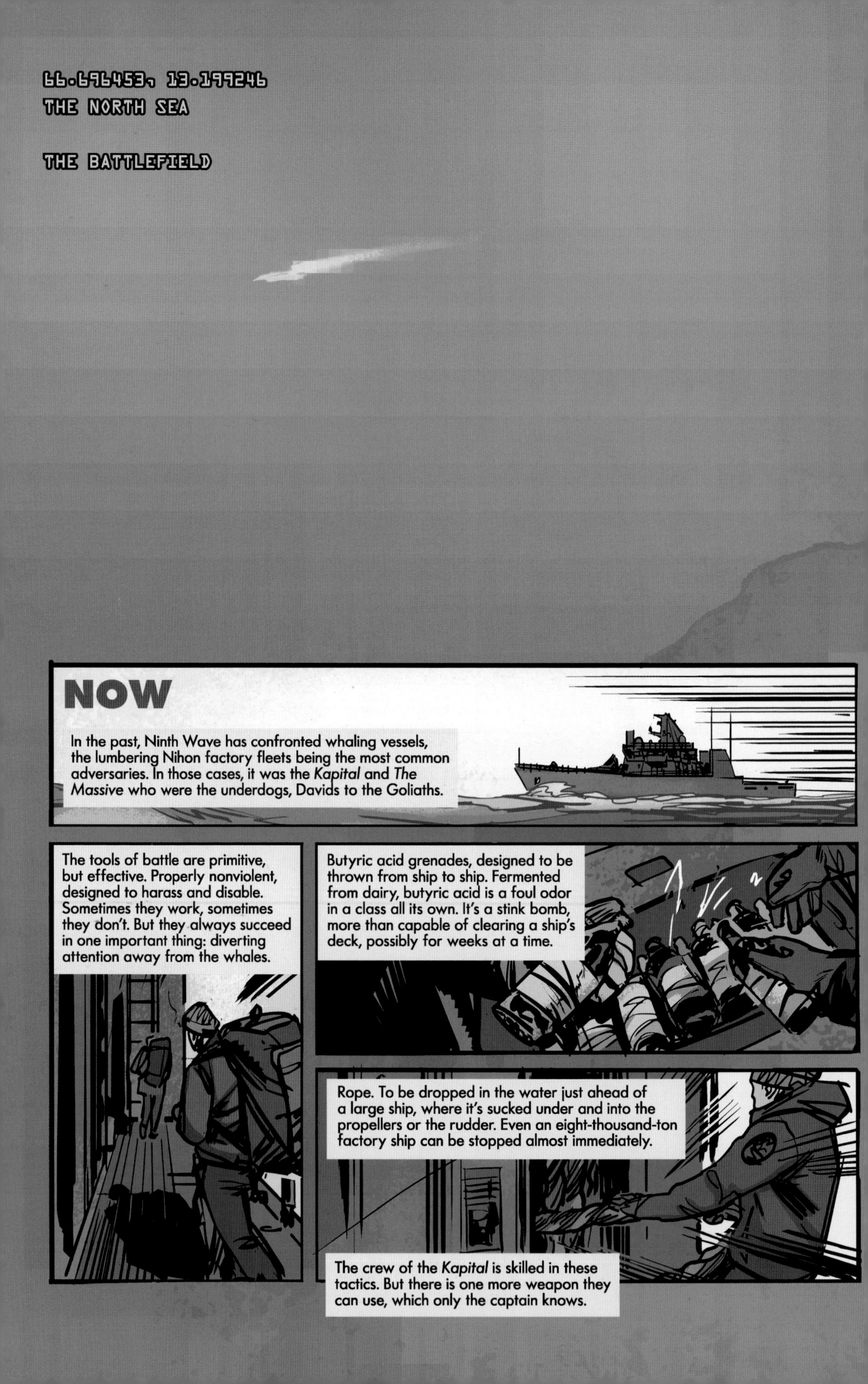
66.696453, 13.199246
THE NORTH SEA
THE BATTLEFIELD
NOW
In the past, Ninth Wave has confronted whaling vessels, the lumbering Nihon factory fleets being the most common adversaries. In those cases, it was the *Kapital* and *The Massive* who were the underdogs, Davids to the Goliaths.
The tools of battle are primitive, but effective. Properly nonviolent, designed to harass and disable. Sometimes they work, sometimes they don't. But they always succeed in one important thing: diverting attention away from the whales.
Butyric acid grenades, designed to be thrown from ship to ship. Fermented from dairy, butyric acid is a foul odor in a class all its own. It's a stink bomb, more than capable of clearing a ship's deck, possibly for weeks at a time.
Rope. To be dropped in the water just ahead of a large ship, where it's sucked under and into the propellers or the rudder. Even an eight-thousand-ton factory ship can be stopped almost immediately.
The crew of the *Kapital* is skilled in these tactics. But there is one more weapon they can use, which only the captain knows.

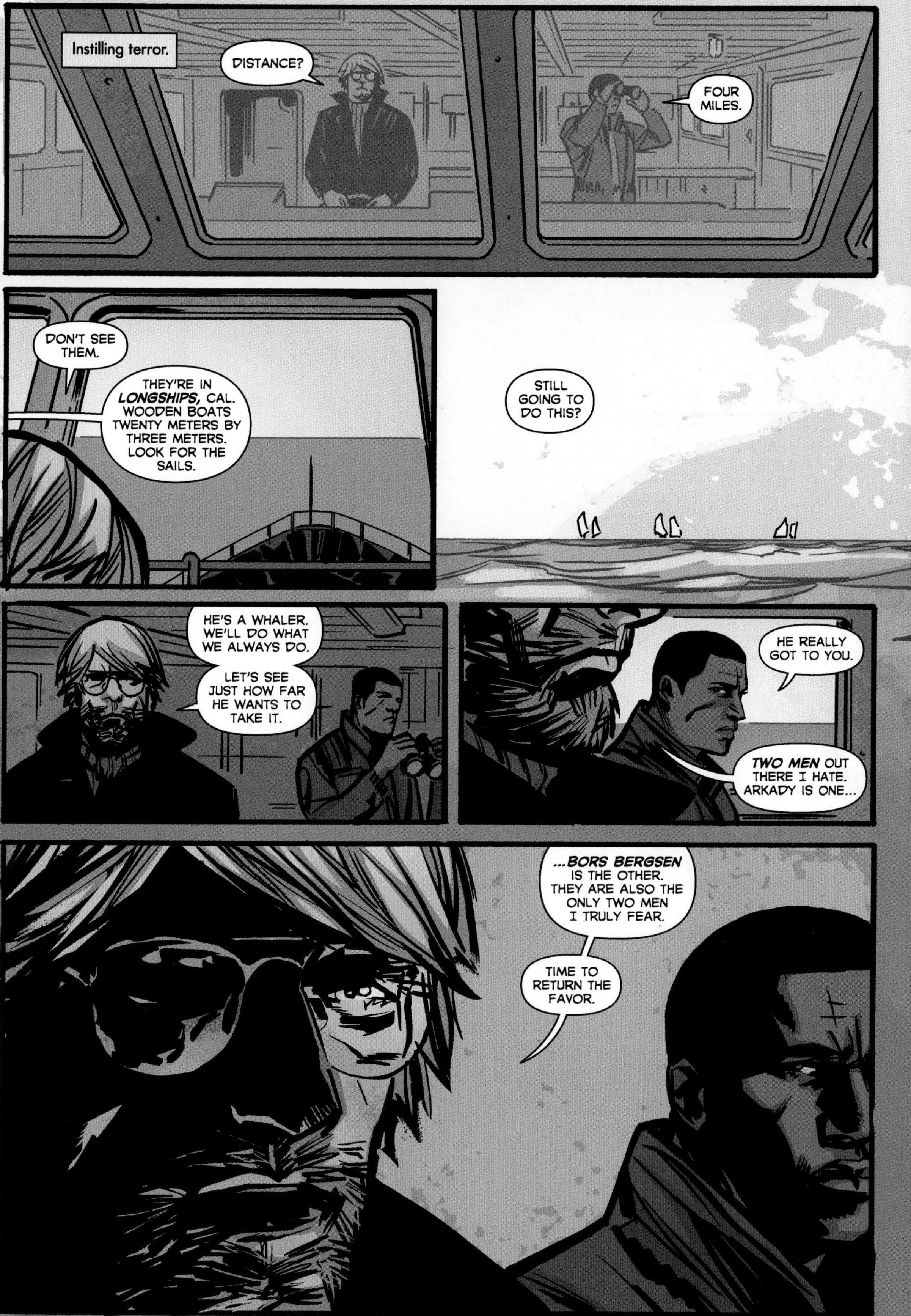
Instilling terror.
DISTANCE?
FOUR MILES.
DON'T SEE THEM.
THEY'RE IN LONGSHIPS, CAL. WOODEN BOATS TWENTY METERS BY THREE METERS. LOOK FOR THE SAILS.
STILL GOING TO DO THIS?
HE'S A WHALER. WE'LL DO WHAT WE ALWAYS DO.
LET'S SEE JUST HOW FAR HE WANTS TO TAKE IT.
HE REALLY GOT TO YOU.
TWO MEN OUT THERE I HATE. ARKADY IS ONE...
...BORS BERGSEN IS THE OTHER. THEY ARE ALSO THE ONLY TWO MEN I TRULY FEAR.
TIME TO RETURN THE FAVOR.

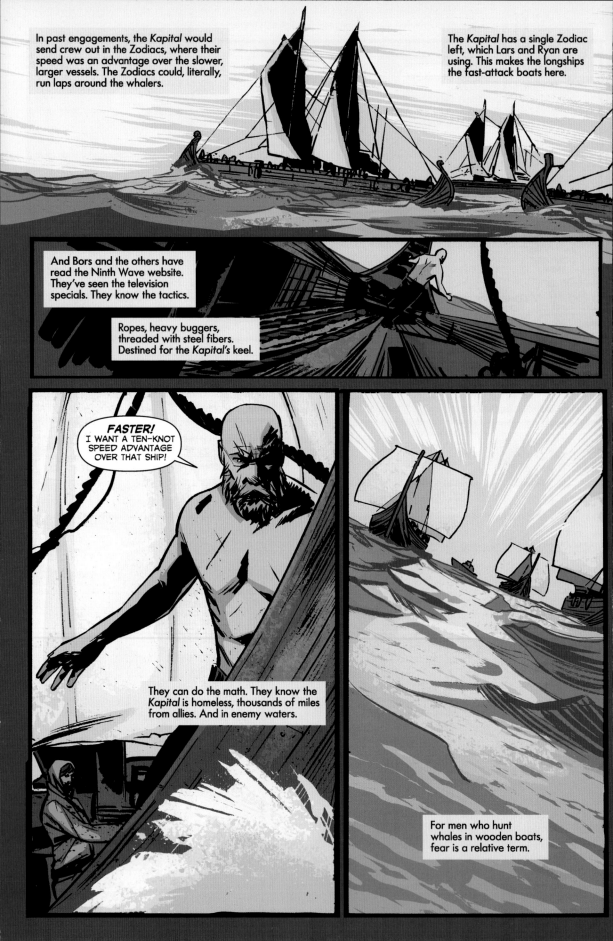

In past engagements, the *Kapital* would send crew out in the Zodiacs, where their speed was an advantage over the slower, larger vessels. The Zodiacs could, literally, run laps around the whalers.

The *Kapital* has a single Zodiac left, which Lars and Ryan are using. This makes the longships the fast-attack boats here.

And Bors and the others have read the Ninth Wave website. They've seen the television specials. They know the tactics.

Ropes, heavy buggers, threaded with steel fibers. Destined for the *Kapital*'s keel.

FASTER! I WANT A TEN-KNOT SPEED ADVANTAGE OVER THAT SHIP!

They can do the math. They know the *Kapital* is homeless, thousands of miles from allies. And in enemy waters.

For men who hunt whales in wooden boats, fear is a relative term.

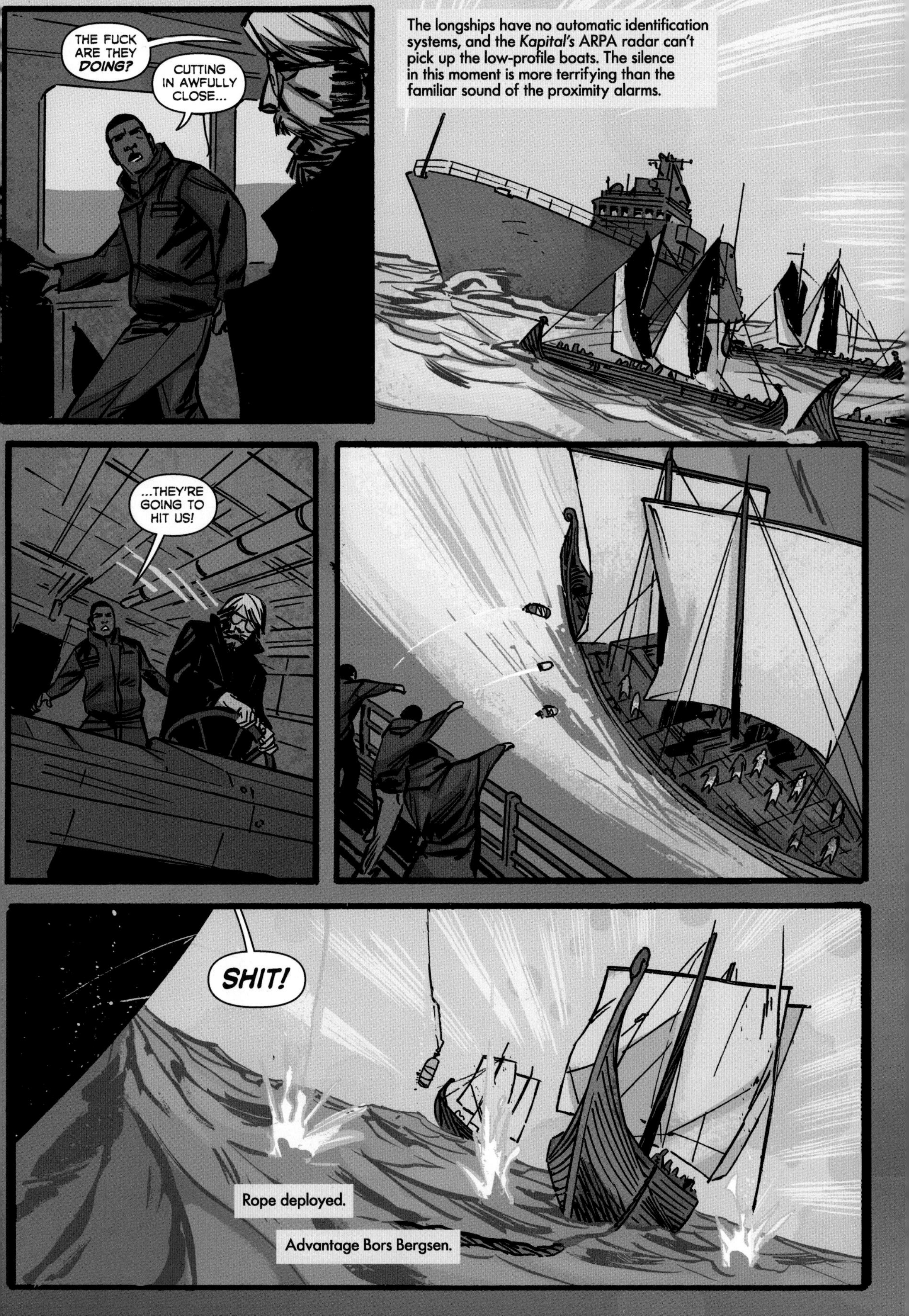
THE FUCK ARE THEY DOING?
CUTTING IN AWFULLY CLOSE...
The longships have no automatic identification systems, and the Kapital's ARPA radar can't pick up the low-profile boats. The silence in this moment is more terrifying than the familiar sound of the proximity alarms.
...THEY'RE GOING TO HIT US!
SHIT!
Rope deployed.
Advantage Bors Bergsen.

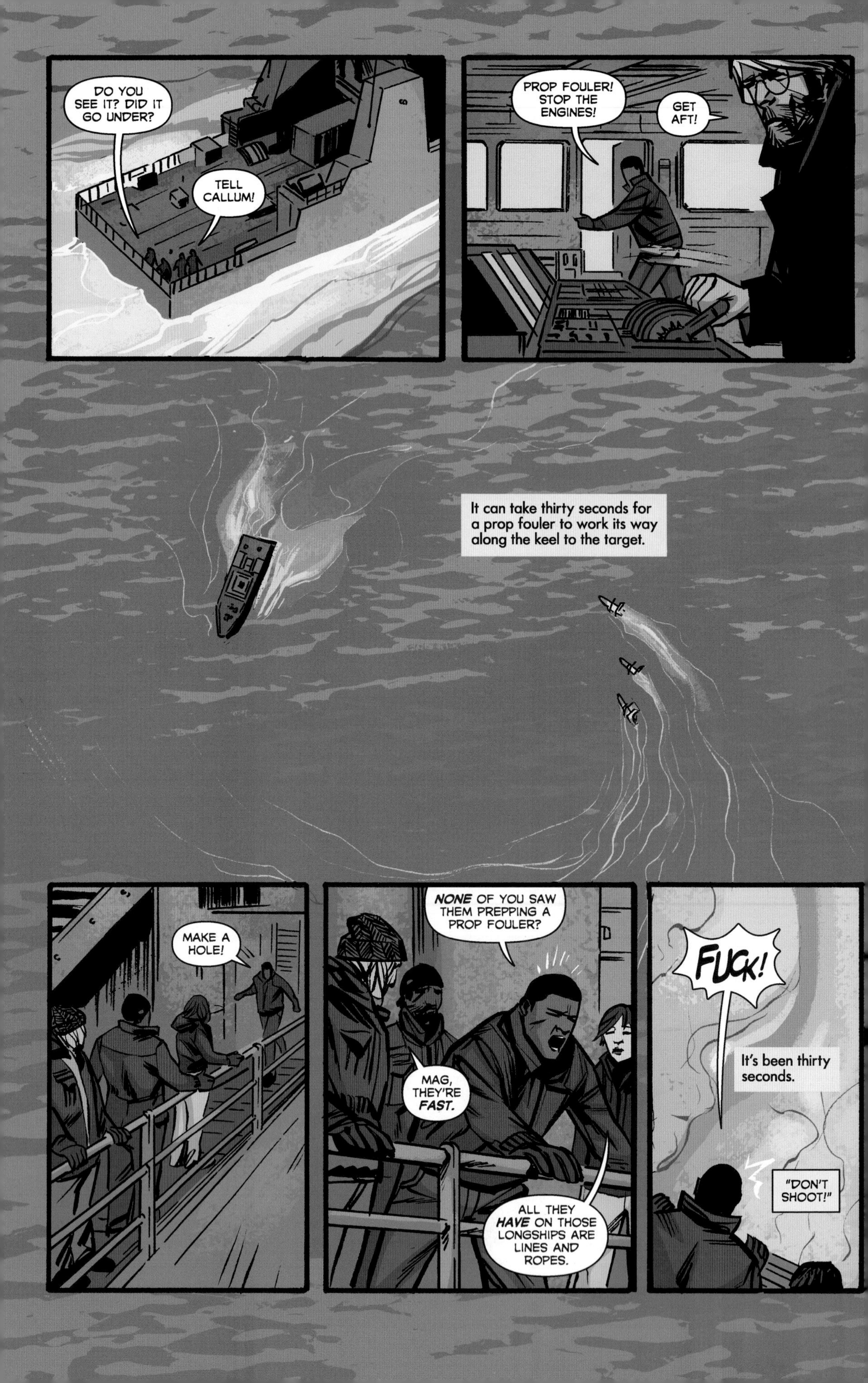
DO YOU SEE IT? DID IT GO UNDER?
TELL CALLUM!
PROP FOULER! STOP THE ENGINES!
GET AFT!
It can take thirty seconds for a prop fouler to work its way along the keel to the target.
MAKE A HOLE!
NONE OF YOU SAW THEM PREPPING A PROP FOULER?
MAG, THEY'RE FAST.
ALL THEY HAVE ON THOSE LONGSHIPS ARE LINES AND ROPES.
FUCK!
It's been thirty seconds.
"DON'T SHOOT!"

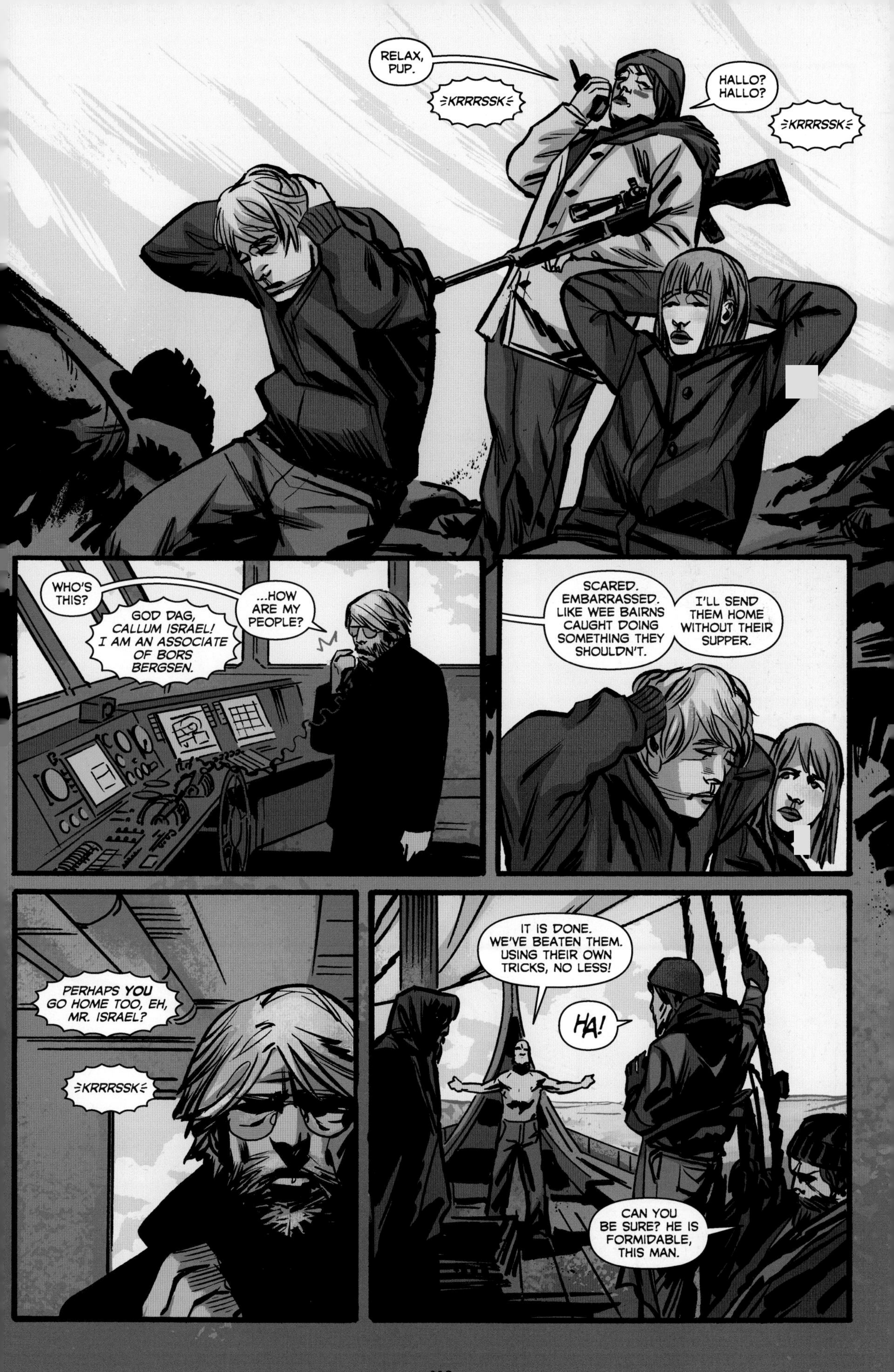
RELAX, PUP.
KRRRSSK
HALLO? HALLO?
KRRRSSK
WHO'S THIS?
GOD DAG, CALLUM ISRAEL! I AM AN ASSOCIATE OF BORS BERGSEN.
...HOW ARE MY PEOPLE?
SCARED. EMBARRASSED. LIKE WEE BAIRNS CAUGHT DOING SOMETHING THEY SHOULDN'T.
I'LL SEND THEM HOME WITHOUT THEIR SUPPER.
PERHAPS **YOU** GO HOME TOO, EH, MR. ISRAEL?
KRRRSSK
IT IS DONE. WE'VE BEATEN THEM. USING THEIR OWN TRICKS, NO LESS!
HA!
CAN YOU BE SURE? HE IS FORMIDABLE, THIS MAN.

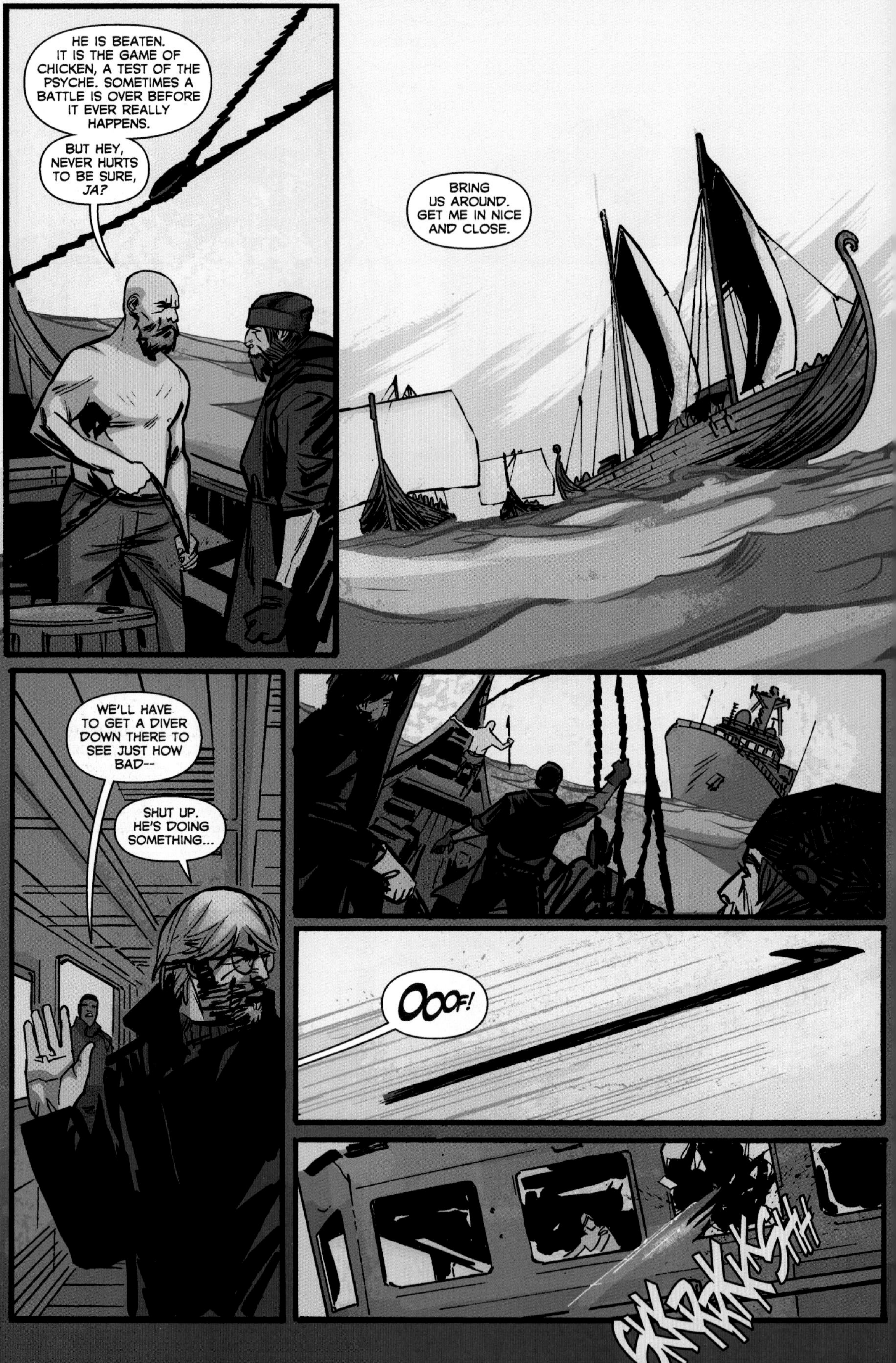
HE IS BEATEN. IT IS THE GAME OF CHICKEN, A TEST OF THE PSYCHE. SOMETIMES A BATTLE IS OVER BEFORE IT EVER REALLY HAPPENS.
BUT HEY, NEVER HURTS TO BE SURE, JA?
BRING US AROUND. GET ME IN NICE AND CLOSE.
WE'LL HAVE TO GET A DIVER DOWN THERE TO SEE JUST HOW BAD--
SHUT UP. HE'S DOING SOMETHING...
OOOF!
SKRKKKSH

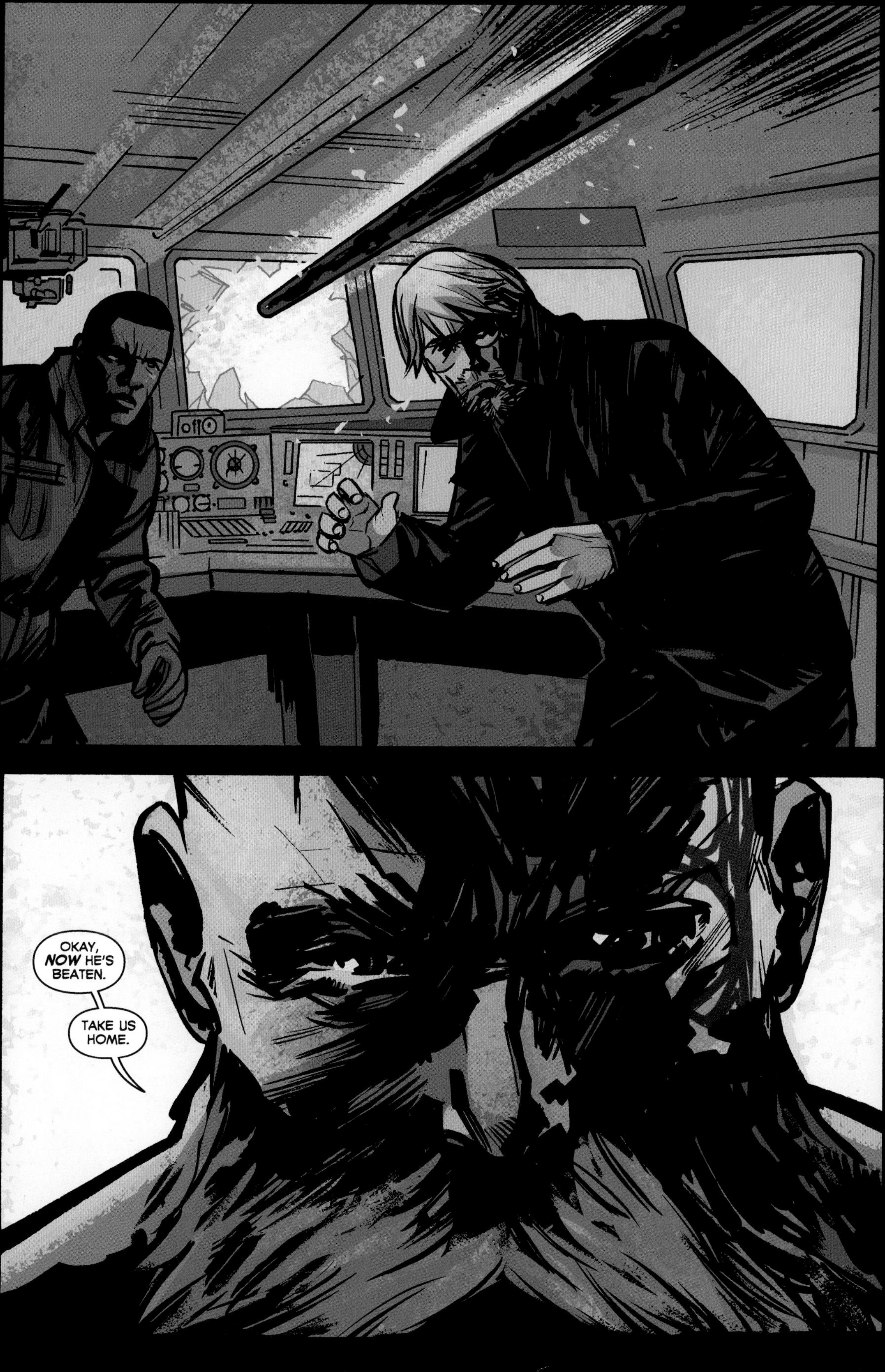
OKAY, *NOW* HE'S BEATEN.
TAKE US HOME.

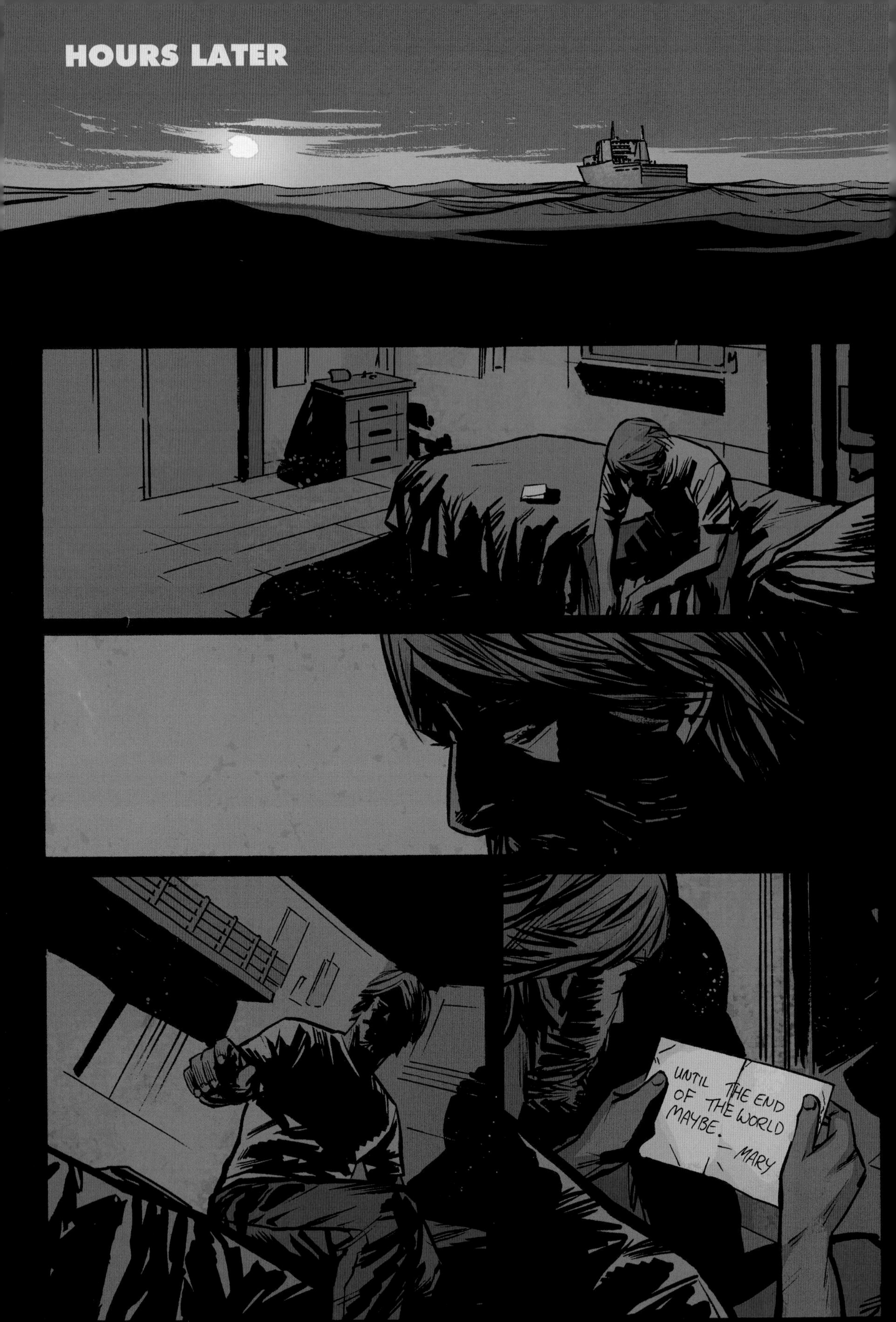
HOURS LATER
UNTIL THE END OF THE WORLD MAYBE.
— MARY

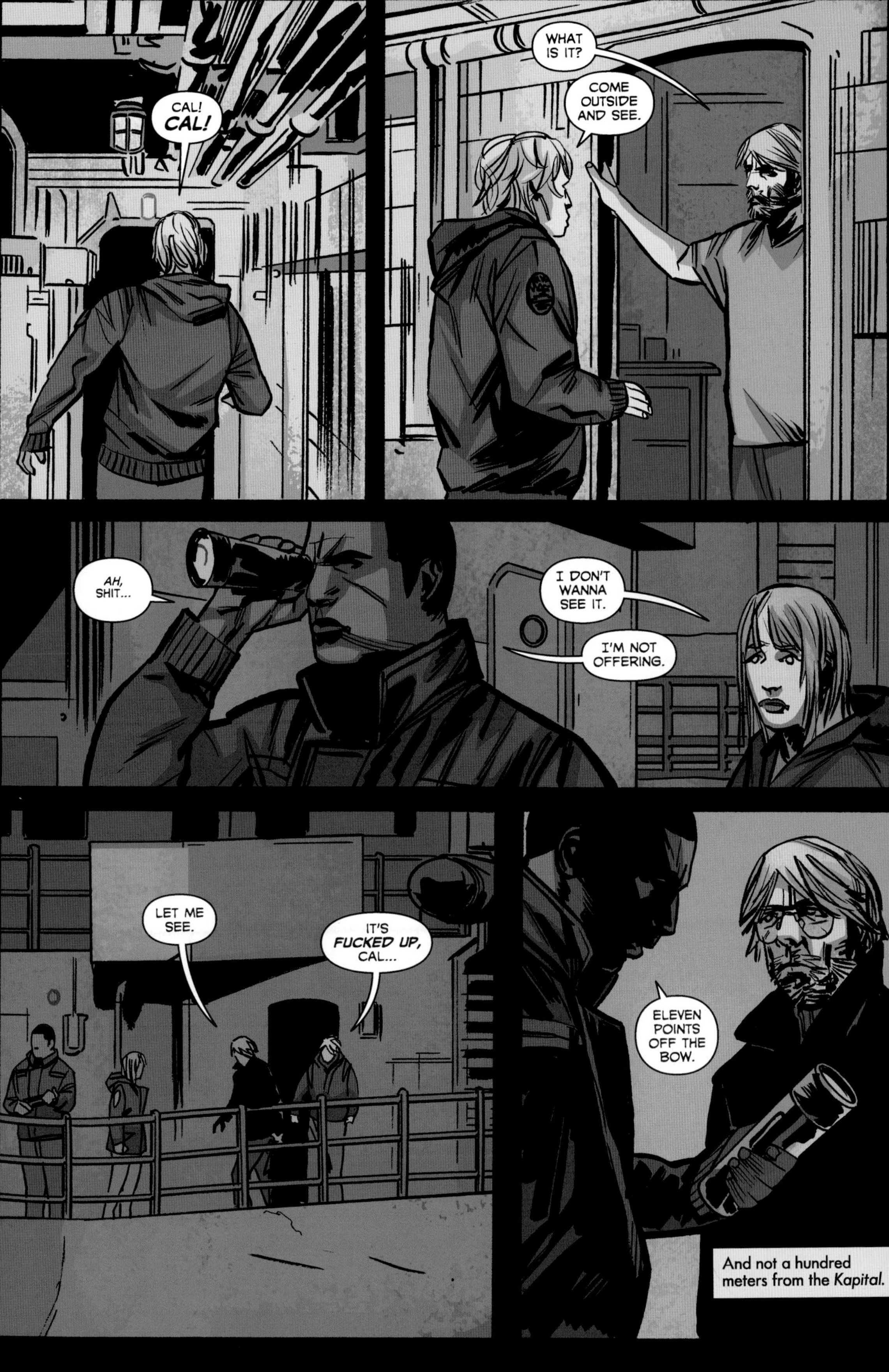
CAL! CAL!
WHAT IS IT?
COME OUTSIDE AND SEE.
AH, SHIT...
I DON'T WANNA SEE IT.
I'M NOT OFFERING.
LET ME SEE.
IT'S FUCKED UP, CAL...
ELEVEN POINTS OFF THE BOW.
And not a hundred meters from the Kapital.

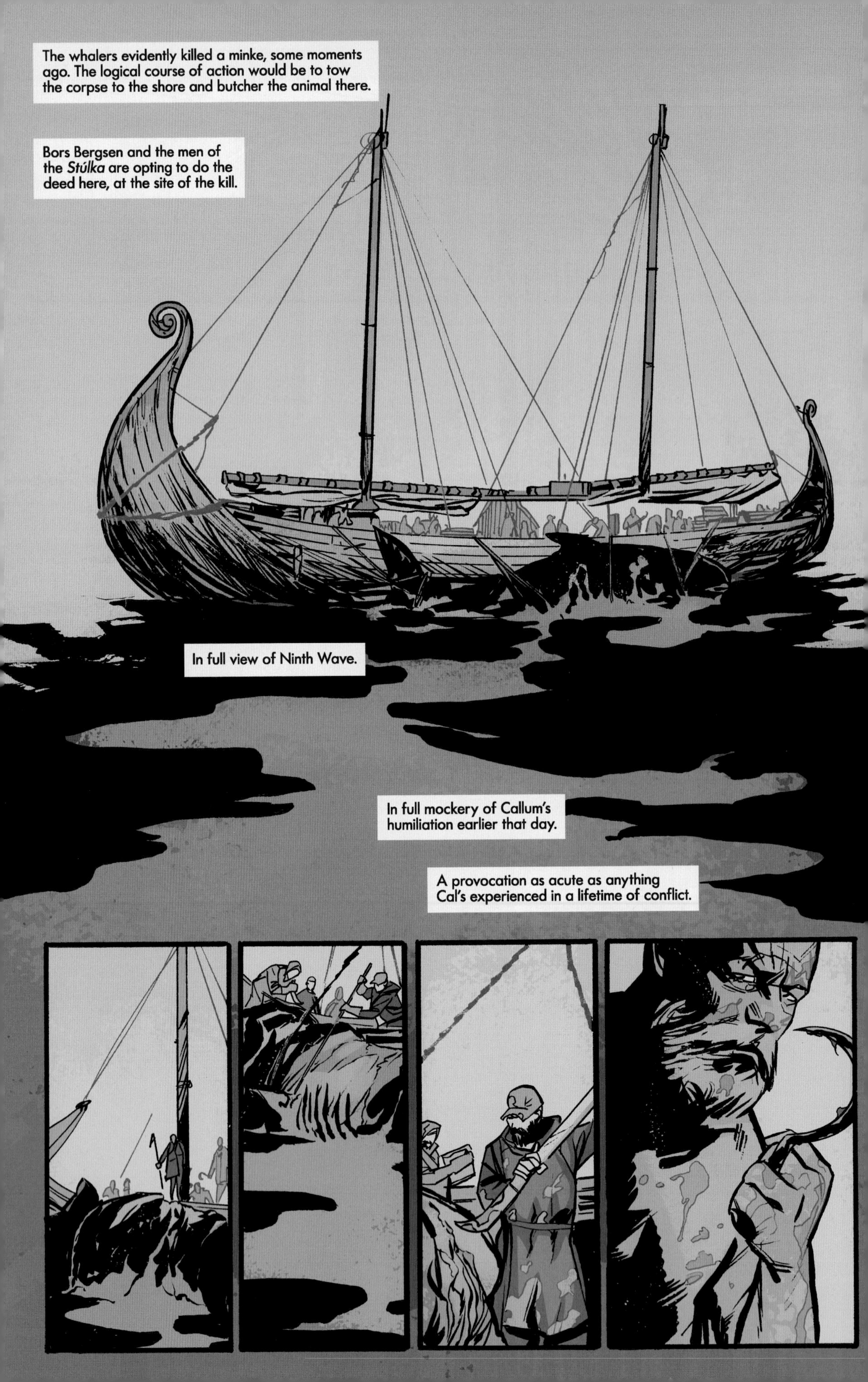

The whalers evidently killed a minke, some moments ago. The logical course of action would be to tow the corpse to the shore and butcher the animal there.
Bors Bergsen and the men of the *Stúlka* are opting to do the deed here, at the site of the kill.
In full view of Ninth Wave.
In full mockery of Callum's humiliation earlier that day.
A provocation as acute as anything Cal's experienced in a lifetime of conflict.

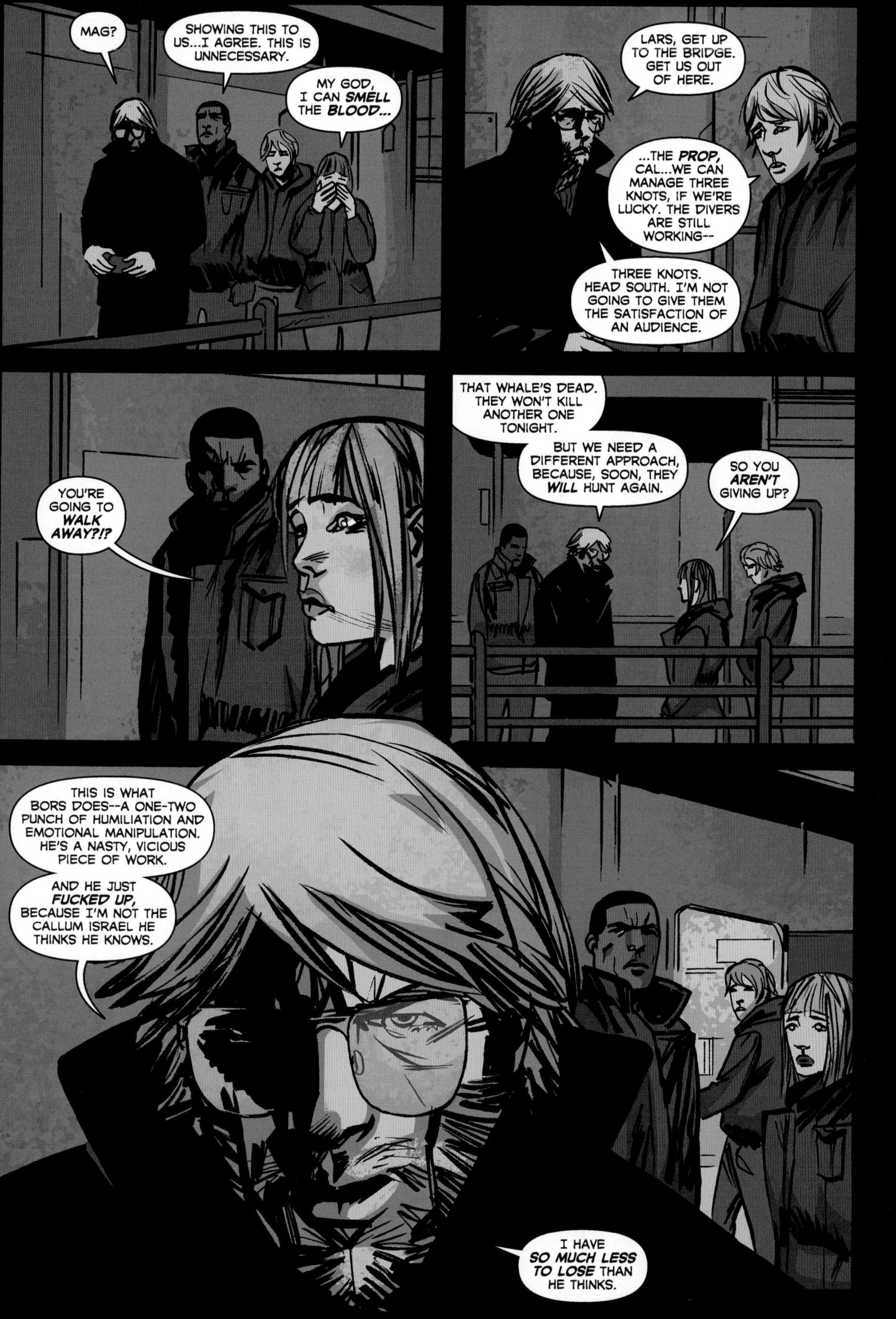
MAG?
SHOWING THIS TO US...I AGREE. THIS IS UNNECESSARY.
MY GOD, I CAN SMELL THE BLOOD...
LARS, GET UP TO THE BRIDGE. GET US OUT OF HERE.
...THE PROP, CAL...WE CAN MANAGE THREE KNOTS, IF WE'RE LUCKY. THE DIVERS ARE STILL WORKING--
THREE KNOTS. HEAD SOUTH. I'M NOT GOING TO GIVE THEM THE SATISFACTION OF AN AUDIENCE.
YOU'RE GOING TO WALK AWAY?!?
THAT WHALE'S DEAD. THEY WON'T KILL ANOTHER ONE TONIGHT.
BUT WE NEED A DIFFERENT APPROACH, BECAUSE, SOON, THEY WILL HUNT AGAIN.
SO YOU AREN'T GIVING UP?
THIS IS WHAT BORS DOES--A ONE-TWO PUNCH OF HUMILIATION AND EMOTIONAL MANIPULATION. HE'S A NASTY, VICIOUS PIECE OF WORK.
AND HE JUST FUCKED UP, BECAUSE I'M NOT THE CALLUM ISRAEL HE THINKS HE KNOWS.
I HAVE SO MUCH LESS TO LOSE THAN HE THINKS.

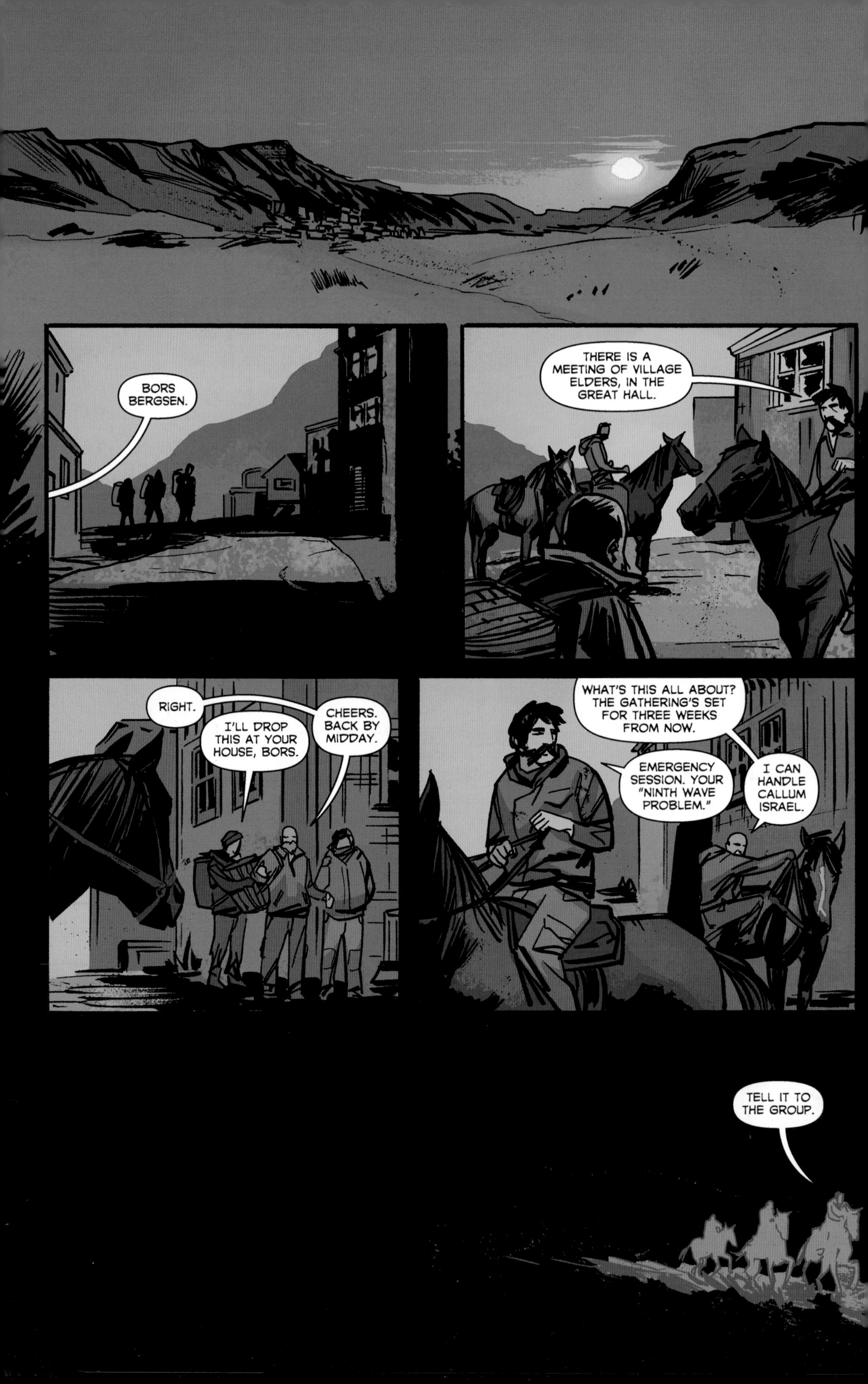
BORS BERGSEN.
THERE IS A MEETING OF VILLAGE ELDERS, IN THE GREAT HALL.
RIGHT.
I'LL DROP THIS AT YOUR HOUSE, BORS.
CHEERS. BACK BY MIDDAY.
WHAT'S THIS ALL ABOUT? THE GATHERING'S SET FOR THREE WEEKS FROM NOW.
EMERGENCY SESSION. YOUR "NINTH WAVE PROBLEM."
I CAN HANDLE CALLUM ISRAEL.
TELL IT TO THE GROUP.

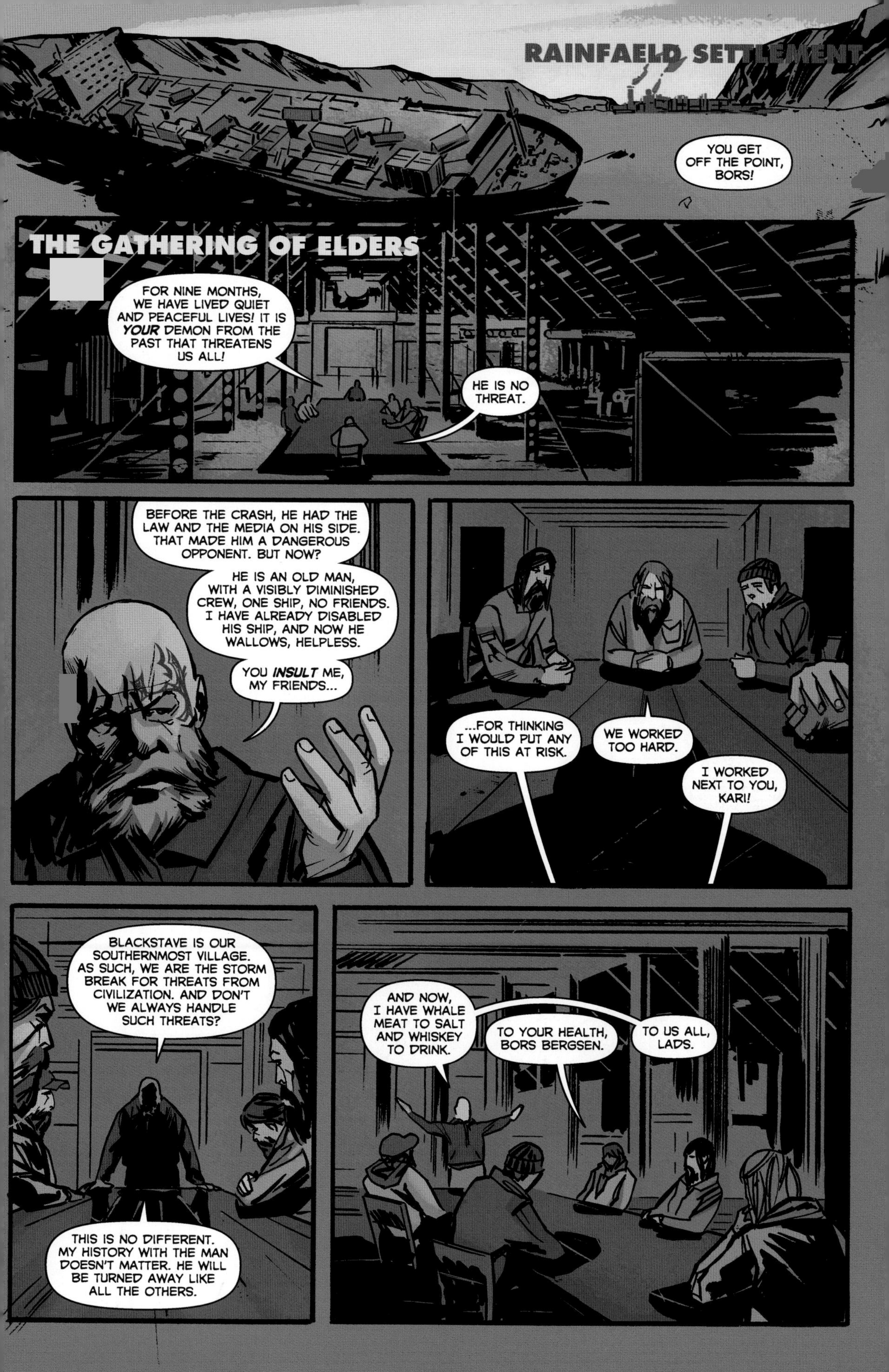
RAINFAELD SETTLEMENT
YOU GET OFF THE POINT, BORS!
THE GATHERING OF ELDERS
FOR NINE MONTHS, WE HAVE LIVED QUIET AND PEACEFUL LIVES! IT IS *YOUR* DEMON FROM THE PAST THAT THREATENS US ALL!
HE IS NO THREAT.
BEFORE THE CRASH, HE HAD THE LAW AND THE MEDIA ON HIS SIDE. THAT MADE HIM A DANGEROUS OPPONENT. BUT NOW?
HE IS AN OLD MAN, WITH A VISIBLY DIMINISHED CREW, ONE SHIP, NO FRIENDS. I HAVE ALREADY DISABLED HIS SHIP, AND NOW HE WALLOWS, HELPLESS.
YOU *INSULT* ME, MY FRIENDS...
...FOR THINKING I WOULD PUT ANY OF THIS AT RISK.
WE WORKED TOO HARD.
I WORKED NEXT TO YOU, KARI!
BLACKSTAVE IS OUR SOUTHERNMOST VILLAGE. AS SUCH, WE ARE THE STORM BREAK FOR THREATS FROM CIVILIZATION. AND DON'T WE ALWAYS HANDLE SUCH THREATS?
THIS IS NO DIFFERENT. MY HISTORY WITH THE MAN DOESN'T MATTER. HE WILL BE TURNED AWAY LIKE ALL THE OTHERS.
AND NOW, I HAVE WHALE MEAT TO SALT AND WHISKEY TO DRINK.
TO YOUR HEALTH, BORS BERGSEN.
TO US ALL, LADS.

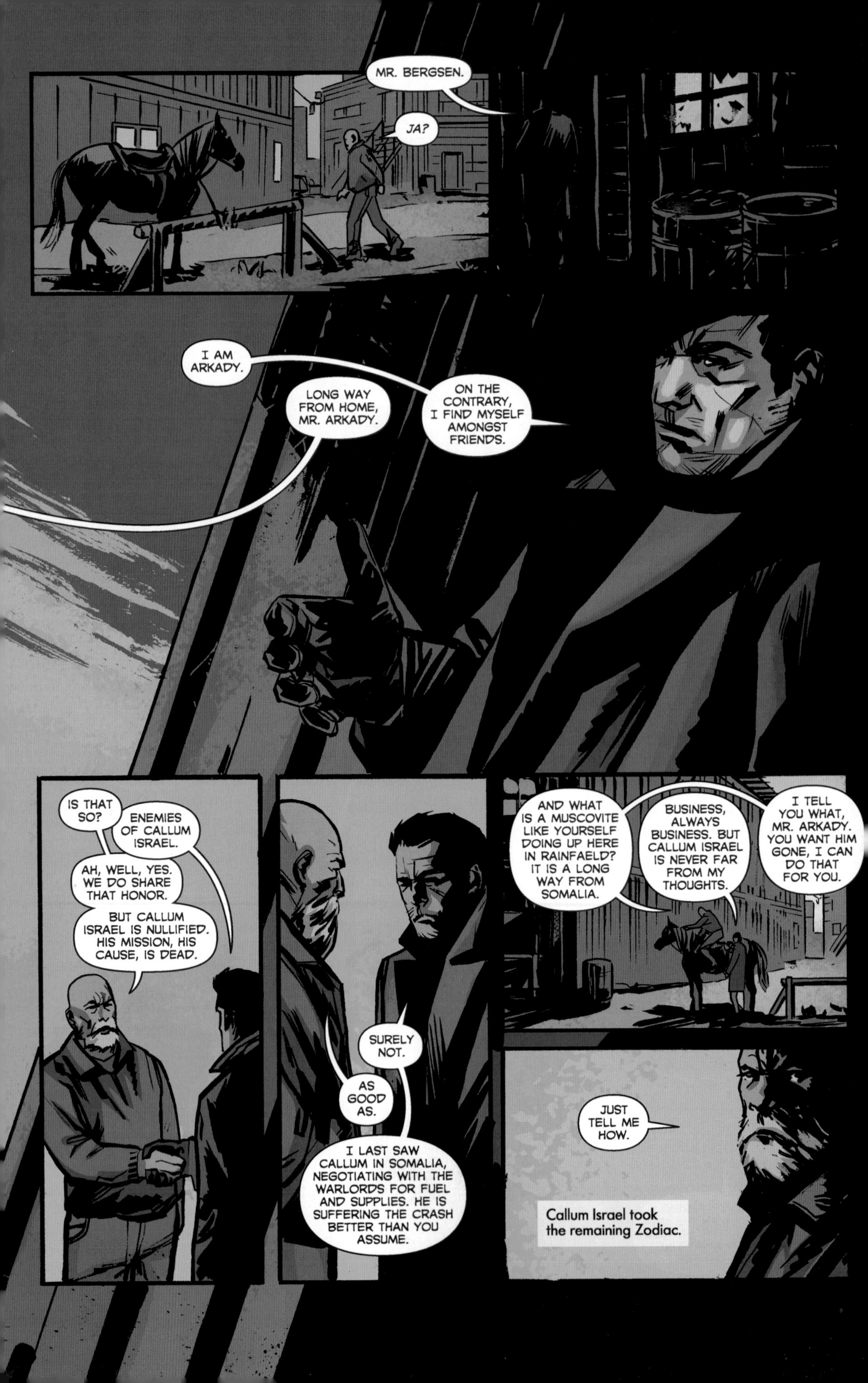
MR. BERGSEN.
JA?
I AM ARKADY.
LONG WAY FROM HOME, MR. ARKADY.
ON THE CONTRARY, I FIND MYSELF AMONGST FRIENDS.
IS THAT SO?
ENEMIES OF CALLUM ISRAEL.
AH, WELL, YES. WE DO SHARE THAT HONOR.
BUT CALLUM ISRAEL IS NULLIFIED. HIS MISSION, HIS CAUSE, IS DEAD.
SURELY NOT.
AS GOOD AS.
I LAST SAW CALLUM IN SOMALIA, NEGOTIATING WITH THE WARLORDS FOR FUEL AND SUPPLIES. HE IS SUFFERING THE CRASH BETTER THAN YOU ASSUME.
AND WHAT IS A MUSCOVITE LIKE YOURSELF DOING UP HERE IN RAINFAELD? IT IS A LONG WAY FROM SOMALIA.
BUSINESS, ALWAYS BUSINESS. BUT CALLUM ISRAEL IS NEVER FAR FROM MY THOUGHTS.
I TELL YOU WHAT, MR. ARKADY. YOU WANT HIM GONE, I CAN DO THAT FOR YOU.
JUST TELL ME HOW.
Callum Israel took the remaining Zodiac.

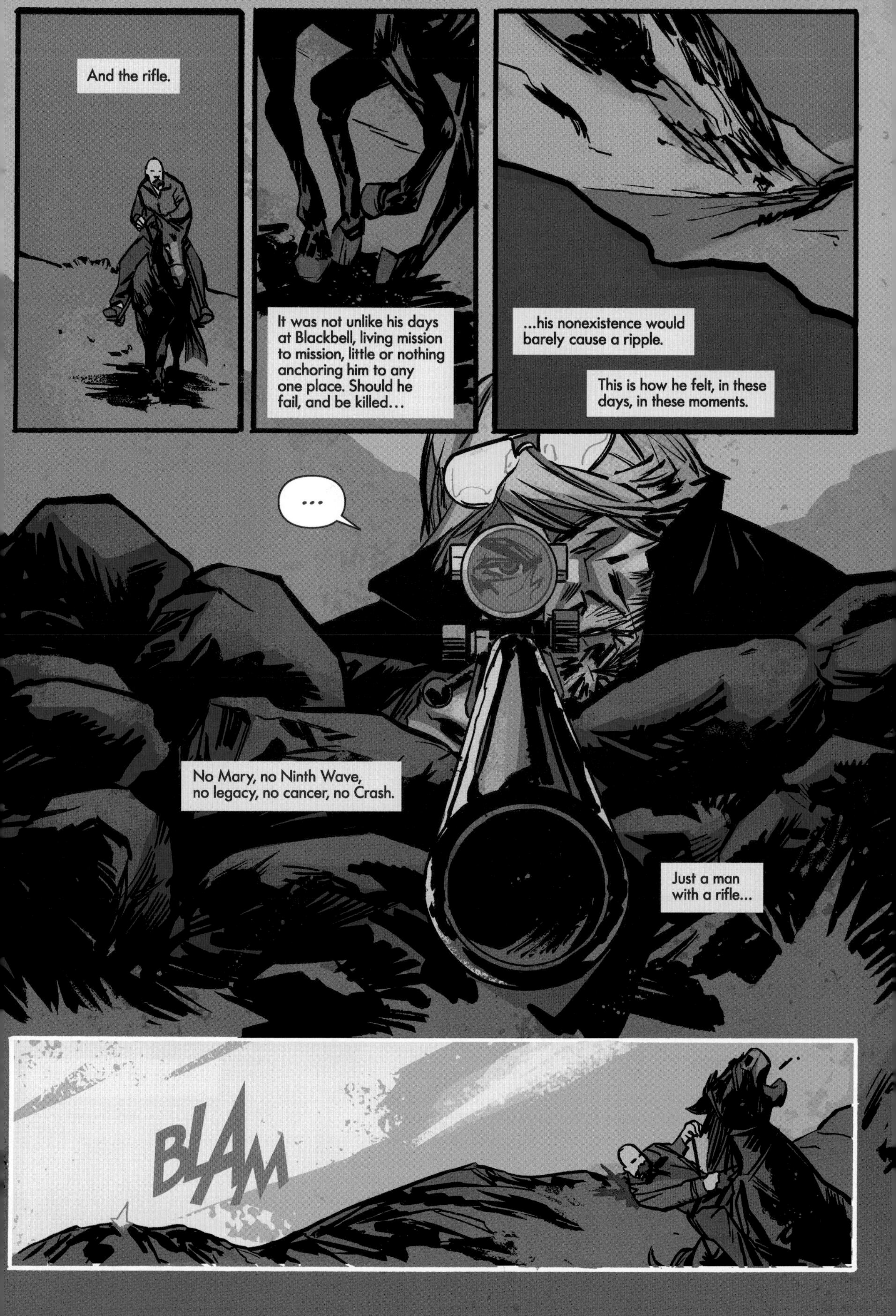
And the rifle.
It was not unlike his days at Blackbell, living mission to mission, little or nothing anchoring him to any one place. Should he fail, and be killed…
...his nonexistence would barely cause a ripple.
This is how he felt, in these days, in these moments.
...
No Mary, no Ninth Wave, no legacy, no cancer, no Crash.
Just a man with a rifle...
BLAM

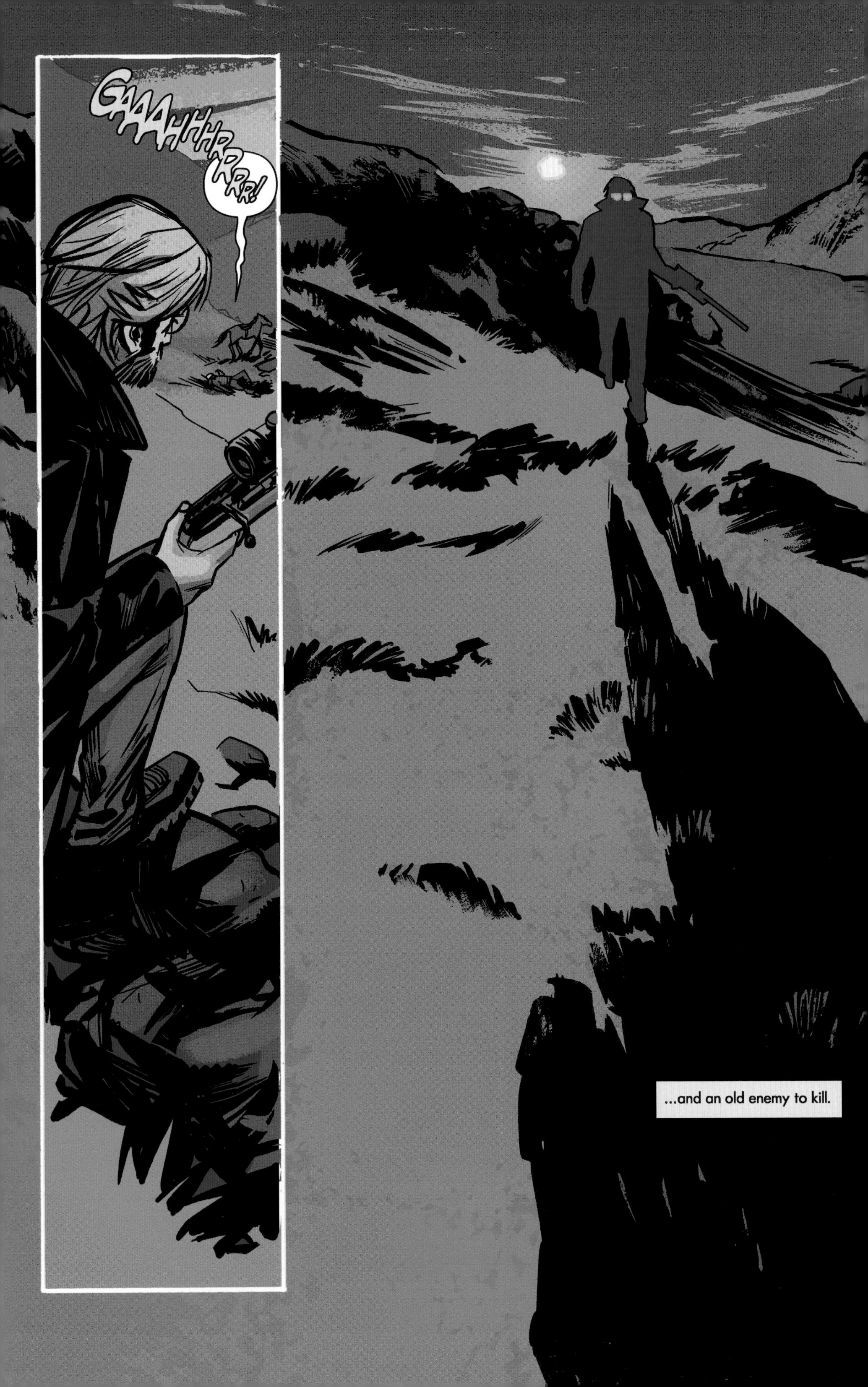
GAAAHHHRRRR!
...and an old enemy to kill.

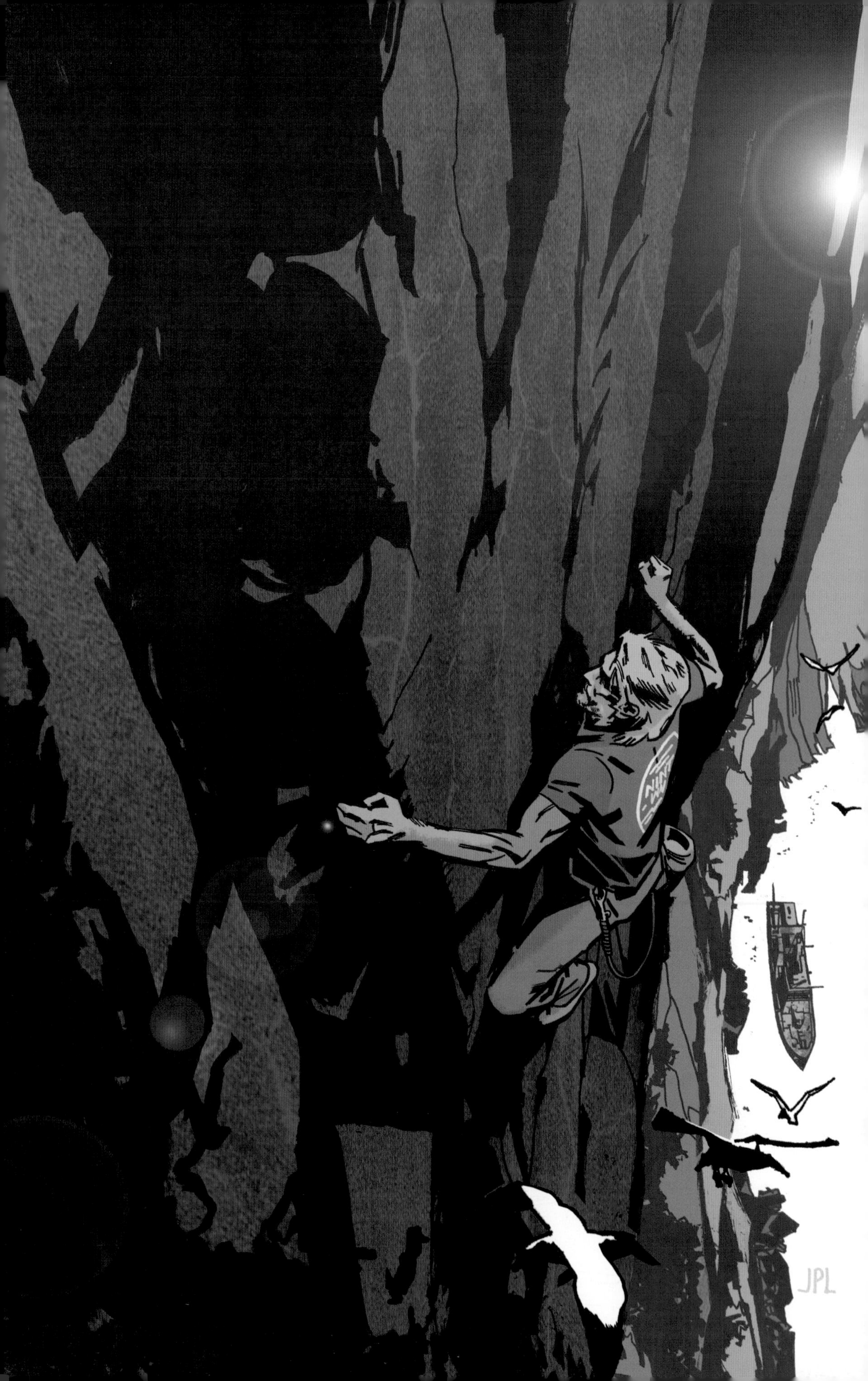
JPL

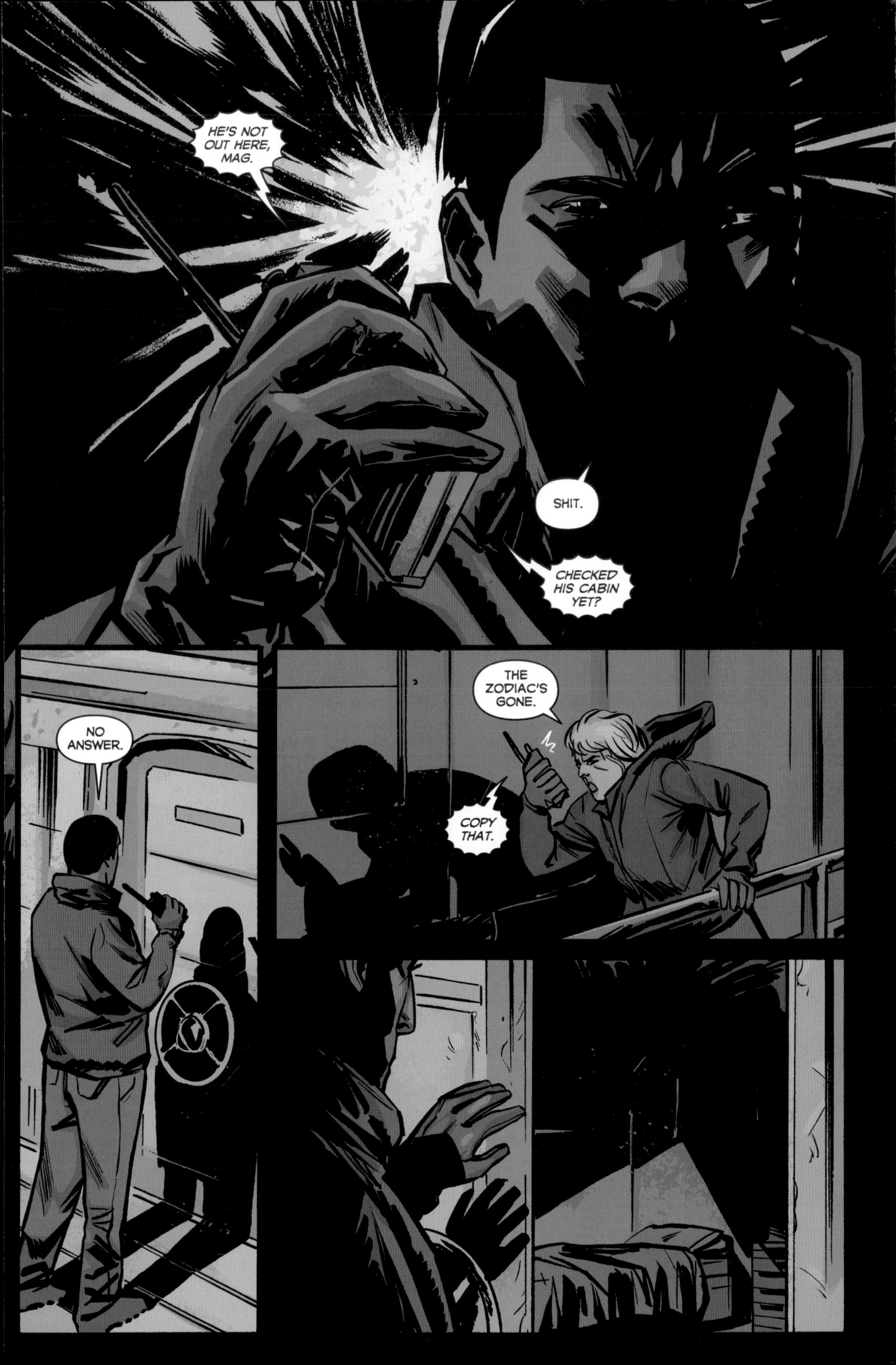
HE'S NOT OUT HERE, MAG.
SHIT.
CHECKED HIS CABIN YET?
NO ANSWER.
THE ZODIAC'S GONE.
COPY THAT.

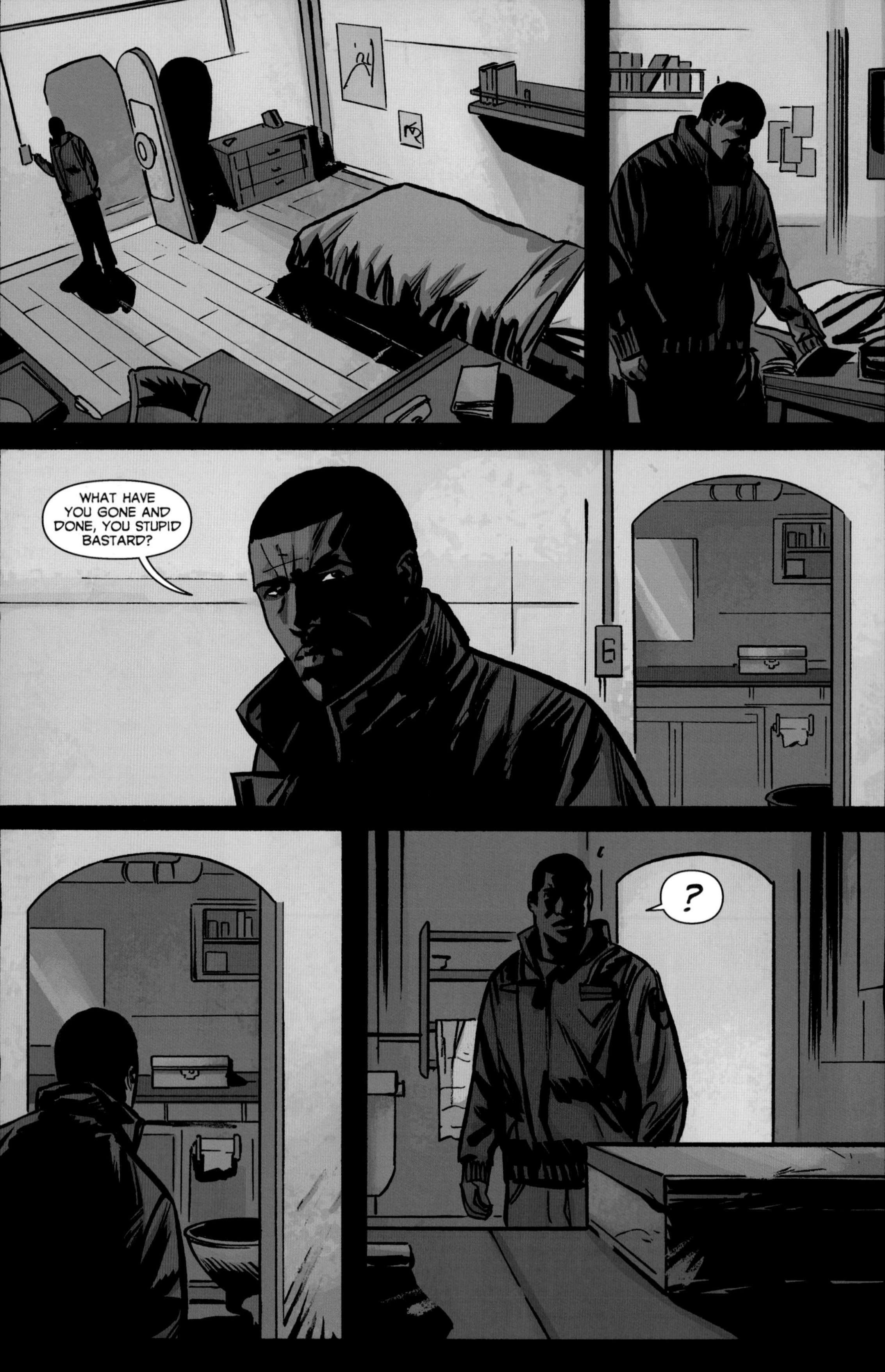
WHAT HAVE YOU GONE AND DONE, YOU STUPID BASTARD?
?

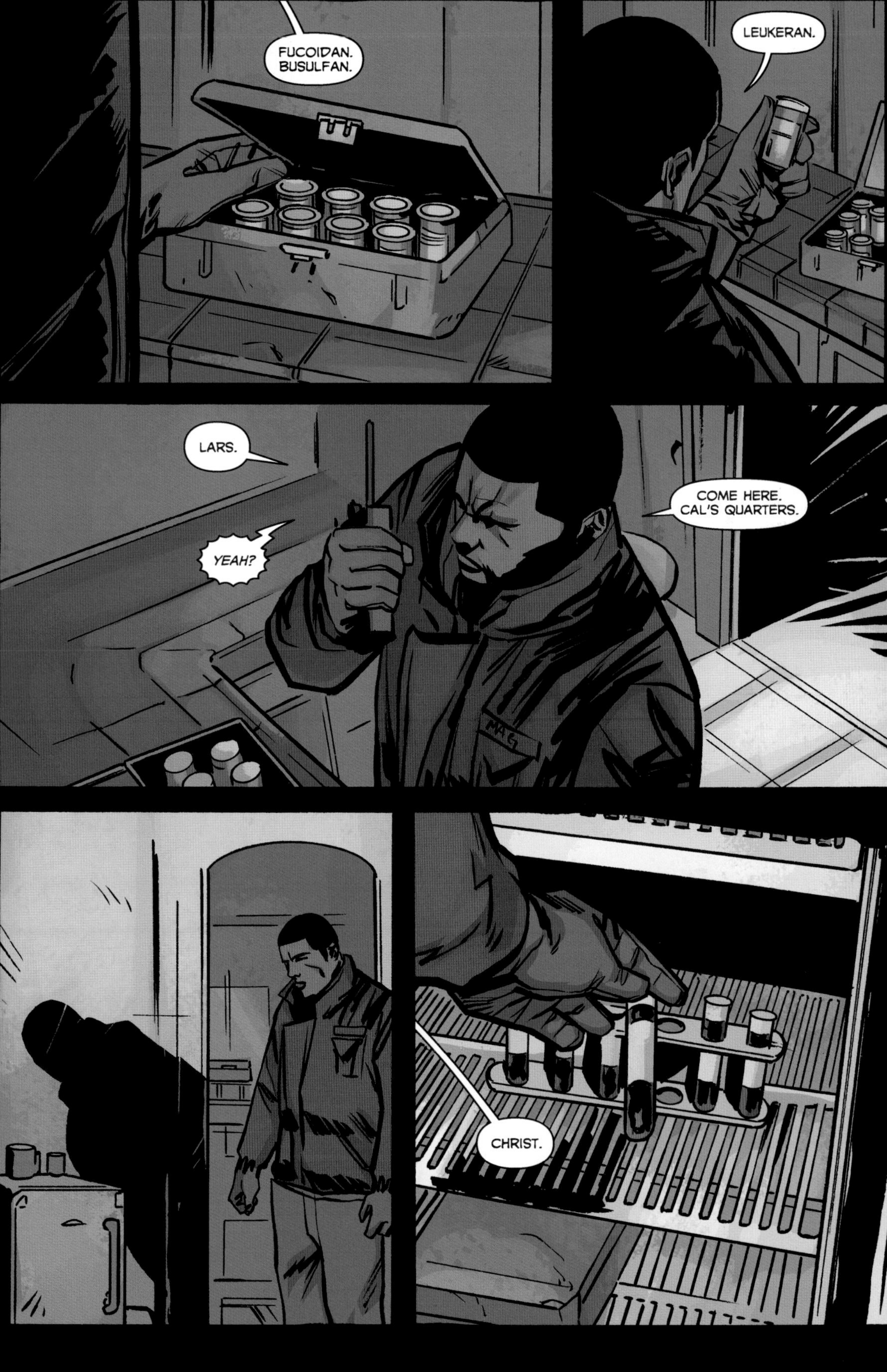
FUCOIDAN. BUSULFAN.
LEUKERAN.
LARS.
YEAH?
COME HERE. CAL'S QUARTERS.
CHRIST.

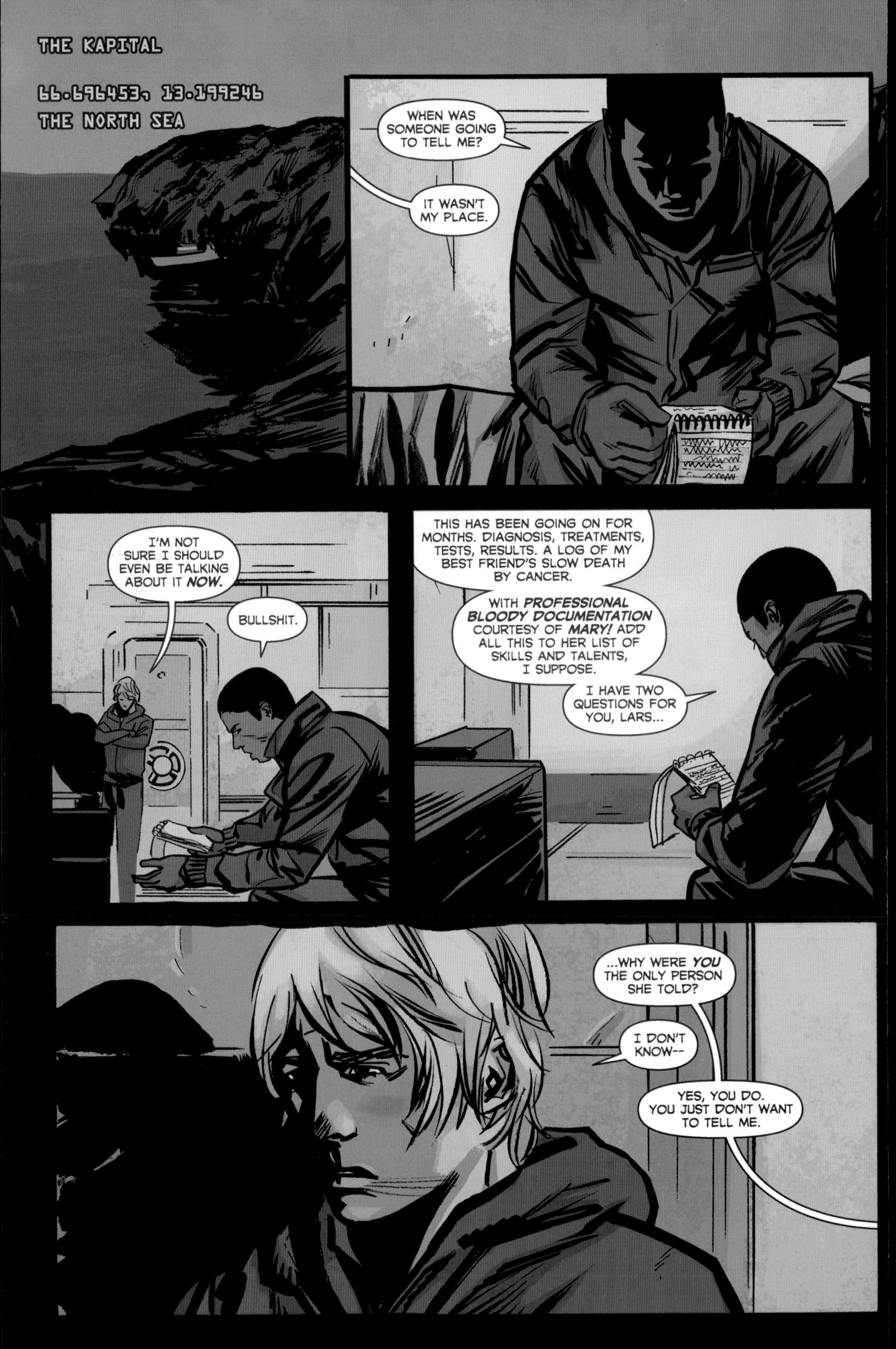
THE KAPITAL
66.696453, 13.199246
THE NORTH SEA
WHEN WAS SOMEONE GOING TO TELL ME?
IT WASN'T MY PLACE.
I'M NOT SURE I SHOULD EVEN BE TALKING ABOUT IT *NOW.*
BULLSHIT.
THIS HAS BEEN GOING ON FOR MONTHS. DIAGNOSIS, TREATMENTS, TESTS, RESULTS. A LOG OF MY BEST FRIEND'S SLOW DEATH BY CANCER.
WITH ***PROFESSIONAL BLOODY DOCUMENTATION*** COURTESY OF ***MARY!*** ADD ALL THIS TO HER LIST OF SKILLS AND TALENTS, I SUPPOSE.
I HAVE TWO QUESTIONS FOR YOU, LARS...
...WHY WERE ***YOU*** THE ONLY PERSON SHE TOLD?
I DON'T KNOW--
YES, YOU DO. YOU JUST DON'T WANT TO TELL ME.

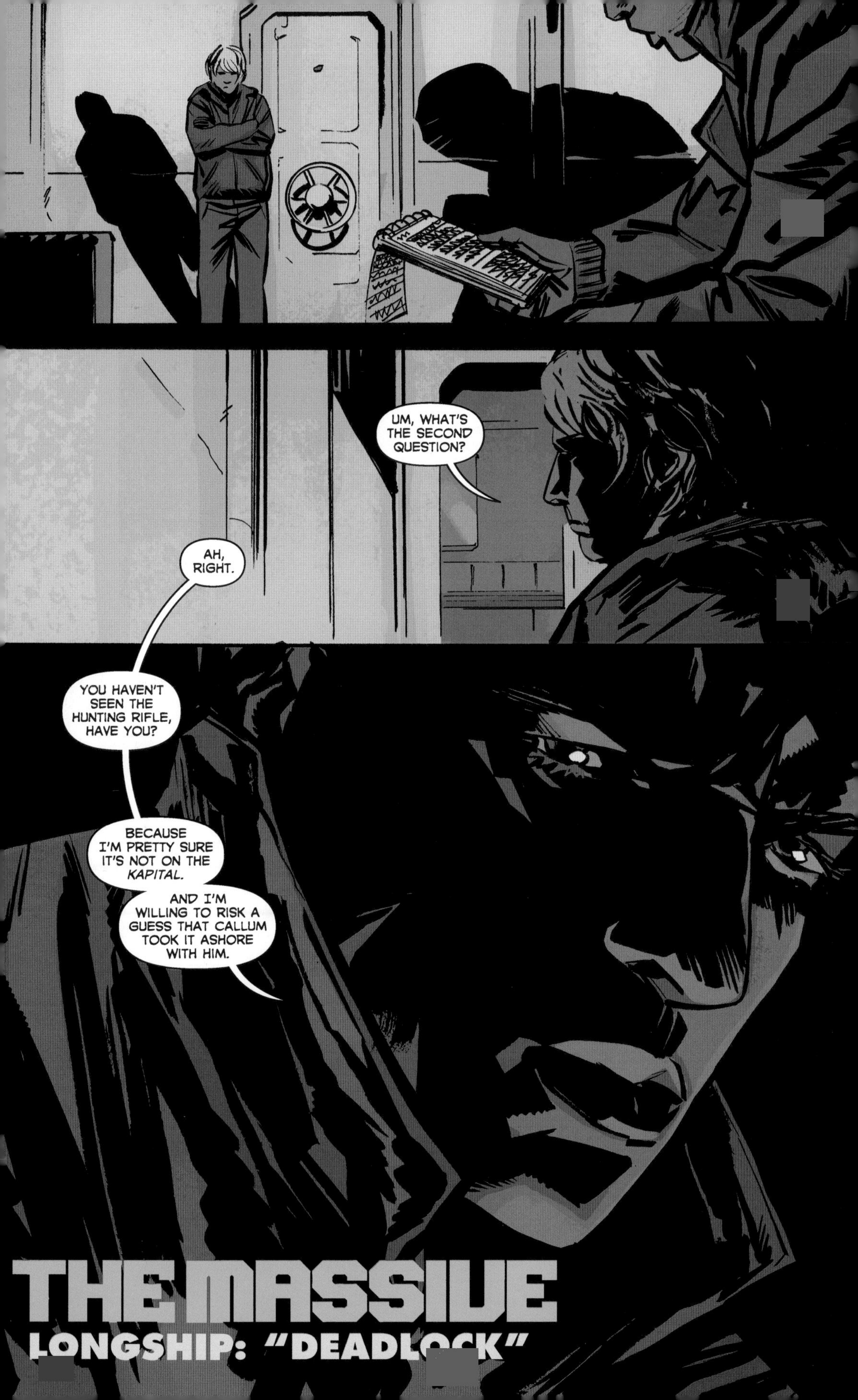
UM, WHAT'S THE SECOND QUESTION?
AH, RIGHT.
YOU HAVEN'T SEEN THE HUNTING RIFLE, HAVE YOU?
BECAUSE I'M PRETTY SURE IT'S NOT ON THE *KAPITAL.*
AND I'M WILLING TO RISK A GUESS THAT CALLUM TOOK IT ASHORE WITH HIM.
THE MASSIVE
LONGSHIP: "DEADLOCK"

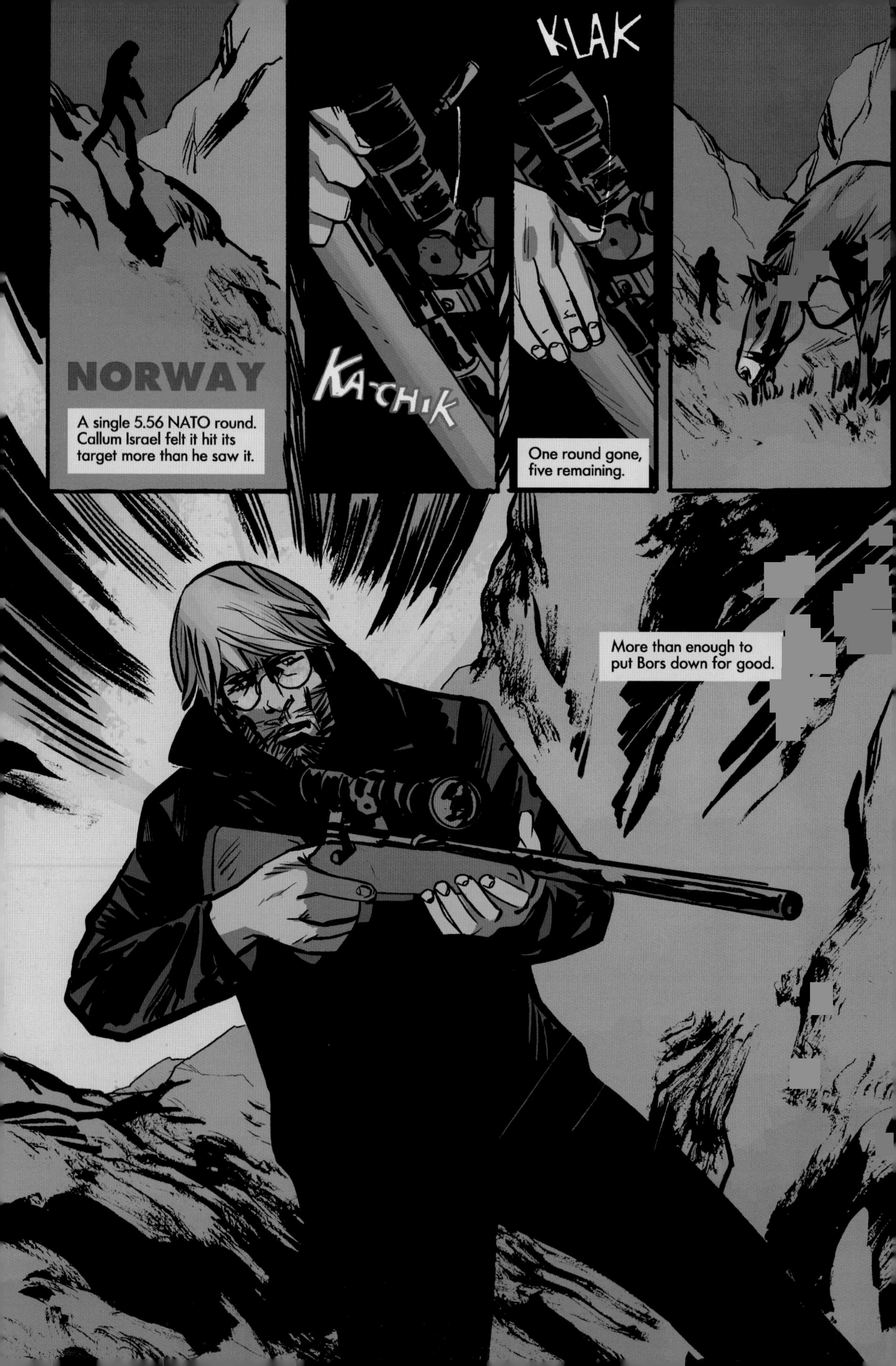
NORWAY
A single 5.56 NATO round. Callum Israel felt it hit its target more than he saw it.
KA-CHIK
KLAK
One round gone, five remaining.
More than enough to put Bors down for good.

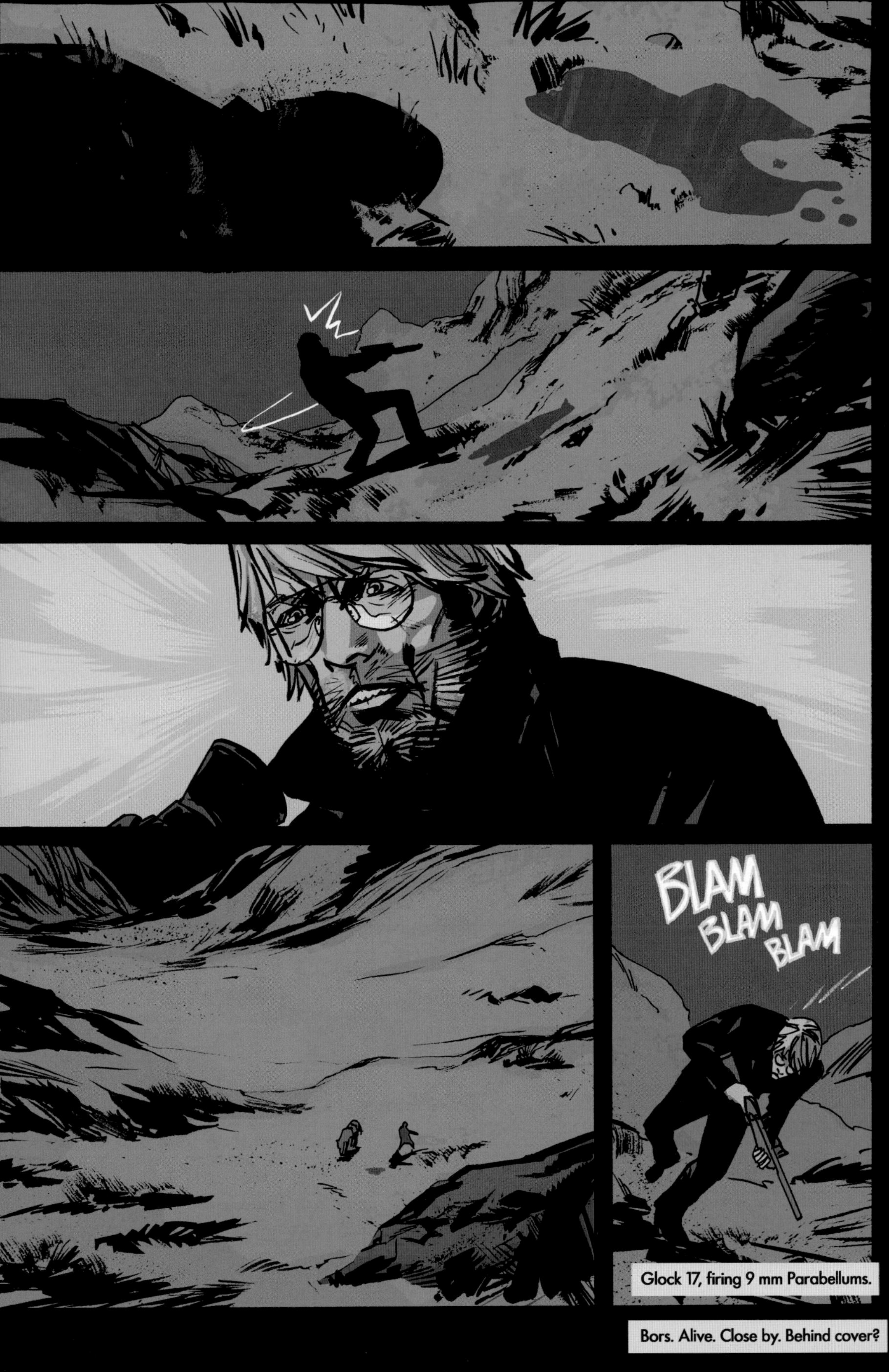
BLAM
BLAM
BLAM
BLAM
Glock 17, firing 9 mm Parabellums.
Bors. Alive. Close by. Behind cover?

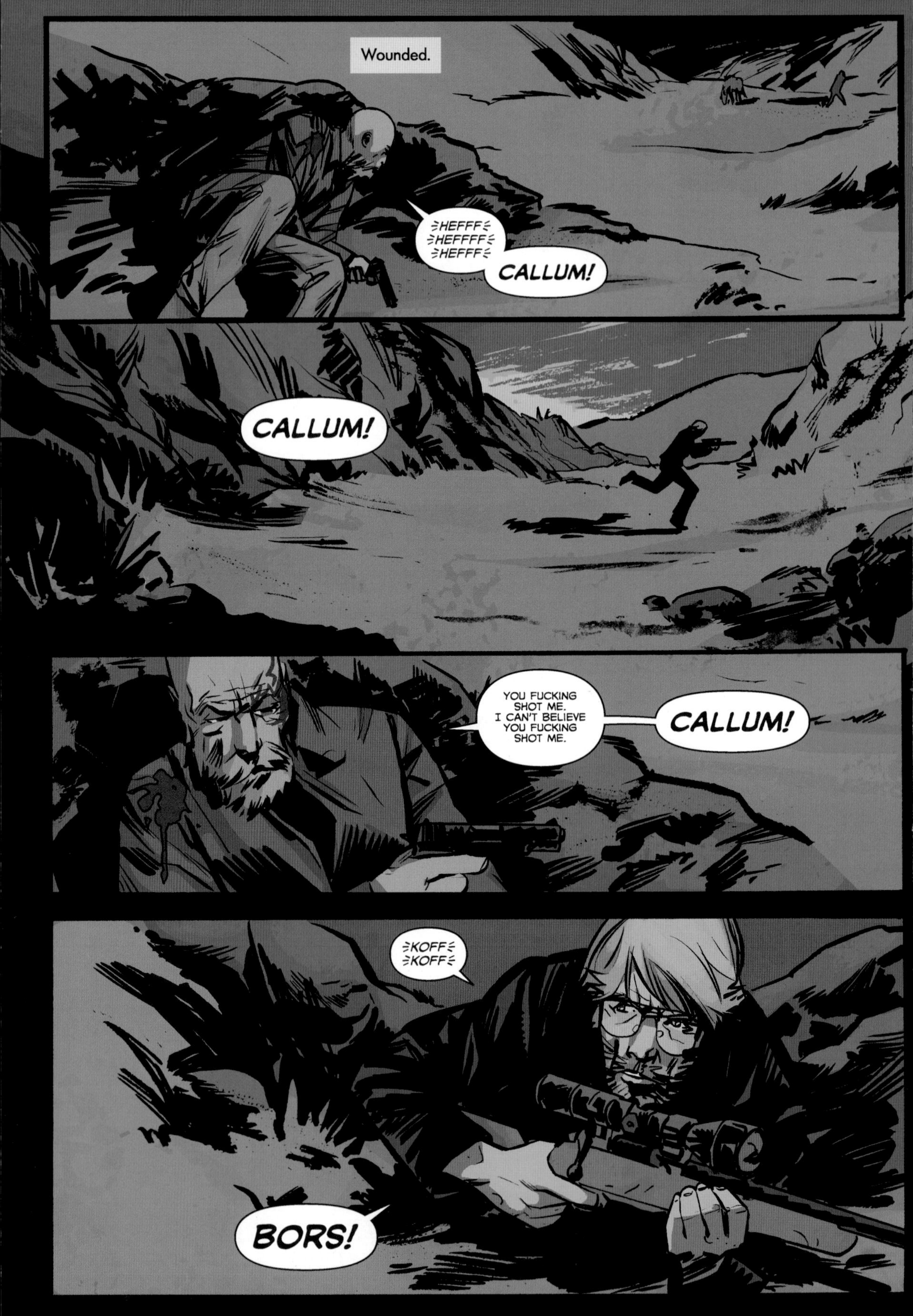
Wounded.
HEFFF HEFFFF HEFFF
CALLUM!
CALLUM!
YOU FUCKING SHOT ME. I CAN'T BELIEVE YOU FUCKING SHOT ME.
CALLUM!
KOFF KOFF
BORS!

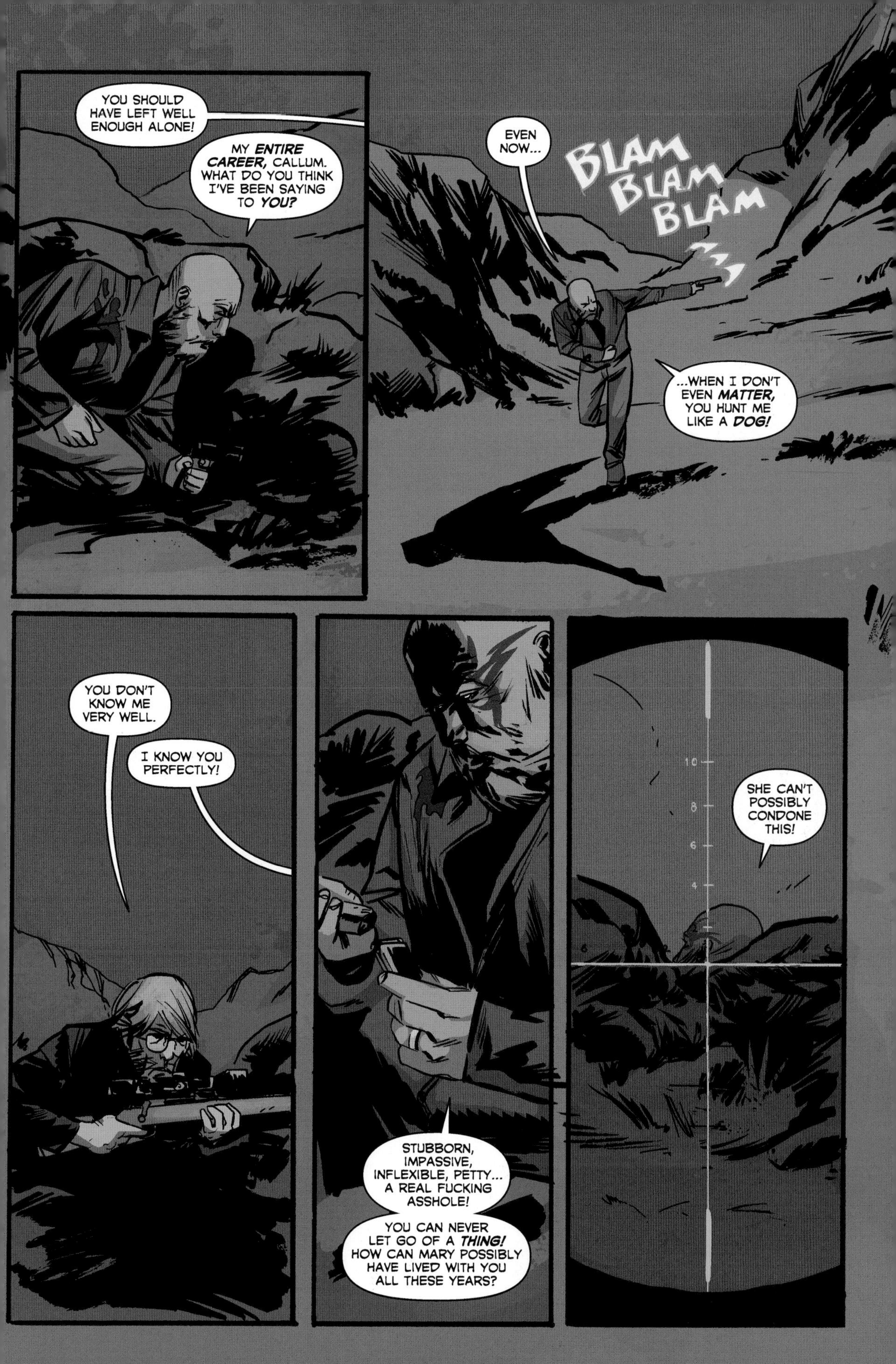
YOU SHOULD HAVE LEFT WELL ENOUGH ALONE!
MY ENTIRE CAREER, CALLUM. WHAT DO YOU THINK I'VE BEEN SAYING TO YOU?
EVEN NOW...
BLAM BLAM BLAM
...WHEN I DON'T EVEN MATTER, YOU HUNT ME LIKE A DOG!
YOU DON'T KNOW ME VERY WELL.
I KNOW YOU PERFECTLY!
STUBBORN, IMPASSIVE, INFLEXIBLE, PETTY... A REAL FUCKING ASSHOLE!
YOU CAN NEVER LET GO OF A THING! HOW CAN MARY POSSIBLY HAVE LIVED WITH YOU ALL THESE YEARS?
10
8
6
4
SHE CAN'T POSSIBLY CONDONE THIS!

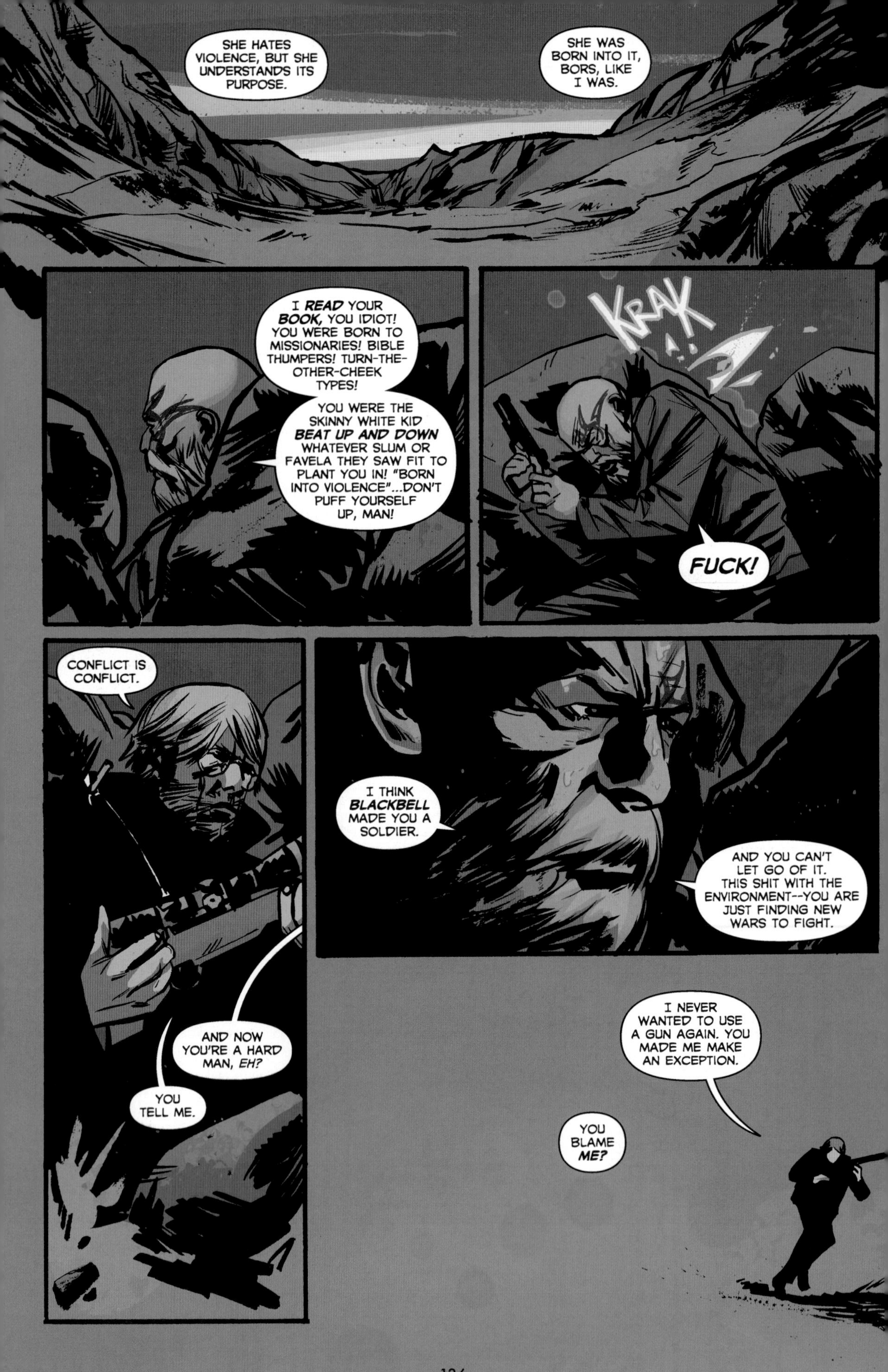
SHE HATES VIOLENCE, BUT SHE UNDERSTANDS ITS PURPOSE.
SHE WAS BORN INTO IT, BORS, LIKE I WAS.
I READ YOUR BOOK, YOU IDIOT! YOU WERE BORN TO MISSIONARIES! BIBLE THUMPERS! TURN-THE-OTHER-CHEEK TYPES!
YOU WERE THE SKINNY WHITE KID BEAT UP AND DOWN WHATEVER SLUM OR FAVELA THEY SAW FIT TO PLANT YOU IN! "BORN INTO VIOLENCE"...DON'T PUFF YOURSELF UP, MAN!
KRAK
FUCK!
CONFLICT IS CONFLICT.
I THINK BLACKBELL MADE YOU A SOLDIER.
AND YOU CAN'T LET GO OF IT. THIS SHIT WITH THE ENVIRONMENT--YOU ARE JUST FINDING NEW WARS TO FIGHT.
AND NOW YOU'RE A HARD MAN, EH?
YOU TELL ME.
I NEVER WANTED TO USE A GUN AGAIN. YOU MADE ME MAKE AN EXCEPTION.
YOU BLAME ME?

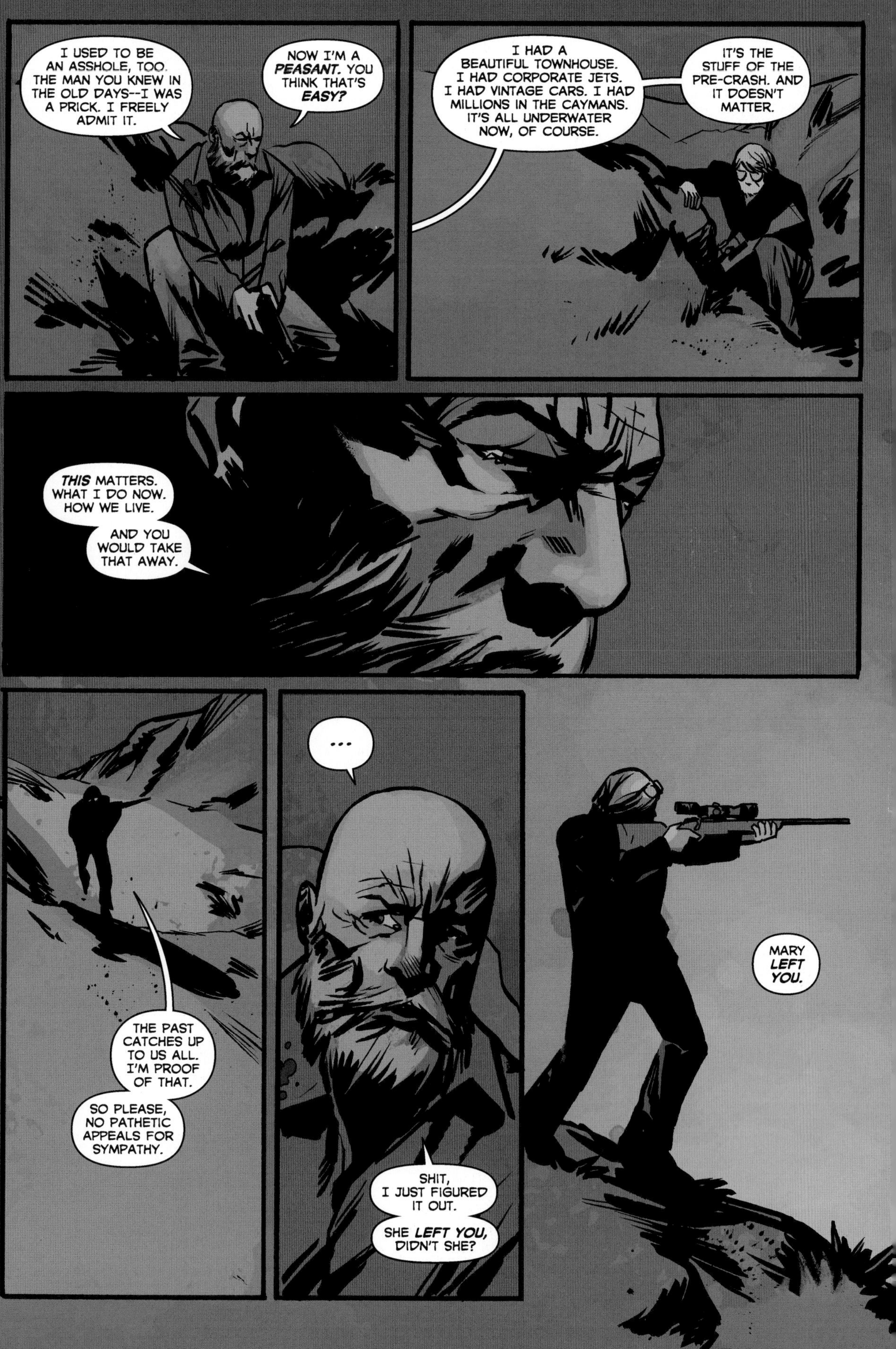

I USED TO BE AN ASSHOLE, TOO. THE MAN YOU KNEW IN THE OLD DAYS--I WAS A PRICK. I FREELY ADMIT IT.
NOW I'M A *PEASANT.* YOU THINK THAT'S *EASY?*
I HAD A BEAUTIFUL TOWNHOUSE. I HAD CORPORATE JETS. I HAD VINTAGE CARS. I HAD MILLIONS IN THE CAYMANS. IT'S ALL UNDERWATER NOW, OF COURSE.
IT'S THE STUFF OF THE PRE-CRASH. AND IT DOESN'T MATTER.
THIS MATTERS. WHAT I DO NOW. HOW WE LIVE.
AND YOU WOULD TAKE THAT AWAY.
THE PAST CATCHES UP TO US ALL. I'M PROOF OF THAT.
SO PLEASE, NO PATHETIC APPEALS FOR SYMPATHY.
...
SHIT, I JUST FIGURED IT OUT.
SHE *LEFT YOU,* DIDN'T SHE?
MARY *LEFT YOU.*

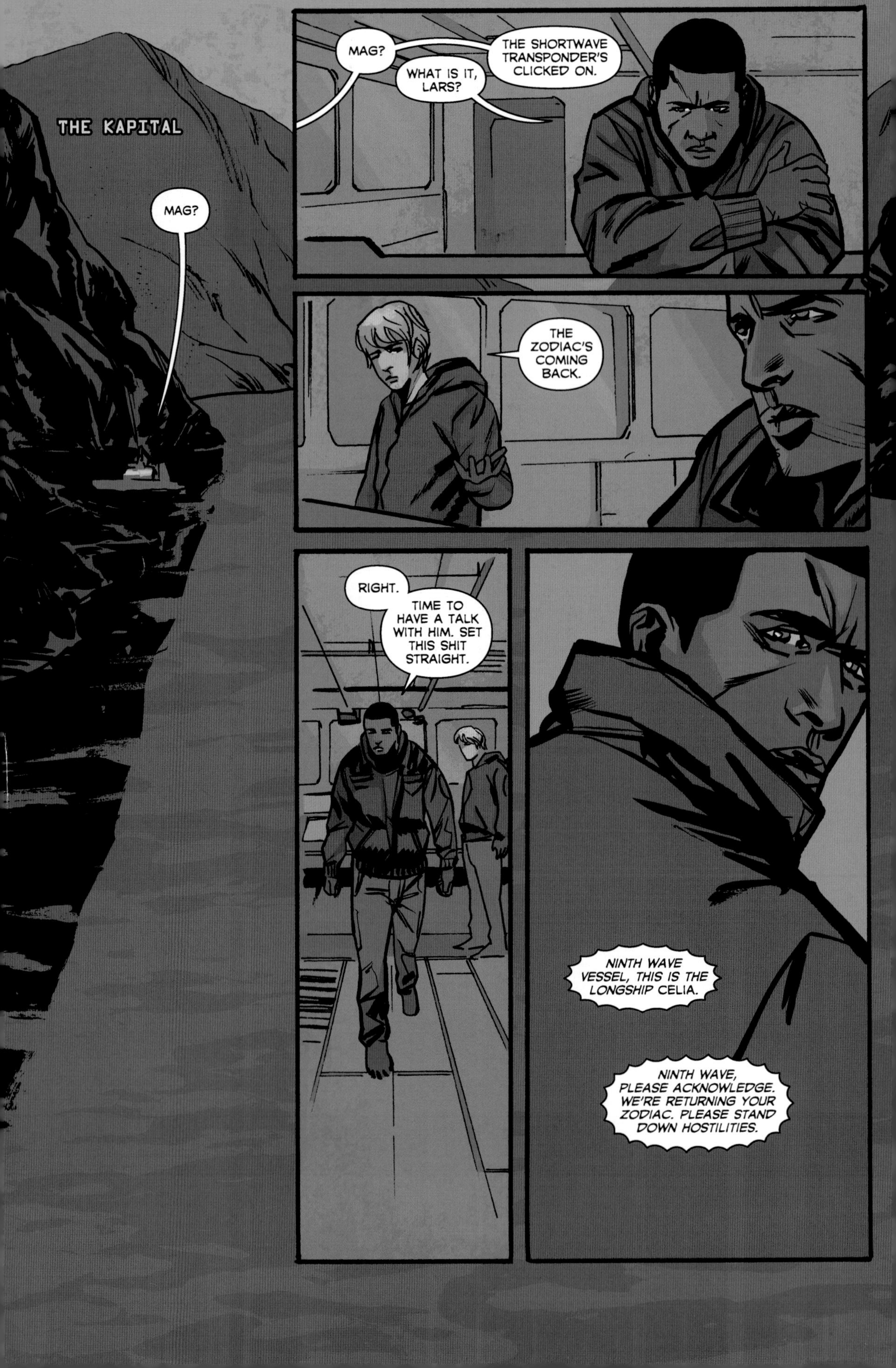
THE KAPITAL
MAG?
MAG?
WHAT IS IT, LARS?
THE SHORTWAVE TRANSPONDER'S CLICKED ON.
THE ZODIAC'S COMING BACK.
RIGHT.
TIME TO HAVE A TALK WITH HIM. SET THIS SHIT STRAIGHT.
NINTH WAVE VESSEL, THIS IS THE LONGSHIP CELIA.
NINTH WAVE, PLEASE ACKNOWLEDGE. WE'RE RETURNING YOUR ZODIAC. PLEASE STAND DOWN HOSTILITIES.

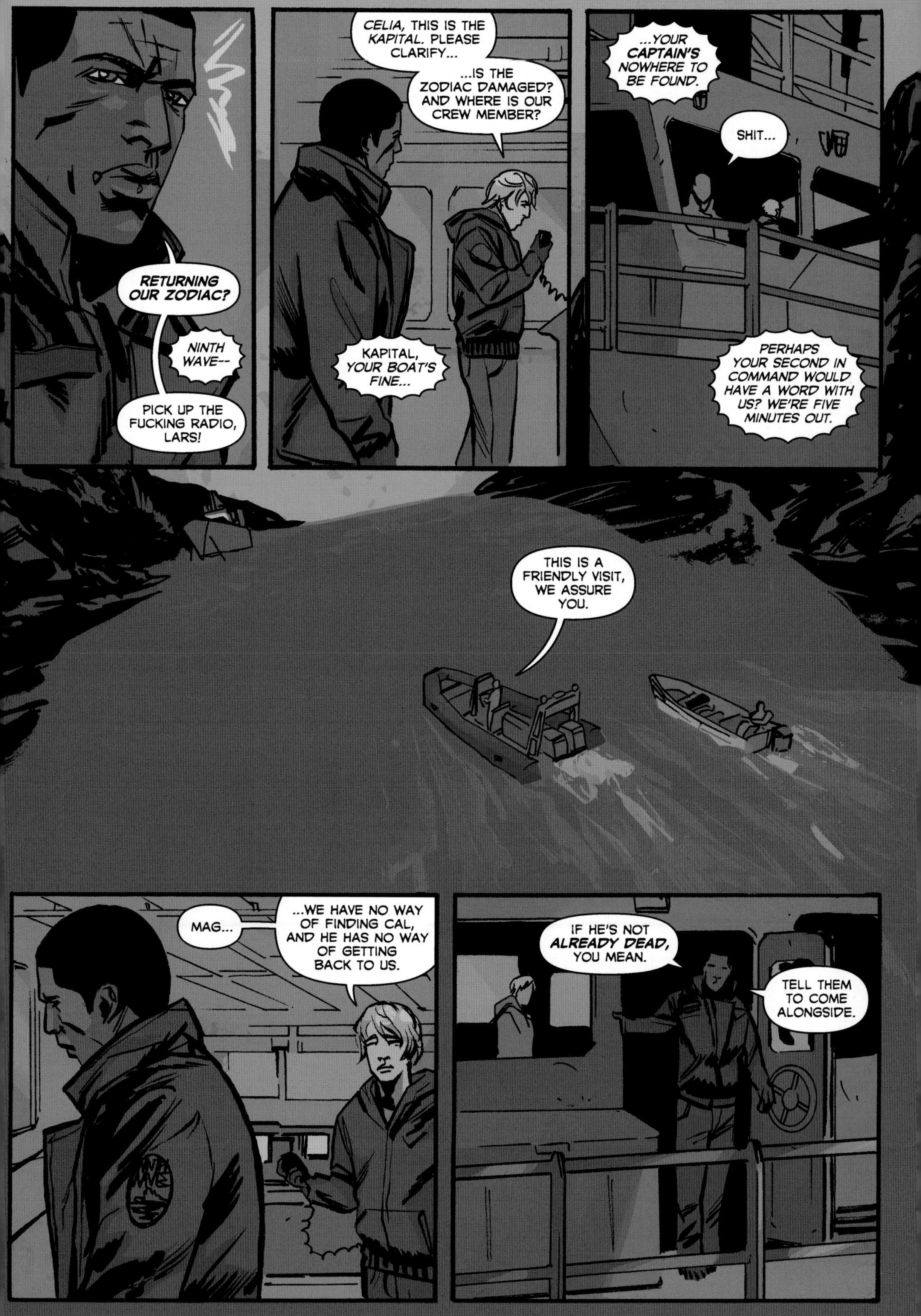
RETURNING OUR ZODIAC?
NINTH WAVE--
PICK UP THE FUCKING RADIO, LARS!
CELIA, THIS IS THE KAPITAL. PLEASE CLARIFY...
...IS THE ZODIAC DAMAGED? AND WHERE IS OUR CREW MEMBER?
KAPITAL, YOUR BOAT'S FINE...
...YOUR CAPTAIN'S NOWHERE TO BE FOUND.
SHIT...
PERHAPS YOUR SECOND IN COMMAND WOULD HAVE A WORD WITH US? WE'RE FIVE MINUTES OUT.
THIS IS A FRIENDLY VISIT, WE ASSURE YOU.
MAG...
...WE HAVE NO WAY OF FINDING CAL, AND HE HAS NO WAY OF GETTING BACK TO US.
IF HE'S NOT ALREADY DEAD, YOU MEAN.
TELL THEM TO COME ALONGSIDE.

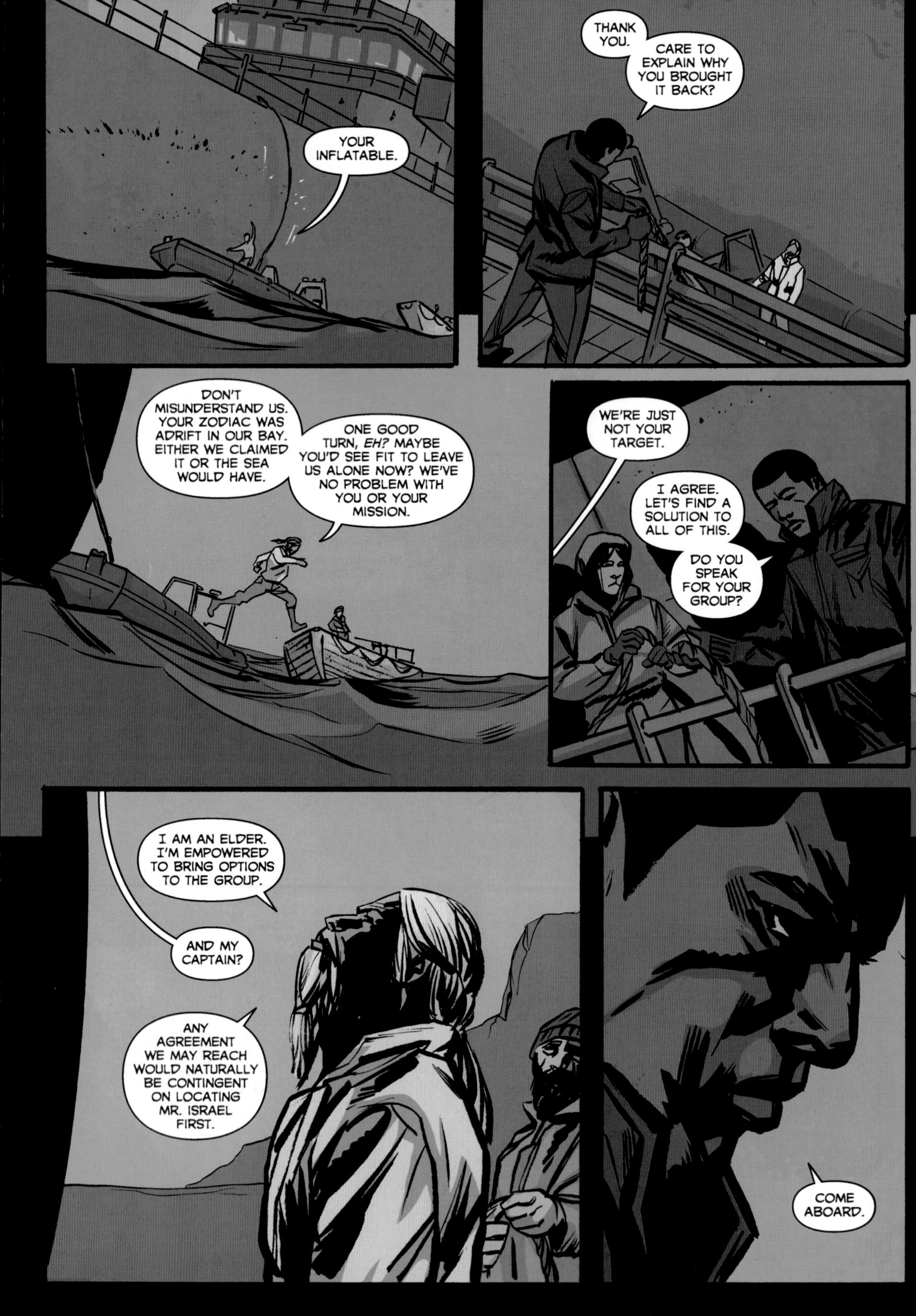

YOUR INFLATABLE.
THANK YOU.
CARE TO EXPLAIN WHY YOU BROUGHT IT BACK?
DON'T MISUNDERSTAND US. YOUR ZODIAC WAS ADRIFT IN OUR BAY. EITHER WE CLAIMED IT OR THE SEA WOULD HAVE.
ONE GOOD TURN, *EH?* MAYBE YOU'D SEE FIT TO LEAVE US ALONE NOW? WE'VE NO PROBLEM WITH YOU OR YOUR MISSION.
WE'RE JUST NOT YOUR TARGET.
I AGREE. LET'S FIND A SOLUTION TO ALL OF THIS.
DO YOU SPEAK FOR YOUR GROUP?
I AM AN ELDER. I'M EMPOWERED TO BRING OPTIONS TO THE GROUP.
AND MY CAPTAIN?
ANY AGREEMENT WE MAY REACH WOULD NATURALLY BE CONTINGENT ON LOCATING MR. ISRAEL FIRST.
COME ABOARD.

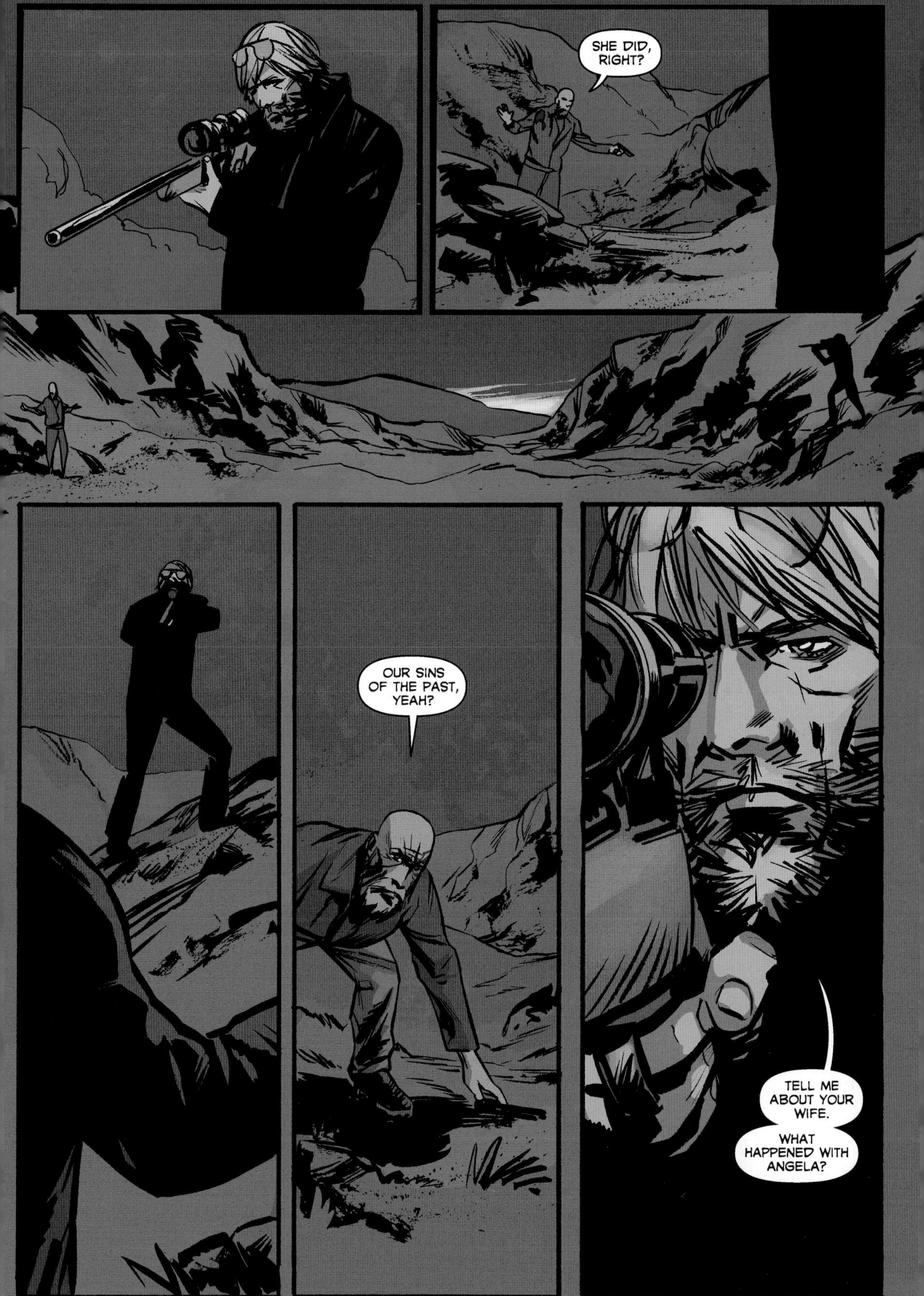
SHE DID, RIGHT?
OUR SINS OF THE PAST, YEAH?
TELL ME ABOUT YOUR WIFE.
WHAT HAPPENED WITH ANGELA?

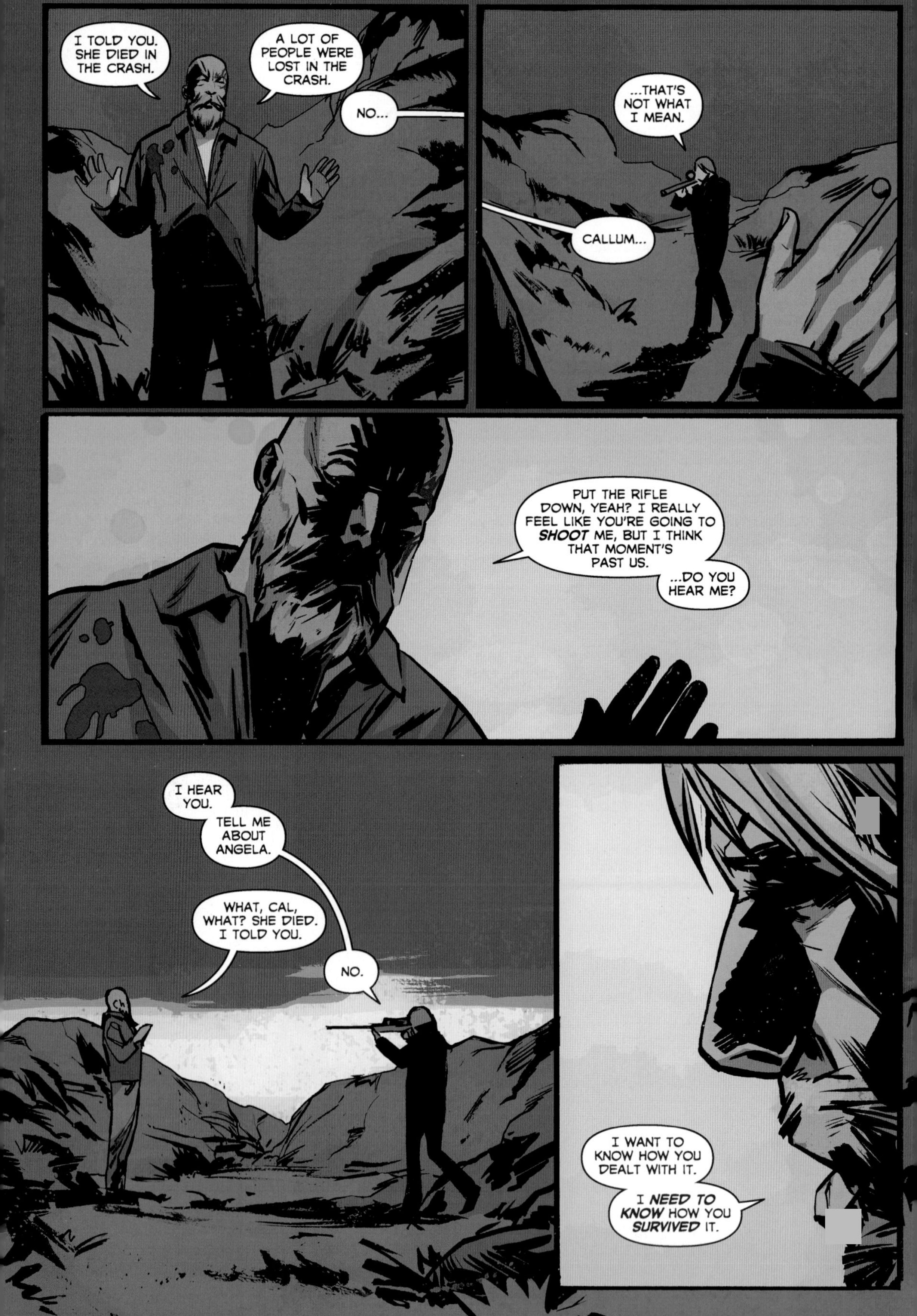
I TOLD YOU. SHE DIED IN THE CRASH.
A LOT OF PEOPLE WERE LOST IN THE CRASH.
NO...
...THAT'S NOT WHAT I MEAN.
CALLUM...
PUT THE RIFLE DOWN, YEAH? I REALLY FEEL LIKE YOU'RE GOING TO **SHOOT** ME, BUT I THINK THAT MOMENT'S PAST US.
...DO YOU HEAR ME?
I HEAR YOU.
TELL ME ABOUT ANGELA.
WHAT, CAL, WHAT? SHE DIED. I TOLD YOU.
NO.
I WANT TO KNOW HOW YOU DEALT WITH IT.
I **NEED TO KNOW** HOW YOU **SURVIVED** IT.

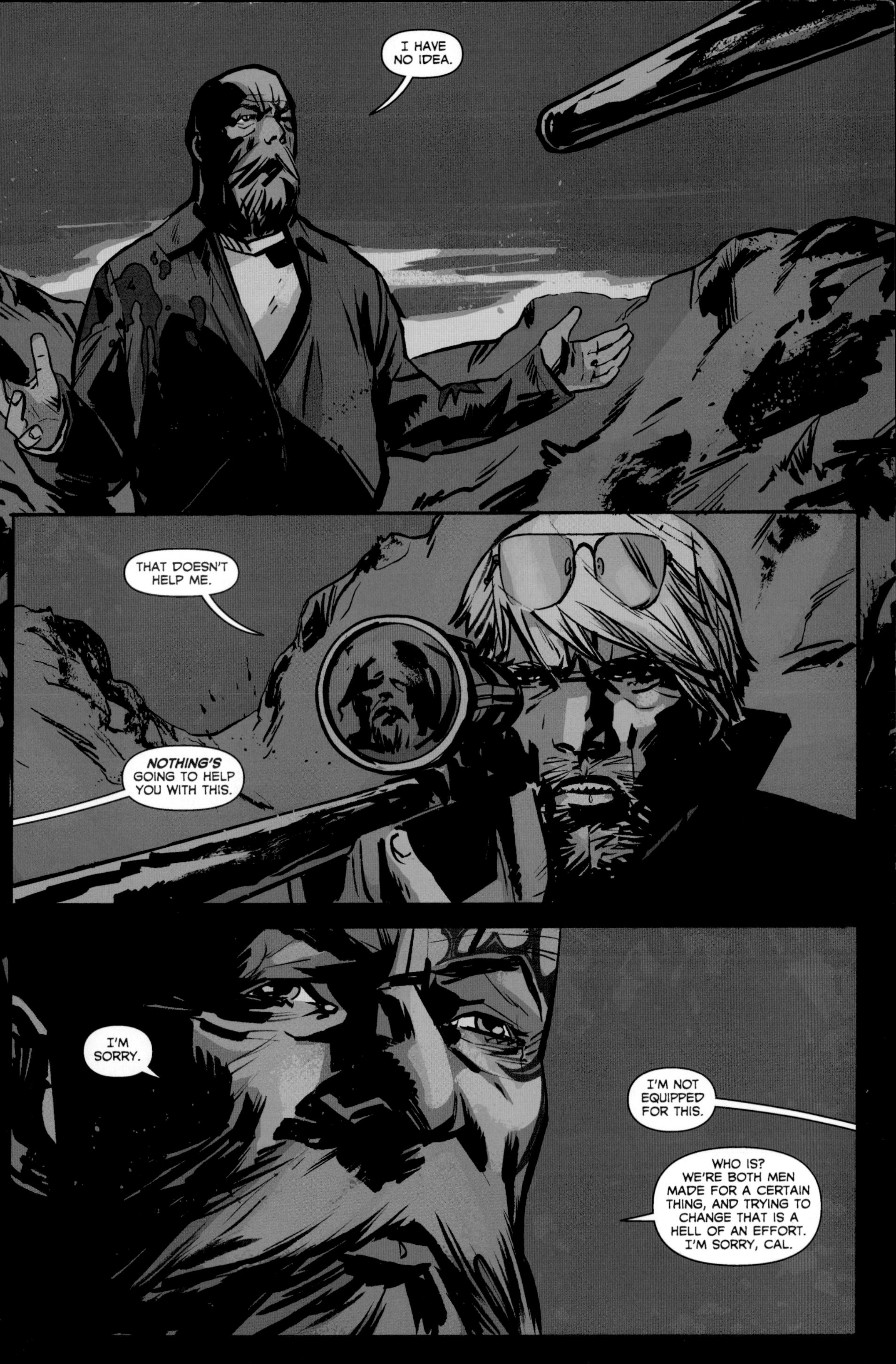
I HAVE NO IDEA.
THAT DOESN'T HELP ME.
NOTHING'S GOING TO HELP YOU WITH THIS.
I'M SORRY.
I'M NOT EQUIPPED FOR THIS.
WHO IS? WE'RE BOTH MEN MADE FOR A CERTAIN THING, AND TRYING TO CHANGE THAT IS A HELL OF AN EFFORT. I'M SORRY, CAL.

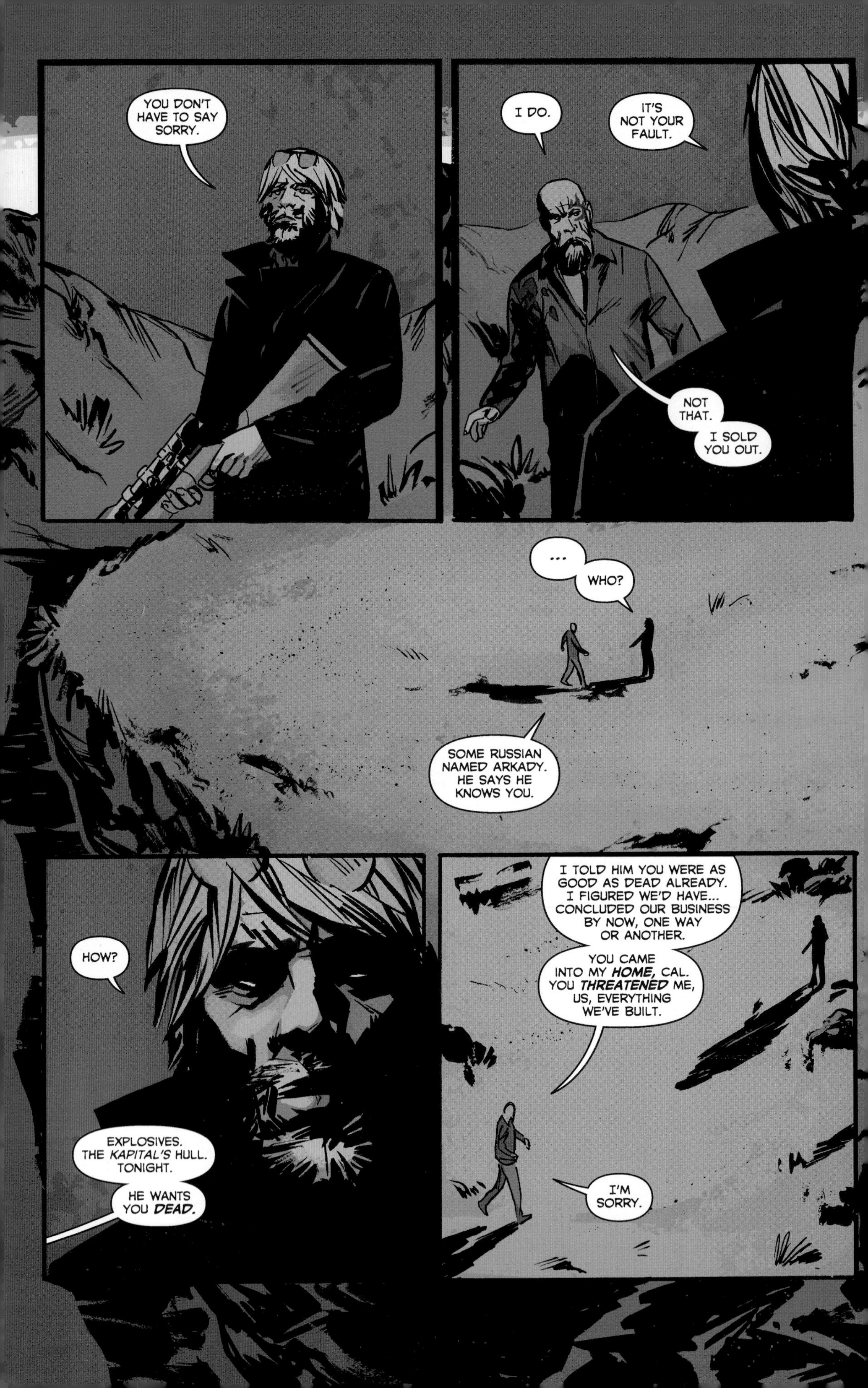

YOU DON'T HAVE TO SAY SORRY.
I DO.
IT'S NOT YOUR FAULT.
NOT THAT.
I SOLD YOU OUT.
...
WHO?
SOME RUSSIAN NAMED ARKADY. HE SAYS HE KNOWS YOU.
HOW?
EXPLOSIVES. THE *KAPITAL'S* HULL. TONIGHT.
HE WANTS YOU ***DEAD.***
I TOLD HIM YOU WERE AS GOOD AS DEAD ALREADY. I FIGURED WE'D HAVE... CONCLUDED OUR BUSINESS BY NOW, ONE WAY OR ANOTHER.
YOU CAME INTO MY ***HOME,*** CAL. YOU ***THREATENED*** ME, US, EVERYTHING WE'VE BUILT.
I'M SORRY.

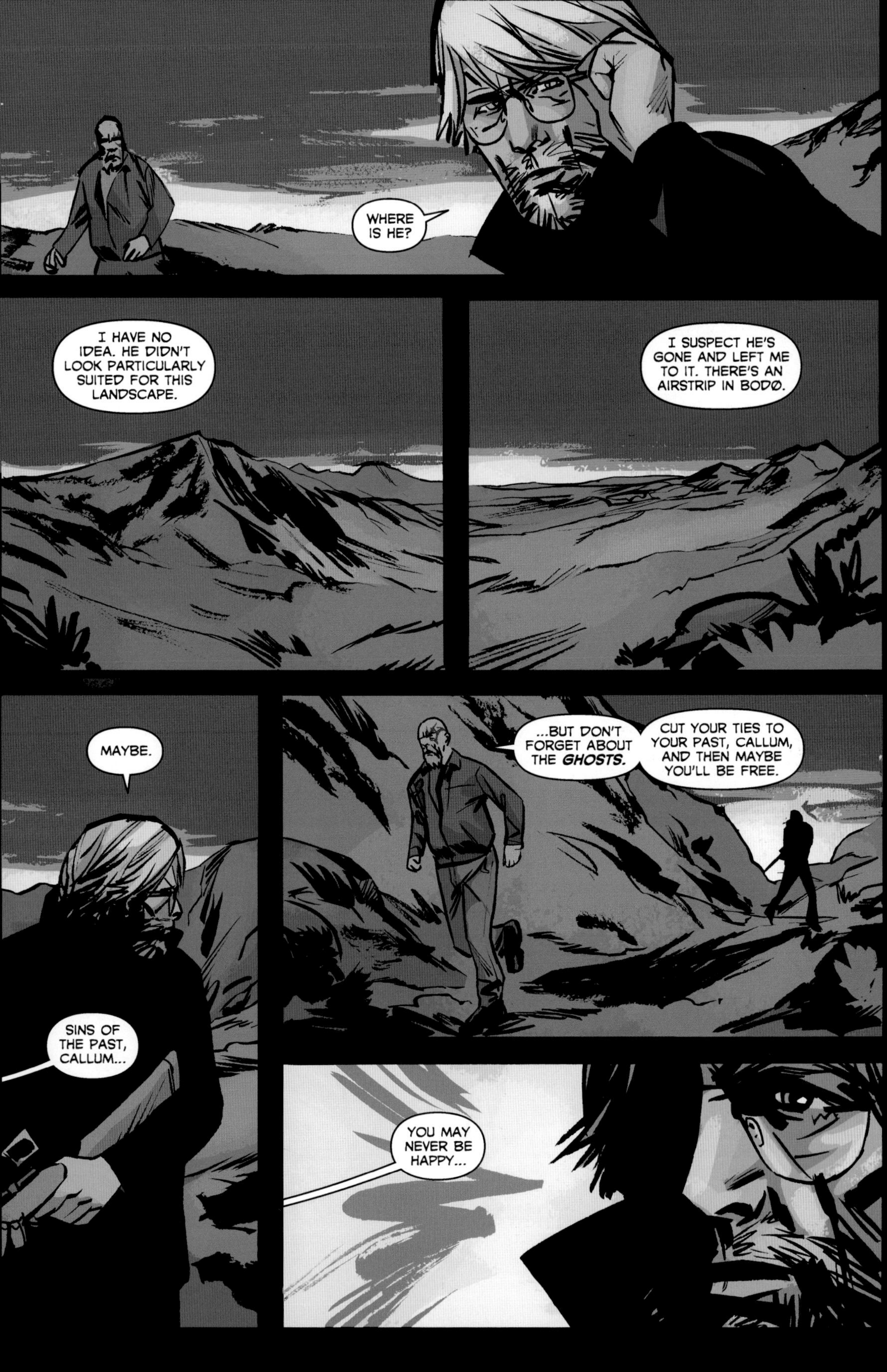
WHERE IS HE?
I HAVE NO IDEA. HE DIDN'T LOOK PARTICULARLY SUITED FOR THIS LANDSCAPE.
I SUSPECT HE'S GONE AND LEFT ME TO IT. THERE'S AN AIRSTRIP IN BODØ.
MAYBE.
CUT YOUR TIES TO YOUR PAST, CALLUM, AND THEN MAYBE YOU'LL BE FREE.
...BUT DON'T FORGET ABOUT THE *GHOSTS.*
SINS OF THE PAST, CALLUM...
YOU MAY NEVER BE HAPPY...

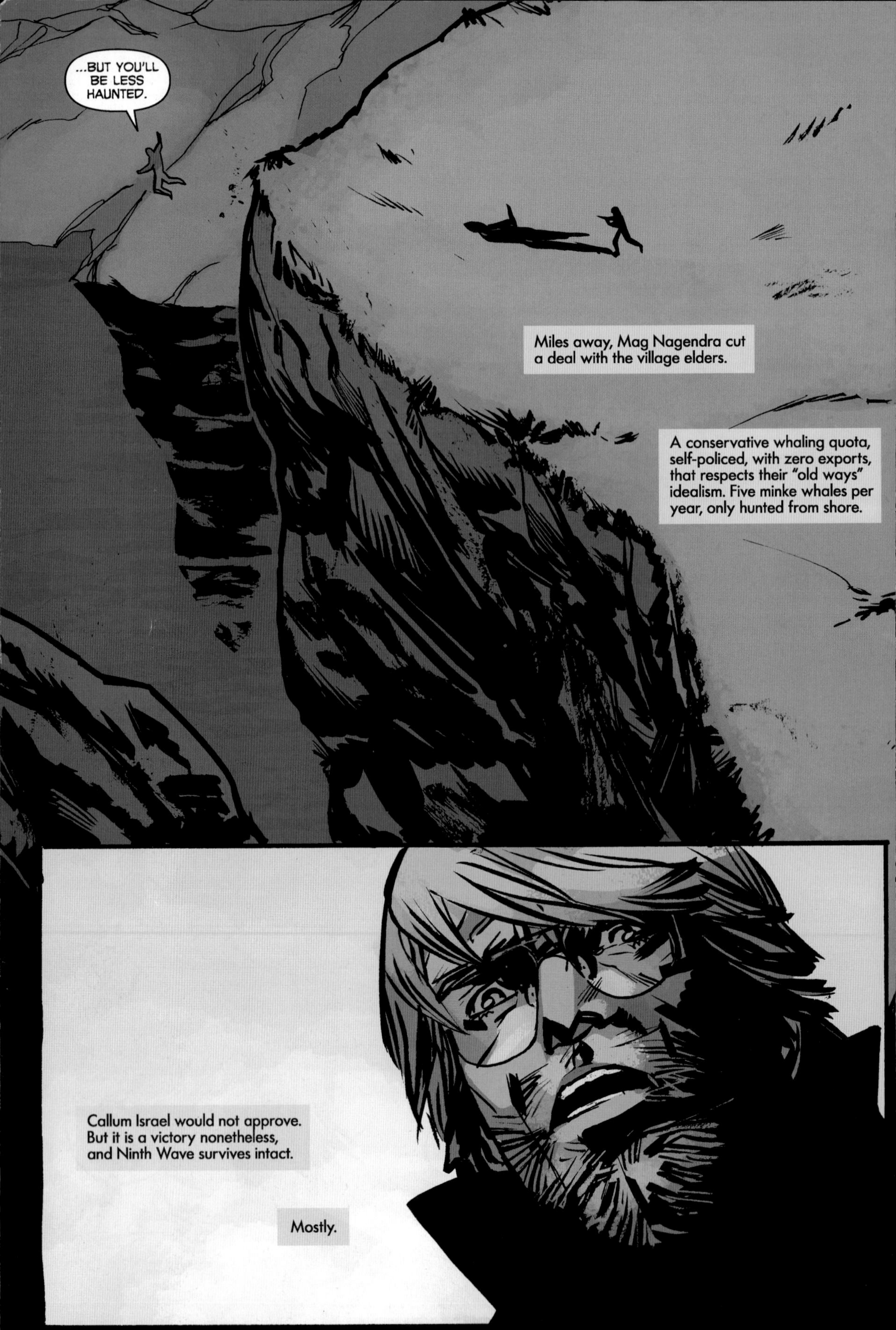
...BUT YOU'LL BE LESS HAUNTED.
Miles away, Mag Nagendra cut a deal with the village elders.
A conservative whaling quota, self-policed, with zero exports, that respects their "old ways" idealism. Five minke whales per year, only hunted from shore.
Callum Israel would not approve. But it is a victory nonetheless, and Ninth Wave survives intact.
Mostly.

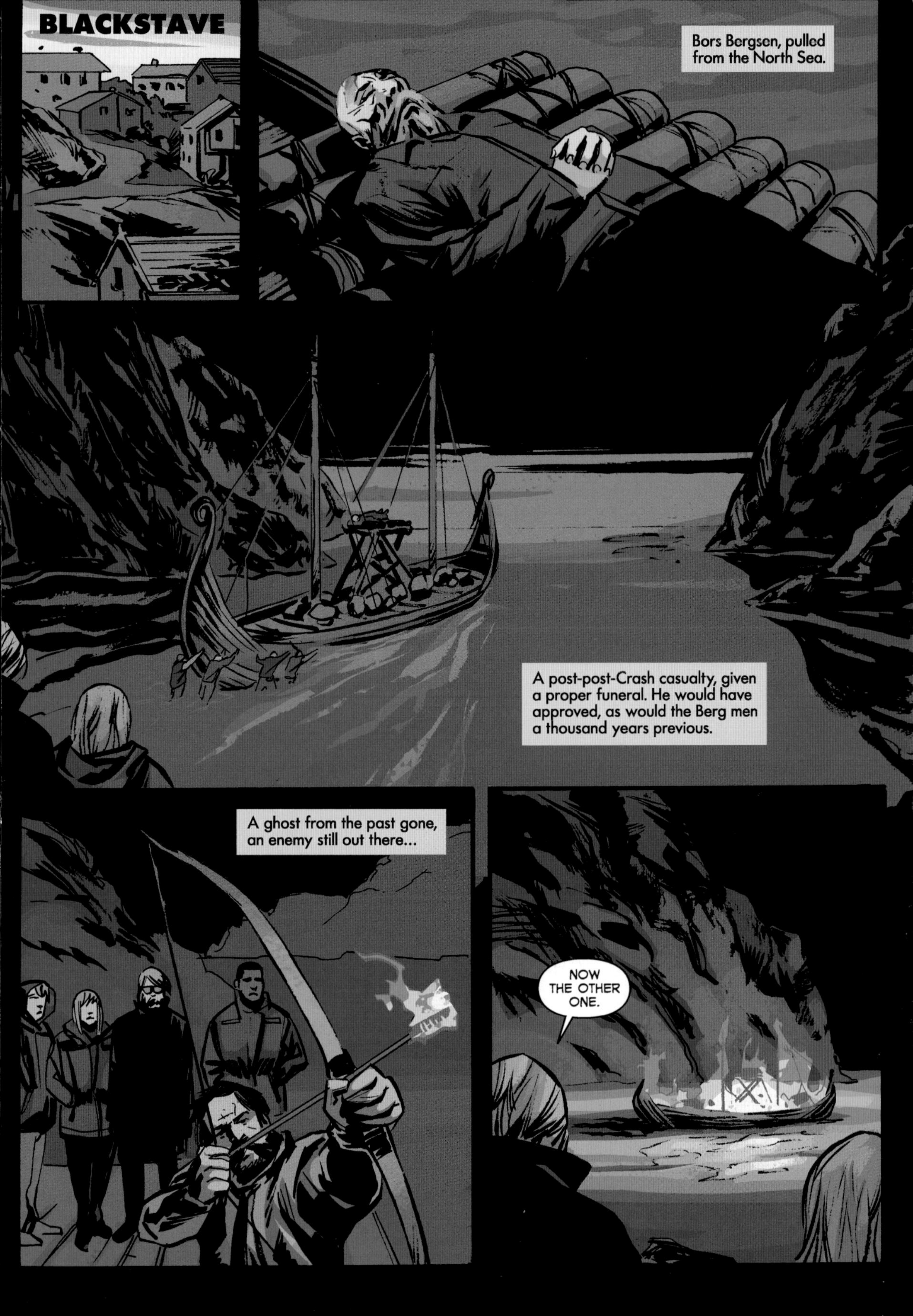
BLACKSTAVE
Bors Bergsen, pulled from the North Sea.
A post-post-Crash casualty, given a proper funeral. He would have approved, as would the Berg men a thousand years previous.
A ghost from the past gone, an enemy still out there...
NOW THE OTHER ONE.

SHE MIGHT COME BACK, CALLUM...

SHE WON'T.

I *KNOW* SHE WON'T.

NOT IN ENOUGH TIME, ANYWAY.

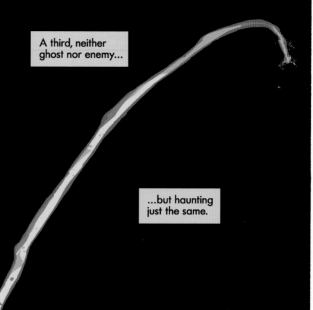

A third, neither ghost nor enemy...

...but haunting just the same.

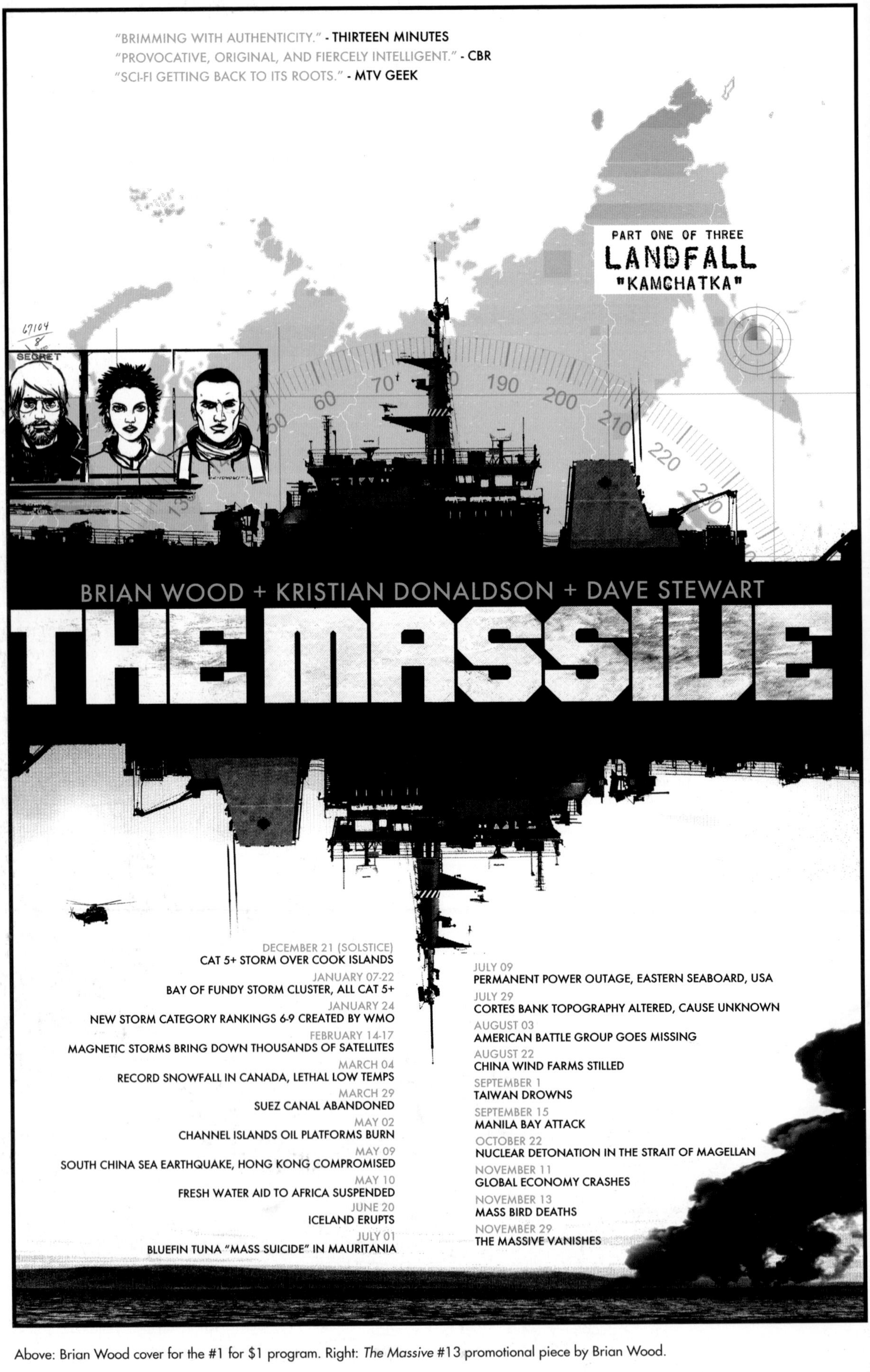
"BRIMMING WITH AUTHENTICITY." - THIRTEEN MINUTES
"PROVOCATIVE, ORIGINAL, AND FIERCELY INTELLIGENT." - CBR
"SCI-FI GETTING BACK TO ITS ROOTS." - MTV GEEK
PART ONE OF THREE
LANDFALL
"KAMCHATKA"
SECRET
BRIAN WOOD + KRISTIAN DONALDSON + DAVE STEWART
THE MASSIVE
DECEMBER 21 (SOLSTICE)
CAT 5+ STORM OVER COOK ISLANDS
JANUARY 07-22
BAY OF FUNDY STORM CLUSTER, ALL CAT 5+
JANUARY 24
NEW STORM CATEGORY RANKINGS 6-9 CREATED BY WMO
FEBRUARY 14-17
MAGNETIC STORMS BRING DOWN THOUSANDS OF SATELLITES
MARCH 04
RECORD SNOWFALL IN CANADA, LETHAL LOW TEMPS
MARCH 29
SUEZ CANAL ABANDONED
MAY 02
CHANNEL ISLANDS OIL PLATFORMS BURN
MAY 09
SOUTH CHINA SEA EARTHQUAKE, HONG KONG COMPROMISED
MAY 10
FRESH WATER AID TO AFRICA SUSPENDED
JUNE 20
ICELAND ERUPTS
JULY 01
BLUEFIN TUNA "MASS SUICIDE" IN MAURITANIA
JULY 09
PERMANENT POWER OUTAGE, EASTERN SEABOARD, USA
JULY 29
CORTES BANK TOPOGRAPHY ALTERED, CAUSE UNKNOWN
AUGUST 03
AMERICAN BATTLE GROUP GOES MISSING
AUGUST 22
CHINA WIND FARMS STILLED
SEPTEMBER 1
TAIWAN DROWNS
SEPTEMBER 15
MANILA BAY ATTACK
OCTOBER 22
NUCLEAR DETONATION IN THE STRAIT OF MAGELLAN
NOVEMBER 11
GLOBAL ECONOMY CRASHES
NOVEMBER 13
MASS BIRD DEATHS
NOVEMBER 29
THE MASSIVE VANISHES

Above: Brian Wood cover for the #1 for $1 program. Right: *The Massive* #13 promotional piece by Brian Wood.

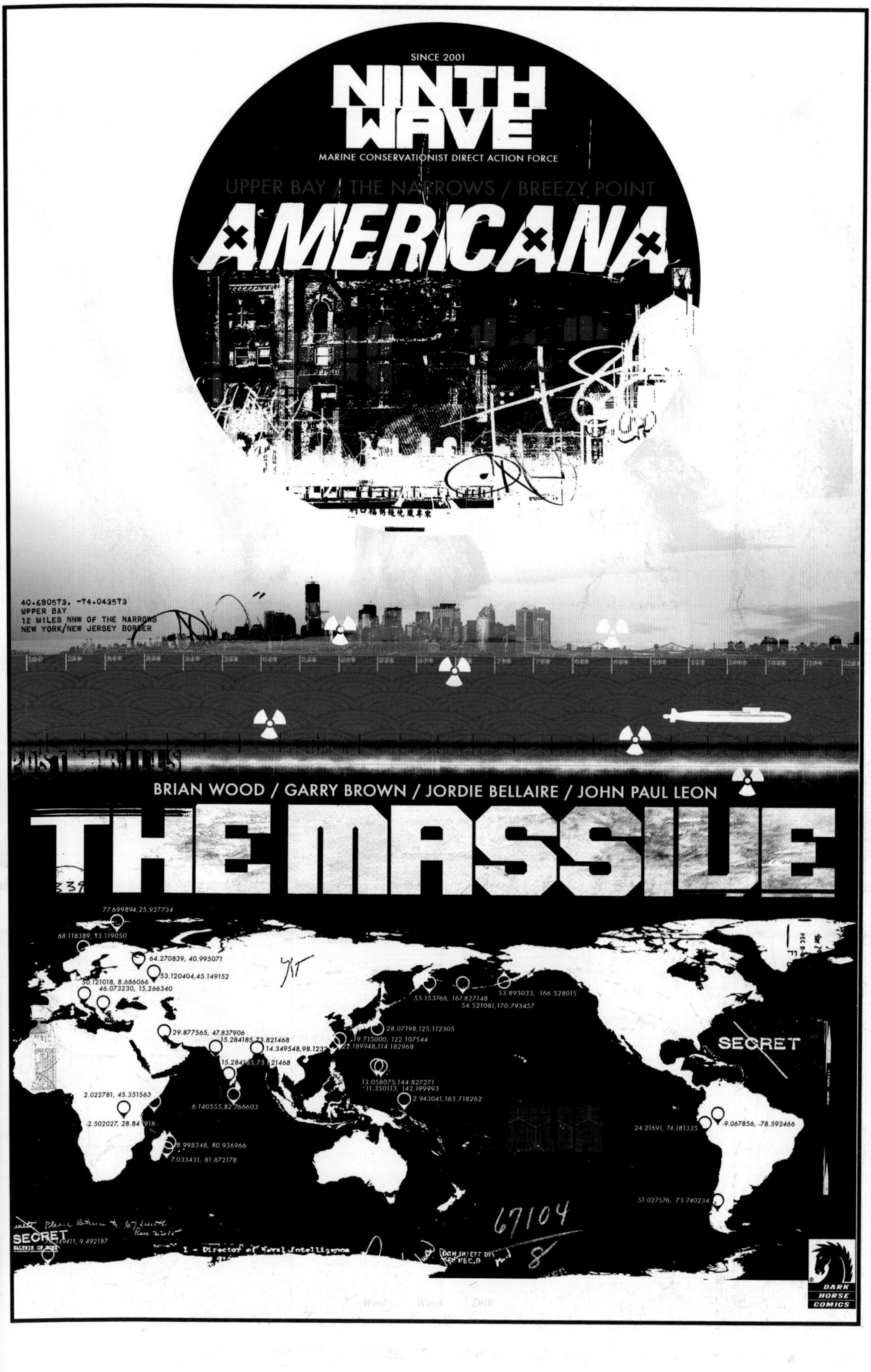

SINCE 2001
NINTH WAVE
MARINE CONSERVATIONIST DIRECT ACTION FORCE
UPPER BAY / THE NARROWS / BREEZY POINT
AMERICANA
40.680573, -74.043573
UPPER BAY
12 MILES NNW OF THE NARROWS
NEW YORK/NEW JERSEY BORDER
BRIAN WOOD / GARRY BROWN / JORDIE BELLAIRE / JOHN PAUL LEON
THE MASSIVE
77.699894, 25.927734
68.118389, 13.119050
64.270839, 40.995071
53.120404, 45.149152
46.073230, 15.266340
55.153766, 167.827148
53.895033, -166.528015
54.521081, 170.793457
28.07198, 125.112305
29.877565, 47.837906
SECRET
2.022781, 45.351563
6.140555, 82.766603
13.058075, 144.827271
2.943041, 163.718262
24.21691, 74.181335
-9.067856, -78.592466
8.998348, 80.936966
7.033431, 81.872178
51.027576, 73.740234
67104
SECRET
1 - Director of Naval Intelligence
DARK HORSE COMICS

MORE FROM *NEW YORK TIMES* BEST-SELLING AUTHOR

BRIAN WOOD

"Someone remembered what comics are for. Meet Brian Wood."
—Warren Ellis

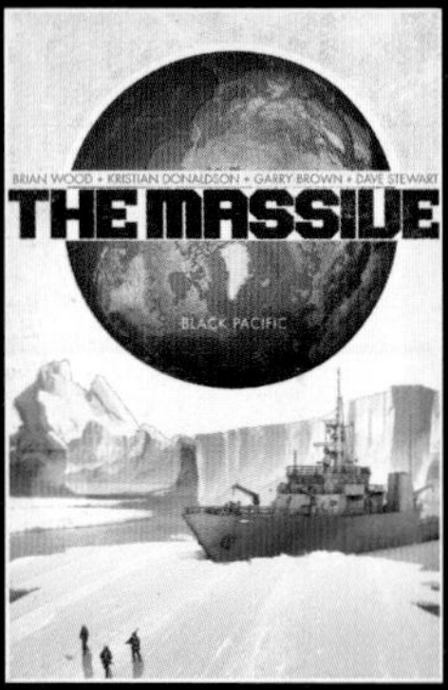
BRIAN WOOD • KRISTIAN DONALDSON • GARRY BROWN • DAVE STEWART
THE MASSIVE
BLACK PACIFIC

THE MASSIVE

Written by Brian Wood
Art by Kristian Donaldson and Garry Brown

In this first volume of Brian Wood's new, sprawling postapocalyptic epic, follow the crew of the *Kapital* from the flooded remnants of Hong Kong to Unalaska, with stops in Antarctica and Mogadishu, as post-Crash ethics and economics are explored across a broken world.

Volume 1: Black Pacific
ISBN 978-1-61655-132-2 | $19.99

Volume 2: Subcontinental
ISBN 978-1-61655-316-6 | $19.99

Volume 3: Longship
ISBN 978-1-61655-446-0 | $19.99

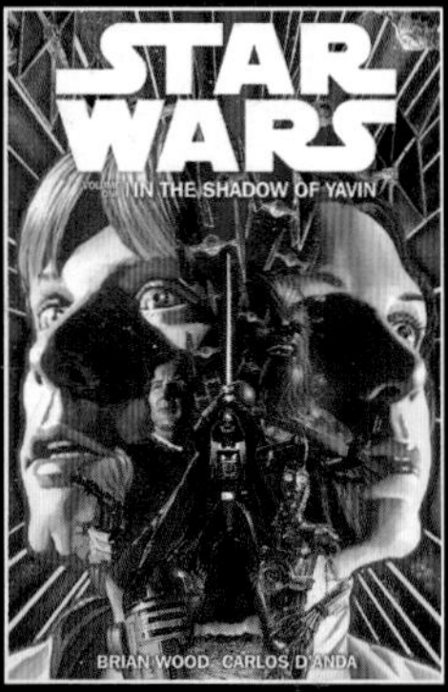
STAR WARS
IN THE SHADOW OF YAVIN
BRIAN WOOD CARLOS D'ANDA

STAR WARS VOLUME 1: IN THE SHADOW OF YAVIN

Written by Brian Wood
Art by Carlos D'Anda, Ryan Odagawa, and Gabe Eltaeb
Cover by Alex Ross

After the destruction of the Death Star, the Rebels are hounded by the Empire. Suspecting a spy in their ranks, Princess Leia forms a secret X-wing squadron—which includes Luke Skywalker—to expose the spy and find a safe home. Meanwhile, Han Solo and Chewbacca are sent on a covert mission!

ISBN 978-1-61655-170-4 | $19.99

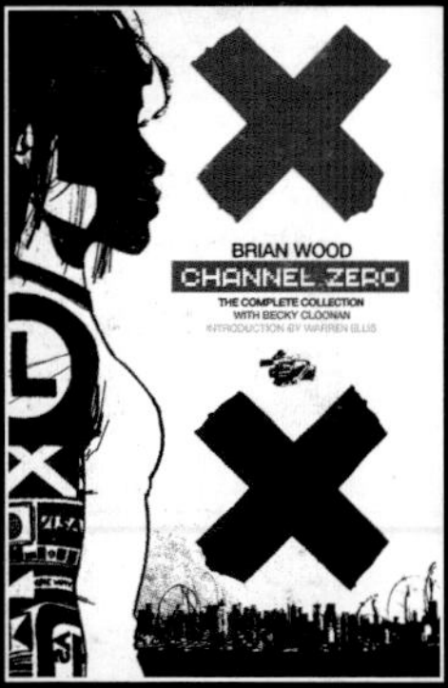
BRIAN WOOD
CHANNEL ZERO
THE COMPLETE COLLECTION
WITH BECKY CLOONAN
INTRODUCTION BY WARREN ELLIS

CHANNEL ZERO

Written by Brian Wood
Art by Becky Cloonan

A blistering take on media control in a repressive future America! *DMZ* and *The Massive* creator Brian Wood launched an all-out assault on the comics medium in 1997 with *Channel Zero*, an influential, forward-thinking series that combined art, politics, and graphic design in a unique way.

ISBN 978-1-59582-936-8 | $19.99

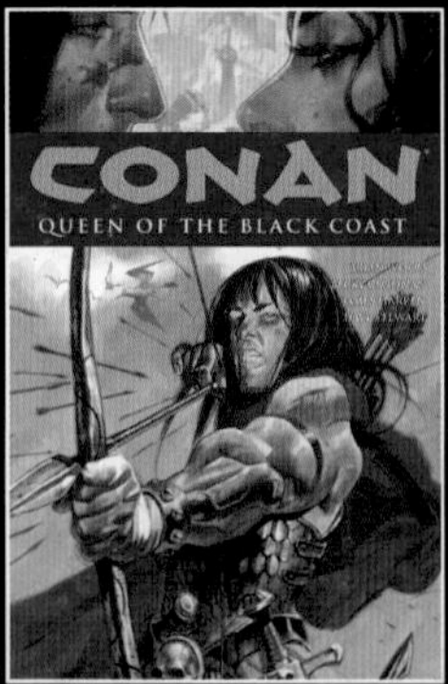
CONAN
QUEEN OF THE BLACK COAST

CONAN VOLUME 13: QUEEN OF THE BLACK COAST

Written by Brian Wood
Art by Becky Cloonan and James Harren

Conan turns his back on the civilized world and takes to the Western Ocean. Finding first danger and then passion in the arms of the pirate queen Bêlit, the Cimmerian begins a new life of pleasure and pillage along the Black Coast, in this epic of romance and terror!

TPB: ISBN 978-1-61655-043-1 | $19.99
HC: ISBN 978-1-61655-042-4 | $24.99

CONAN VOLUME 14: THE DEATH

Written by Brian Wood
Art by Becky Cloonan, Vasilis Lolos, and Declan Shalvey

Conan returns to Cimmeria to track down an impostor destroying villages in his name, only to discover a tragic connection to his own past!

TPB: ISBN 978-1-61655-123-0 | $19.99
HC: ISBN 978-1-61655-122-3 | $24.99